A Book Of

FINANCIAL MANAGEMENT

For
M.B.A. (Semester - II)
Also Useful for PGDBM (Semester - II)
As Per Pune University's Revised Syllabus
Effective from June 2013

Dr. Nachiket M. Vechalekar
Associate Dean – Post Graduate Programmes
IndSearch
Pune 411 004

NIRALI PRAKASHAN
Advancement of knowledge

FINANCIAL MANAGEMENT

First Edition : December 2013

© : Author

The text of this publication, or any part thereof, should not be reproduced or transmitted in any form or stored in any computer storage system or device for distribution including photocopy, recording, taping or information retrieval system or reproduced on any disc, tape, perforated media or other information storage device etc., without the written permission of Authors with whom the rights are reserved. Breach of this condition is liable for legal action.

Every effort has been made to avoid errors or omissions in this publication. In spite of this, errors may have crept in. Any mistake, error or discrepancy so noted and shall be brought to our notice shall be taken care of in the next edition. It is notified that neither the publisher nor the authors or seller shall be responsible for any damage or loss of action to any one, of any kind, in any manner, therefrom.

ISBN 978-93-83750-57-3

Published By :
NIRALI PRAKASHAN
Abhyudaya Pragati, 1312, Shivaji Nagar,
Off J.M. Road, PUNE – 411005
Tel - (020) 25512336/37/39, Fax - (020) 25511379
Email : niralipune@pragationline.com

Printed By :
Repro Knowledgecast Limited,
Thane

DISTRIBUTION CENTRES
PUNE

Nirali Prakashan
119, Budhwar Peth, Jogeshwari Mandir Lane
Pune 411002, Maharashtra
Tel : (020) 2445 2044, 66022708, Fax : (020) 2445 1538
Email : bookorder@pragationline.com

Nirali Prakashan
S. No. 28/27, Dhyari,
Near Pari Company, Pune 411041
Tel : (020) 24690204 Fax : (020) 24690316
Email : dhyari@pragationline.com
             bookorder@pragationline.com

MUMBAI
Nirali Prakashan
385, S.V.P. Road, Rasdhara Co-op. Hsg. Society Ltd.,
Girgaum, Mumbai 400004, Maharashtra
Tel : (022) 2385 6339 / 2386 9976, Fax : (022) 2386 9976
Email : niralimumbai@pragationline.com

DISTRIBUTION BRANCHES

NAGPUR
Pratibha Book Distributors
Above Maratha Mandir, Shop No. 3, First Floor,
Rani Jhanshi Square, Sitabuldi, Nagpur 440012,
Maharashtra, Tel : (0712) 254 7129

BENGALURU
Pragati Book House
House No. 1, Sanjeevappa Lane, Avenue Road Cross,
Opp. Rice Church, Bengaluru – 560002.
Tel : (080) 64513344, 64513355,
Mob : 9880582331, 9845021552
Email:bharatsavla@yahoo.com

JALGAON
Nirali Prakashan
34, V. V. Golani Market, Navi Peth, Jalgaon 425001,
Maharashtra, Tel : (0257) 222 0395
Mob : 94234 91860

KOLHAPUR
Nirali Prakashan
New Mahadvar Road,
Kedar Plaza, 1st Floor Opp. IDBI Bank
Kolhapur 416 012, Maharashtra. Mob : 9855046155

CHENNAI
Pragati Books
9/1, Montieth Road, Behind Taas Mahal, Egmore,
Chennai 600008 Tamil Nadu, Tel : (044) 6518 3535,
Mob : 94440 01782 / 98450 21552 / 98805 82331, Email : bharatsavla@yahoo.com

RETAIL OUTLETS
PUNE

Pragati Book Centre
157, Budhwar Peth, Opp. Ratan Talkies,
Pune 411002, Maharashtra
Tel : (020) 2445 8887 / 6602 2707, Fax : (020) 2445 8887

Pragati Book Centre
Amber Chamber, 28/A, Budhwar Peth,
Appa Balwant Chowk, Pune : 411002, Maharashtra,
Tel : (020) 20240335 / 66281669
Email : pbcpune@pragationline.com

Pragati Book Centre
676/B, Budhwar Peth, Opp. Jogeshwari Mandir,
Pune 411002, Maharashtra
Tel : (020) 6601 7784 / 6602 0855

PBC Book Sellers & Stationers
152, Budhwar Peth, Pune 411002, Maharashtra
Tel : (020) 2445 2254 / 6609 2463

MUMBAI
Pragati Book Corner
Indira Niwas, 111 - A, Bhavani Shankar Road, Dadar (W), Mumbai 400028, Maharashtra
Tel : (022) 2422 3526 / 6662 5254, Email : pbcmumbai@pragationline.com

www.pragationline.com   info@pragationline.com

Preface

Financial management is that specialised function of general management, which is related to the procurement of finance and its effective utilisation for the achievement of common goals of the organisation. It is devoted to a cautious use of capital and a careful selection of sources of capital, in order to enable a spending unit to move in the direction of reaching its goals.

Financial management is one of the most critical and important activities for the professional business manager. It is a fact that the consequences of all important management decisions, financial and otherwise, are immediately and/or eventually will be reflected in the financial performance of the business organisation.

It therefore is a great pleasure to present the book on 'Financial Management' written as per the revised syllabus of University of Pune for MBA [Semester II] and PGDBM [Semester II] and other management programmes effective from the academic year 2013-14. I am grateful to the entire academic fraternity for giving an overwhelming response to the earlier editions of this book.

In this new edition, the topics are re-arranged as per the sequence given in the syllabus of the University of Pune so that it will be easy for the users of this book to refer them. Additional numerical problems with solutions are added wherever necessary and case studies have also been added in some topics. Efforts have been made to keep the language as simple as possible so that even the beginners of this subject can understand the various concepts easily.

I am extremely grateful to Mr. Dinesh bhai Furia and Mr. Jignesh Furia of Nirali Prakashan and their entire team for all the support and encouragement given for the completion of this book. I am also grateful to my family members who have always encouraged me to write this book.

I request the readers of this book to give their valuable suggestions required for further improvement in the book.

Dr Nachiket M. Vechalekar,
Associate Dean – PGP,
IndSearch, Pune: 411004
Email: nmvechalekar@yahoo.co.in

Syllabus ...

Financial Management
(M.B.A. : Semester II)

1. **Environment of Business Finance** (3 + 2)
   Introduction, Definition of Financial Management, Goals of Financial Management, Modern approaches to Financial Management, Finance and other related disciplines, Functions of Finance Manager, Key Strategies of Financial Management.

2. **Techniques of Financial Analysis** (8 + 2)
   Meaning, Nature, Objectives and Limitations of Financial Analysis, Tools of Analysis and interpretation, Fund Flow Statement Analysis (Working Capital basis), Cash Flow Statement Analysis - (Cash basis), Ratio Analysis (Interpretations of ratios only)

3. **Capital Budgeting** (8 + 2)
   Meaning, Definition and Types of Evaluating the Project on the basis of Payback period, NPV, IRR, PI, ARR.

4. **Working Capital Management** (8 + 2)
   Nature and Scope, Components of Working Capital, Operating Cycle, Types of Working Capital, Determination of Working Capital, Assessment of Working Capital Requirement, Working Capital Financing.

5. **Capital Structure and Firm Valuation** (8 + 2)
   Meaning, Factors affecting the Capital Structure, Capital and Measurement in Cost of Capital, Measurement of Specific Costs: WACC. Assumptions of Capital Structure theories, NI, NOI and MM Approach.

Financial Management
(P.G.D.B.M. : Semester II)

1. **Concept of Financial Management** - Scope and Functions - Financial Planning and Forecasting - Risk and Return - Portfolio Investment - CAPM. (3 + 2)

2. **Capitalization** - Under and Over capitalization - Capital structure - Computation of Cost of Capital - Trading on Equity and various types of Leverages - Management of Profits - Dividend Policy, Procedural and Legal Formalities involved in the Payment of dividends - Bonus Shares. (8 + 2)

3. **Capital Budgeting** - Nature and Significance - Time value of money - Methods of evaluating Capital Expenditure Proposals. (8 + 2)

4. **Financial Statement Analysis** including Ratio Analysis - Funds Flow and Cash Flow Statements. (8 + 2)

5. **Working Capital Management** - Types of Working Capital - Working Capital Budget - Operating Cycle - Components of Working Capital - Cash, Receivables and Inventory. (8 + 2)

Contents ...

1. Environment of Business Finance — 1.1 – 1.22

2. Techniques of Financial Analysis — 2.1 – 2.96

3. Capital Budgeting — 3.1 – 3.40

4. Working Capital Management — 4.1 – 4.70

5. Capital Structure and Firm Valuation — 5.1 – 5.46

6. Management of Profits (For P.G.D.B.M. only) — 6.1 – 6.16

Multiple Choice Questions — MCQ.1 – MCQ.14

Chapter 1...
Environment of Business Finance

Contents ...
1.1 Introduction
1.2 Definition of Financial Management
1.3 Modern Approaches to Financial Management
1.4 Goals of Financial Management
1.5 Functions of a Finance Manager
1.6 Finance and Other Related Disciplines
1.7 Key Strategies of Financial Management
1.8 Risk and Return
1.9 Capital Asset Pricing Model
- Points to Remember
- Questions for Discussion
- Questions from Previous Pune University Examinations

Learning Objectives ...
After studying this topic, you should be able to,
1. Know the Meaning of Financial Management
2. Distinguish between the Traditional and Modern Concepts of Financial Management
3. Understand the Scope, Objectives and Functions of Financial Management
4. Know the Interface between Financial Management and Other Disciplines
5. Grasp the various Financial Management Strategies

1.1 Introduction

Management is an activity which is concerned with planning and controlling of different activities, in order to achieve a specific objective. If we apply the concept of management to financial management, it will mean that it is planning and controlling of financial resources of a firm with a specific objective. Financial Management is still a comparatively new discipline and hence there are several controversies about various theories and concepts. The subject of financial management has assumed greater importance today, as the financial strategies required to survive in a competitive environment, have become extremely crucial today.

1.2 Definition of Financial Management

The term *'financial management'* can be defined as *the management of flow of funds and it deals with financial decision-making*. It is basically concerned with raising of funds and the utilisation of funds in the most optimum manner so as to maximise the return for the owner.

Since raising of the funds and the best possible utilisation of the same is a very crucial part of the success of an organisation, financial management as a functional area has got a place of prime relevance in every firm. All business decisions have financial implications and therefore financial management is inevitably related to almost every aspect of business operations.

1.3 Modern Approaches to Financial Management

In order to understand the concepts of financial management in a better manner, it is necessary to understand the difference between the traditional and modern concept of financial management.

Though financial management is a relatively new discipline, finance as a function has been known to business organisations even in ancient times. The traditional concept of financial management can be summarised as mentioned below:

(a) Finance function was mainly concerned with raising funds for various requirements like diversification, expansion and so on. It was not considered to be a regular part of managerial functions.

(b) Attention was given to the long term funds only. The concept and day-to-day management of working capital was not considered.

(c) Sources used for raising funds were mainly equity shares, debentures and preference shares. The knowledge of legal framework necessary for raising funds through these sources was considered essential.

Modern Concept of Financial Management

Due to increasing competition and growth in business as well as occurrence of trade cycles, the scope of the finance function expanded. It was no longer a fund raising activity only. The finance function became more analytical and decision oriented. Apart from fund raising, utilisation of funds became of paramount importance. A Finance Manager became a professional manager and he had to seek the answers to the following questions.

(a) What is the projection of the requirements of funds for the organisation? How should this amount be raised?

(b) How to utilise the funds in an optimum manner in order to maximise the returns of the shareholders?

1.4 Goals of Financial Management

Financial management is concerned with the following activities:
1. Raising of funds
2. Investment of funds
3. Other decisions like dividend decisions.

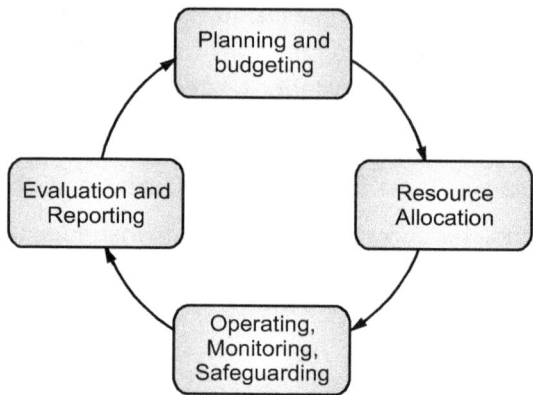

Fig 1.1: Financial Management Cycle

1. **Raising of Funds:** A finance manager has to take a crucial decision regarding the selection of source for raising of funds. Funds can be raised from owned sources as well as from borrowed sources, with the right balance between the owned funds and borrowed funds.

   These sources have their own peculiar features and characteristics. While owned funds do not have any obligation such as repayment at maturity and interest payments, borrowed funds have both these obligations. However, borrowed funds are comparatively cheaper, however will have a risk element always. This risk is known as financial risk, i.e. risk of insolvency due to landing in a debt trap. Equity shares, preference shares and retained earnings are owned sources of raising funds while debentures and term loans are borrowed sources of raising of funds. There is a need for striking a right balance between the owned funds and borrowed funds. These sources have their own peculiar features and characteristics. The main difference between them is that in case of borrowed funds, there is a commitment of fixed amount in the form of interest payments as well as repayment of principal amount. In case of ownership funds, these commitments are not there and hence they are considered to be risk free sources.

   A business organisation normally has a combination of both the types of funds. There should be a balance between the two types of funds so that there will be a balance

between the risk and profitability. While planning the debt-equity mix, various factors should be considered. These are cash flow analysis.
- EBIT-EPS analysis
- Debt-equity ratio
- Financial and operating leverage
- Capital market situation
- Capital structure models
- Cost of funds
- Management perception of control.

A finance manager must tap new financial instruments for raising finance and therefore should be aware of financial engineering.

To summarise, three crucial aspects should be taken into consideration before financing decisions are taken.

(a) Requirement of funds during long term and short term.

(b) Deciding about optimum combination of owned funds and borrowed funds for raising the funds.

(c) Determination of the financing pattern for long term and short term requirements of the funds.

2. **Investment of Funds:** Another important decision that is to be taken by the finance manager is about the investment of the funds. Resources at the command of the firm are always scarce and there are several demands on the same. It is therefore necessary for the finance manager to provide a framework for taking appropriate decisions.

Investing decisions are normally related to the following areas.

(a) **Fixed Assets:** Investment in fixed assets is made with a long term perspective and the main objective behind this decision is to enhance the earning capacity of the organisation. Investments in fixed assets also called capital budgeting decisions are normally irreversible and involve heavy amounts. Therefore capital budgeting decisions are to be taken with utmost care and only after ensuring that the projected benefits will be more than the projected costs.

(b) **Working Capital:** Working capital is required for the day-to-day requirements of a business organisation. It is defined as the excess of current assets over current liabilities. Current assets are basically created with an intention to convert them into cash or other current assets within a period of one year, while current liabilities are the liabilities which are expected to mature within a period of one year and paid either from existing current assets or by creating new current liabilities. A Finance Manager has to take decisions regarding the amount of funds to be invested in the working capital. He has to ensure that there is neither excess working capital nor shortage of the same. For this, he has to take several decisions like how much inventory is to be kept, how much credit is to be allowed to customers etc. He also has to prepare the estimate of working capital and arrange for the same through various sources.

3. **Dividend Decisions:** Another major area of decision making by a finance manager is known as the dividend decisions. Dividends are paid out of divisible profits of a company. These profits can either be retained as reserves or distributed as dividends to the shareholders.

A Finance manager has to comply with the legal provisions and consider the financial aspects also. Though there is no legal restriction on the rate of dividends, there are several considerations which are to be complied with before dividend decisions are taken. These include:

- cash flow positions
- capital structure planning
- shareholders' expectations

There should be a balance between a liberal and conservative dividend policy. Reactions of the shareholders are also to be considered. Similarly, the likely impact on the prices of the shares is also to be taken into consideration.

A Finance manager must also decide about the declaration of bonus as a policy of the company. Since the dividend decisions have long term implications, utmost care must be taken. Several considerations like cash flow positions, capital structure planning, shareholders' expectations etc. are to be taken into consideration before finalising the dividend policy.

Keeping in mind various areas of importance of financial management, the financial manager has to take numerous decisions as seen above. It is therefore necessary to understand what the goal of financial decision making is. These goals can be listed as given below:

1. **Maximisation of Profits:** Any commercial organisation is established for profits. Therefore maximisation of profits is considered to be the primary goal of financial management. This goal advocates that when there is any issue of decision making, the objective which will maximise the profits should be selected. The profit is measured according to accepted accounting principles. The argument in favour of this objective is that the profit is a parameter for measuring the performance of a

business organisation and hence profit maximisation is the most appropriate objective of financial decision making. It is argued that if every firm tries to maximise profits, there will be maximising of the social welfare of the society. If all the firms keep this target, the resources of the economy will be used for the most productive uses, resulting in efficient utilisation of the same.

However, it has been observed that there are flaws in the profit maximisation concept. It is said that profit maximisation cannot be the goal of financial decision making as the interests of various stakeholders should also be taken into consideration. Profit maximisation ignores the interests of other stakeholders except the shareholders.

The arguments against profit maximisation can be summarised as given below:

(a) The profit maximisation objective aims at maximisation of profits only and ignores other aspects. For example, it ignores the financing aspects this means that in order to earn maximum profits, it may ignore financing options and a firm may be tempted to borrow beyond its capacity to finance an investment proposal.

(b) Risk factors are also ignored if the profit maximisation objective is to be pursued. Even risky investment proposals may be undertaken to earn higher profits and it can bring the firm in trouble.

(c) Profit maximisation does not take into consideration the time value of money.

(d) The profit maximisation concept is considered to be vague. Exactly which profits a firm wants to maximise? Whether accounting profits or cash profits? Pre-tax profits or post tax profits? Long term profits or short term profits? These questions remain unanswered and hence the concept is considered to be quite vague.

(e) This objective aims at maximisation of profits but it remains vague as to whether shareholders' interests are to be protected or not. It remains to be seen whether this profit will be distributed among the shareholders so that their wealth will also be maximised. This question remains unanswered. It is also said that this goal is shortsighted and in an anxiety to maximise profits, the long term impacts may be ignored. Ethical and moral considerations may also be overlooked in order to maximise the profits as the firm may try to achieve the objective by hook or by crook.

This is the reason why wealth maximisation objective of financial management is gaining more importance. The rationale of this goal is discussed in the following paragraphs.

2. **Wealth Maximisation:** The wealth maximization may be described as the prime objective of financial management. Shareholders are the main stakeholders in a firm and are the owners of the firm as per relevant laws. It is natural for a firm to strive for the maximisation of the wealth of the shareholders. All decisions should be taken by keeping this objective in mind.

   It is necessary to understand the concept of the wealth of shareholders. The wealth of shareholders is measured in terms of the value of shares of a firm. In case, the shares of a firm are not quoted on stock exchange and hence no market value is available, the wealth can be measured in terms of earnings per share and the intrinsic value of the share.

   Wealth in financial management is measured in terms of economic value which is the present value of future cash flows which result from a particular decision regarding capital investment.

   When a firm takes a decision regarding any capital investment, it is based on the *net present value* generated from that decision. The net present value is calculated by discounting the future cash flows at an appropriate rate of discount and deducting them from the initial investment made in the project. Decision regarding capital investment is taken if the net present value comes positive. Therefore the concept of wealth is based on cash flows rather than the accounting profits.

   When the net present value is positive, it is reflected in the overall performance of the firm and the shareholders get the benefits in the form of increased dividends and appreciation in the market value of their shares. Thus economic value of the shareholders' wealth is finally the market value of the shares of the company.

   The objective of maximisation of wealth of shareholders implies that all the financial decisions should be taken by keeping the shareholders' interest in mind. The decisions should result in higher dividends and increased market price of shares that will benefit the shareholders. Thus, it will be necessary for the management to allocate the scarce resources for the most efficient use and thereby maximise the returns to the shareholders.

   Few points that need to be considered in this regard are discussed below. This objective of financial management is quite acceptable as it is realistic and recognises the importance of the stakeholders. It is but natural that as the shareholders supply the capital and in fact they are the owners of the firm, their interests should get priority and get protected. However, some questions arise regarding the measurement of wealth of shareholders. The first one is concerned with the measurement of wealth, if the shares of the firm are not quoted on a stock exchange, how does one measure the wealth of the shareholders? In such cases the earning per share as well as the intrinsic value of the share should be taken into consideration. If the earnings per share are constantly increasing and the intrinsic value is also constantly higher than the face value, it can be concluded that the wealth of shareholders is growing.

Another consideration is that the share prices are dependent on several factors. Performance of a firm is one of the factors and not the only factor. Market price of a share is influenced by the overall economic and political scenario in the country and by speculative transactions. Hence it is very difficult to decide whether the market price has appreciated due to the good financial performance of a firm or whether due to other factors.

One more consideration that goes against this objective is that shareholders are not the only the stakeholders in a firm. There are also others like creditors, suppliers, employees as well as the members of the general public. At times there might be a conflict of interests between the interests of shareholders and interests of the other stakeholders.

Despite the above limitations, it can be concluded that as compared to the profit maximisation objective, the objective of wealth maximisation can be considered to be superior as it takes into account the present value of the future expected cash flows arising out of an investment decision and hence it is more realistic and objective.

1.5 Functions of a Finance Manager

The functions of a finance manager may be classified into two groups:

(A) Executive Finance Functions and

(B) Incidental Finance Functions.

Executive finance functions require administrative skill in planning, execution and control of financial activities while incidental finance functions do not require any specialised administrative skill and mostly cover routine work that is necessary to carry out the executive decisions.

(A) Executive Finance Functions

Executive finance functions of a manager include all those financial decisions of importance which require specialised administrative skill.

Some of the executive functions are given below:

1. **Financial Forecasting:** The first and foremost function of financial management is to forecast the financial needs of the organisation. This is generally done by the executive chief or by the office in charge of the finance department in a large scale enterprise, with the help of various budgets such as the sales budget, the production budget. Profit and Loss Account and Balance Sheet and other related data is used to do so.

2. **Investment Policy Decisions or Establishing Asset-Management Policies:** In order to estimate and arrange for cash requirements of an enterprise, it is necessary to decide how much cash will be invested in fixed (non-cash) assets and how much in short term or current assets which are normally convertible into cash within a year. This also includes the kind and coverage of insurance that a company may carry.

   The investment decision involving fixed assets is known as *capital budgeting*. The financial decision regarding the current assets is known as *working capital management*.

   The investment policy of fixed and current assets is popularly known as *asset - management policy*. Establishing a sound asset management policy is a pre-requisite to successful financial management. Here the financial manager requires the cooperation of marketing executives and the production manager in making decisions concerning with the carrying of inventories of finished goods and credit policies and of raw materials and factory supplies, purchases.

3. **Dividend Policy Decision or Allocation of Net Profit:** How does one allocate the net profits of the concern, is yet another issue before a financial manager.

   After paying all taxes, the available net profits of the organisation can be allocated for three purposes:

   (a) For paying dividends to the shareholders of the company as a return for their investment.

   (b) For distributing bonus to the employees and company's contribution to other profit sharing plans.

   (c) Retention of profits for the expansion of business.

4. **Cash Flows and Requirements:** It is the prime responsibility of the financial manager to see that an adequate supply of cash is available at the proper time for the smooth running of the business. A good financial executive should ensure that cash inflows and outflows must be continuous and uninterrupted.

   Inflow of cash originates in sales and cash outflows or cash requirements are closely related to volume of sales. Here the financial manager has to decide how much cash he must retain to meet the current obligations so that there would be no idle cash balance earning for the company.

   The financial manager must maintain a balance between inflow and outflow of cash to pay his bills on time. The more he keeps cash in reserve to protect the company against risks associated with his inability to pay bills on time, the more he loses returns on idle cash. It is certainly a dilemma of liquidity vs. profitability.

5. **Deciding upon Borrowing Policy:** Every organisation plans for the expansion of business for which it requires additional resources. Personal resources being limited, cash must be arranged by borrowing money either from commercial banks and other financial institutions or by floating new debentures or by issuing new shares.

   The financial manager will have to decide the financing mix or capital structure or leverage. It means he should take a decision that may carry an ideal proportion of debt and equity capital. The financial manager must choose the proportion he would like to maintain, keeping in mind various relevant points such as cost of different types of capital return expected, the financial risks involved and so on.

6. **Negotiations for New, Outside Financing:** The finance function does not stop with the decision to undertake outside financing, it extends towards negotiations with outside financing agencies, to arrange for it. Finances are needed by an establishment to meet its short term and long term requirements.

   The financial manager must assess short and long term financial requirements of the organisation and start negotiations for raising these funds.

7. **Checking upon Financial Performance:** It is necessary for the financial manager to check the financial performance of the funds invested in the business.

(B) Incidental Finance Functions

Incidental finance functions are clerical or routine in nature and are necessary for the execution of decisions taken by the executives. Some of the important incidental finance functions are:

(a) Supervision of cash receipts and disbursements and safeguarding of cash balance.

(b) Proper custody and safeguarding of the important and valuable papers, securities and insurance policies.

(c) Taking care of all mechanical details of financing.

(d) Record keeping and reporting.

(e) Cash planning and credit management.

The above incidental functions are self explanatory and the chief finance executive is mainly responsible for taking decisions regarding these functions.

Incidental and routine functions are performed by people at lower levels. The involvement of the chief finance executive in incidental functions is limited to:

- set up the rules of procedure to be followed,
- select forms to be used,
- establish standards for carrying out the functions effectively,
- revise the performance, to check whether the instructions are being followed correctly.

1.6 Finance and Other Related Disciplines

Financial Management is an integral part of the overall management of a business organisation. Financial Management is thus influenced heavily by other disciplines like Accounting, Taxation, Economics, Marketing, Manufacturing and materials and so on.

The following paragraphs attempt to explain the relationship between Financial Management and other disciplines.

(I) Financial Management and Accounting

Accounting is a vital discipline and is an important input in financial decision-making. Accounting generates vital information relating to the various activities of a firm. Financial statements like Profit and Loss Account and Balance Sheet are generated through the accounting system.

Financial Management uses this information for analysing and interpretation of the financial statements through techniques like Ratio Analysis, Cash Flow and Funds Flow statements. Various branches of accounting like Cost Accounting and Management Accounting also contribute in the function of financial decision making by generating vital data.

For example, if a firm wants to make a decision regarding sources of raising funds through owned funds or borrowed funds, the required information regarding projections of cash flows can be gathered from the accounting information. Thus, decisions regarding the financial planning, debt equity mix, forecasting, and capital expenditures and so on can be taken with the help of accounting.

Finance and Accounting are connected in this manner.

(II) Financial Management and Economics

Economics is also a very vital discipline and hence is closely related to the financial management of a business organisation.

Economics is divided into two branches, i.e. Macroeconomics and Microeconomics. Macroeconomics takes a broad view and looks to the overall economy rather than individual components of the economy. This branch of economics takes a broad view of the banking system, financial markets including capital and money market, fiscal and monetary policies of the Government.

A study of these factors helps the finance manager to formulate policies and strategies of a firm. Through the study, the finance manager is able to understand the implications of the monetary and fiscal policies of the Government on the costs and profits of the firm. Similarly, it will help him to understand the economic environmental factors, which will affect his decision-making. For example, the rate of inflation in the economy will help in the pricing strategies as well as in planning the debt equity mix. The growth rate of the GDP will help him to prepare financial plans and forecasting through projections.

On the other hand, microeconomics basically is concerned with more minute details of the economy. It studies the economic decisions of individuals and organisations. To put it differently, microeconomics helps business firms to have effective business operations. For example, microeconomics will help a firm to formulate profit maximisation strategies through balancing between the demand and supply. Similarly, it will also help a business firm to understand the optimum mix of the production factors including product and pricing strategies. The concept of marginal costs and marginal revenue can help a finance manager to take various decisions like replacement of an asset, expanding the existing production capacity and so on.

Thus, it is clear from the above discussion that the study of economics is absolutely necessary for a financial manager in a number of ways. The study of economics will help him to study the environment in a better way and also in decision making.

(III) Financial Management and Taxation

Taxation, direct and indirect is another important field, which a finance manager must study. Direct taxes include income tax and wealth tax while indirect taxes include Central Excise Act or tax, Customs Act or tax, Central Sales Tax and VAT. The payment of all these taxes is mandatory and it involves huge amount of cash flows. Therefore, 'Tax Planning' becomes necessary to reduce the impact of these taxes.

A finance manager should know about the due dates of payment of these taxes, which will help him to plan for the cash outflows so that unnecessary penalties and fines can be avoided.

(IV) Financial Management and Marketing

A study of marketing and sales management is also necessary for a finance manager. Though expert knowledge is not required in the field of marketing, a finance manager should know various marketing concepts like marketing research, media planning, product life cycle, channel of distribution and selection, sales forecast and so on. This will help him in budgeting in an effective way.

1.7 Key Strategies of Financial Management

(A) Introduction

The objective of any business firm is to maximise the wealth of its shareholders. For achieving this, it is necessary that the firm is managed effectively and efficiently. Effective and efficient Management implies use of the scarce resources in an efficient manner. For this, it is essential to have effective coordination and control of the various activities of the firm to enable it to achieve its objectives. However, for effective coordination and control, planning is required and anticipating what is likely to happen in the future is important. Financial planning and budgeting facilitate a systematic approach for attaining effective management performance.

Various aspects of financial planning and forecasting are discussed in the following paragraphs. Financial Planning starts at the top of the organisation with strategic planning. Since strategic decisions have financial implications, a firm must start its budgeting process within the strategic planning process. Failure to link and connect budgeting with strategic planning can result in budgets that are "dead on arrival."

Strategic planning is a formal process for establishing goals and objectives over the long run. Strategic planning involves developing a mission statement that captures why the organisation exists and plans how the organisation will thrive in the future.

Strategic objectives and corresponding goals are developed based on a very thorough assessment of the organisation and the external environment. Finally, strategic plans are implemented by developing an Operating or Action Plan.

(B) Financial Planning – Meaning and Importance

Financial planning is a part of a larger planning system in the business firm. Actually the planning process begins with the determination of the goals or objectives of a firm. In order to achieve the goal, various strategies are formed and for implementing the strategies, various policies and plans are formulated. Financial planning is one of them, i.e. it is a part and parcel of a larger planning system.

Financial planning indicates a firm's growth, performance, investments and requirements of funds during a given period of time, normally three to five years. It involves the preparation of:

- Projected or pro-forma Profit and Loss Account
- Balance Sheet
- Funds Flow Statements
- Cash Flow Statements

While it is relatively easy to prepare the statements mentioned above on the basis of history of the organisation, preparing them on a projected basis really requires a lot of skill and judgment besides thorough knowledge of the environment of the business firm. A long-range financial plan represents blue print of what a firm proposes to do in the future.

A number of questions like, how many assets a firm would hold in the next three to five years? How much would be the requirement of funds? From which sources should the funds be raised? What will the profit/loss position in the future be? How much growth will be there in sales in the future? can be answered with the help of financial planning.

It should be remembered that whenever a financial plan is prepared for a long-term duration, it is to be based on certain assumptions.

Normally a financial plan covers the following aspects.

- **Economic Environment:** Economic environment of a business firm is extremely important for preparing a financial plan. A financial planner has to make his planning on certain assumptions regarding the economic environment.

For example, assumptions need to be made regarding the inflation rate in the future, rate of interest, growth rate of the GDP, monetary and fiscal policies of the Government, exchange rate, deficit financing of the Government, growth of the economy and so on. A projection of these factors for at least the next 5 years is required for preparation of the financial plan.

- **Sales Forecasting:** For most of the major financial decisions, sales forecast is the starting point and hence it is important to prepare a sales forecast.
- **Projected Statements:** The most important aspect of financial planning is the Projected Profit and Loss Account and Balance Sheet.
- **Projection of Assets:** A part of financial planning is the projection regarding the requirement of assets. It is necessary for the firms to know the requirement of working capital and that of the fixed assets through capital expenditures.
- **Pattern of Financing:** A firm has to plan the pattern of financing to be adopted for its requirements. It is essential to have a proper mix of debt and equity. The financial plan shows the proposed pattern of financing through various sources.
- **Cash Budget:** A cash budget is the projection of cash receipts and payments over a particular period of time and the expected balance of cash at the end of the budget period.

(C) Elements of Financial Planning

Various elements of the financial plan have been mentioned briefly in the above paragraphs. A detailed description of these elements is given in the following paragraphs.

[I] Sales Forecast

The forecast of sales is typically the starting point of preparation of the financial plan. The reason behind this is, the several variables are dependent on sales and hence it becomes necessary to prepare a sales forecast.

The sales forecast is normally prepared by the marketing department of a firm though the finance manager is also a party to it. The sales forecast can be prepared for short, medium or long term depending on the requirements. Sales forecast is also prepared product wise.

It is absolutely essential to prepare the sales forecast as accurately as possible because the accuracy of the financial plan will depend on the accuracy of the sales forecast.

For preparing the sales forecast, there are several methods. These methods are as follows:

   (i)   Analysis of past sales
   (ii) Dependent factor method
   (iii) Market research method
   (iv) Estimates given by the sales force

(v) Method based on expert's judgement
(vi) Test Marketing results
(vii) Time Series Projection methods
(viii) Quantitative methods.

[II] Projected Profit and Loss Account

The projected Profit and Loss Account shows the projected profits or losses, for the time horizon which may vary from 1 year to 5 years. Projected Profit and Loss Account can be prepared by any of the following methods.

(a) Percentage of Sales Method: This method is based on the assumption that the percentage of various expenses to sales will remain the same in the future as it was in the past. Estimated sales for the future are worked out and various items of expenses are worked out on the basis of percentage of sales.

(b) Budgeted Expenses Method: The method based on percentage of sales, is sometimes too rigid as it links all items of expenses to sales. In fact there might be certain items, which may not have a direct relationship with sales. Therefore, the budgeted expenses method is an improvement over the first one.

The budgeted expenses method prescribe estimate of all items of expenses on the basis of expected developments in the future for which the projected Profit and Loss Account is prepared. It is expected that the Management takes proper care in estimating various items of expenses and takes more effort in doing so. This method seems to be more logical as compared to the first method.

(c) Combination Method: This method is a combination of both the above mentioned methods. Items of expenses, which have a direct relationship with sales are estimated on the basis of the percentage of sales.

For example, cost of goods sold, selling expenses and expenses like commission to salesmen may be linked to sales and can be estimated on the basis of percentage to sales. On the other hand, other items may be projected individually by projecting future developments.

Thus, the merits of both the methods can be combined in this method and hence it is more practical.

[III] Projected Balance Sheet

For the preparation of the Projected Balance Sheet, various items of assets and liabilities are to be estimated. Assets can be broadly divided into:

- Fixed assets, which are not for resale.
- Current assets, which are expected to be converted into cash or other current assets within a period of one year.
- Investments, which are made in the securities of other companies.

Fixed assets can be projected on the basis of planned capital expenditure in the future years. Plans of diversification and expansion should also be taken into consideration. If the firm is not embarking on any program of expansion or diversification, the figures of fixed assets will not change much as compared to the past.

As regards to the current assets, they can be linked with the sales. On the basis of percentage to sales method, items of expenditures can be estimated and on this basis current assets can be estimated.

Current liabilities can also be projected on the basis of percentage to sales method. Investments can be projected by using the specific information applicable to them.

Reserves and surplus can be projected by adding the projected earnings from the projected profit and loss account to the reserves and surplus figure of the previous period. As regards, to the equity, preference shares and loan funds, they can be projected either on the basis of the previous values or on the basis of the projected requirements in the future.

[IV] Cash Budget

One of the integral parts of the financial plan is preparation of the Cash Budget. A cash budget is actually the projections of cash receipts and cash payments and will show the expected cash balance at the end of the period.

A cash budget is an estimate of cash receipts and cash payments prepared for each month. In this budget all expected payments, receipts, revenue and capital are taken into consideration.

The main purpose of a cash budget is to predict the receipts and payments in cash so that the firm will be able to find out the cash balance at the end of the budget period. This will help the firm to know whether there will be surplus cash or deficit at the end of the budget period. It will help them to plan for either investing the surplus or raise necessary amount to finance the deficit.

Cash Budget is prepared in various ways, but the most popular form of the same is by the method of Receipt and Payment method. This method is illustrated in the following illustration.

Illustration: [Cash Budget]

ABC Co. wishes to arrange overdraft facilities with its bankers during the period April 2012 to June 2012 when it will be manufacturing mostly for the stock. Prepare a Cash Budget for the above period from the following data, indicating the extent of the bank facilities the company will require at the end of each month.

Particulars	Sales (₹)	Purchases (₹)	Wages (₹)
February 2012	1, 80,000	1, 24,800	12, 000
March	1, 92,000	1, 44,000	14, 000
April	1, 08,000	2, 43,000	11, 000
May	1, 74,000	2, 46,000	10, 000
June	1, 26,000	2, 68,000	15, 000

Additional Information:

1. 50% of the credit sales are realized in the month following the sales and remaining 50% in the second month. Creditors are paid in the month following the month of purchases. There are no cash sales or cash purchases. Cash at bank [overdraft] estimated on 1st April 2012 is ₹ 25,000.

Solution:

Working Notes:

Collection from debtors:
- April:
- 50% of sales of February ₹ 90, 000} Total ₹ 1, 86,000
- 50% of sales of March ₹ 96, 000}
- Total for April ₹ 186000
- May
- 50% of sales of March ₹ 96, 000} Total ₹ 1, 50,000
- 50% of sales of April   ₹ 54, 000}
- Total for May ₹ 1,50,000
- June
- 50% of sales of April ₹ 54, 000} Total ₹ 1, 41,000
- 50% of sales of May ₹ 87, 000}
- Total for June ₹ 1,41,000

Cash Budget April – June 2012

Particulars	April ₹	May ₹	June ₹
[A] Opening Balance [Overdraft]	25, 000	56, 000	[47, 000]
[B] Expected Receipts Collections from debtors	1, 86,000	1, 50,000	1, 41,000
[C] Total Cash Available [A + B]	2, 11,000	2, 06,000	94,000
[D] Expected Payments			
(i) Payment to creditors	1, 44,000	2, 43,000	2, 46,000
(ii) Wages	11,000	10,000	15,000
[E] Total Payments	1, 55,000	2, 53,000	2, 61,000
[F] Closing Balance [C – E]	56,000	[47,000]	[1, 67,000]

(D) Strategic Financial Planning

A finance manager of a firm has to perform important functions of generation of funds or raising of funds and allocation of the funds, or investing the funds. The objective of a firm is to maximise the wealth of the shareholders as they are the owners of the firm and hence their interests should be protected. It is therefore necessary for the financial manager to take

decisions, which will increase the wealth of shareholders of the firm. In view of this, strategic financial planning will imply that:
- The firm should accept only those investments that generate positive net present value and thus, increase the current value of the firm's share.
- The firm's capital structure should be optimum, which will ensure that the weighted average cost of capital is minimum.
- A balance is struck between the dividend declaration and the profits ploughed back to the reserves.

(E) Financial Forecasting and Modelling

Financial forecasting is an integral part of financial planning. One of the important functions of Management is forecasting. It is easy to analyse, what happened in the past but real skill is required for preparing a forecast for the future.

Forecasting is based on the past trends. A financial planning model establishes relationship between financial variables and targets and facilitates the financial forecasting and planning process. Relationships can be established between sales and other items of incomes and expenditures. Similarly, relationships can be established between the projected capital expenditures and other items.

A financial model also helps in examining the consequences of alternative financial strategies. A financial model has the following three components.
- Firstly the firm's current financial statements and growth prospects are taken into consideration. The growth prospects of a firm depend on several factors like:
  - Market conditions.
  - The strength of products of the firm.
  - The stage of life cycle in which the product currently is.
  - Existing market share of the firm.
  - Growth rate of the economy.
- After considering the financial statements and the growth prospects, the next step is to define the relationship between financial variables and develop appropriate equations. For example, a relationship can be established between sales and other items like working capital and fixed assets.

  Similarly a pay-out ratio for dividend can be established on the basis of the profit available for distribution. For example, it may be decided that 40% of the divisible profits is to be distributed as dividends. On that basis forecast of dividend can be prepared.
- The third stage in financial modeling is preparing projected financial statements. In other words, this is the output of the financial model. The output shows the investments and funds requirement given and the sales growth objectives and relationship between financial variables.

1.8 Risk and Return

Introduction

Financial Management provides answers to three important questions. These questions are what is the amount of funds required for the business? How the funds will be raised? How the funds will be invested? In taking appropriate decisions in relation to these questions, a finance professional has to take into consideration two important aspects i.e. risk and return. A manager has to find out how much risk he is taking and how much return he is expecting from a particular decision. In raising funds from various sources, risk and return has to take into consideration while even in investing funds, risk and return are involved.

Decisions which will balance risk and return will create value for the shareholders of a firm. Therefore the concepts of risk and return have assumed significant importance in the modern finance theory. In fact it can be said that they are the pillars of the modern finance theory. A detailed study of these concepts has thus become of paramount importance for any finance professional. The aim of this chapter is to discuss various aspects of risk and return and also discuss various theories associated with these concepts.

Concept of Return

The important question is what is return? How it is measured? Let us try to find out answers to these questions. Suppose, an investor has purchased 10 equity shares of a company at a price of ₹ 1000 each. This means that the investment made by him is ₹ 10000. If the company declares a dividend of 10%, the investor will earn ₹ 100 per share, which means he will get total ₹ 1000 as dividend. The rate of return will be therefore ₹ 1000/Rs.10000 X 100 = 10%. It should be remembered that the dividend is always paid on the par value i.e. face value. In this example, ₹ 1000 is the face value and hence the return received by him is 10%. However if suppose the shares are listed on the stock exchange and the market value of each share is ₹ 1050, the total market value of the investments will be ₹ 1050 X ₹ 10 = ₹ 10500 and the rate of return will be ₹ 1000/Rs.10500 X 100 = 9.52%. This means that the rate of return has fallen due to rise in the market price. On the other hand, if the market price of shares falls, the rate of return will increase. The amount of dividend is always paid on the face value and hence the return fluctuates as per the market price. Now suppose, the investor sells these shares after one year for ₹ 15000, he will gain ₹ 5000 which is the difference between the purchase price and the selling price. This gain is called as capital gain. Thus the investor will get dividend as well as capital gain. Hence his total income will be dividend of ₹ 1000 + ₹ 5000 = ₹ 6000. If this gain is computed in percentage, the gain will be ₹ 6000/10000 = 60%. However if the market price goes down as compared to the face value, there will be a loss which means the return from capital gain will be negative.

Risk

Risk is present everywhere. Risk is there in everyday life. When a finance manager selects an investment avenue or a marketing manager finalises an advertising campaign or a production manager selects a plant and machinery, there is always an uncertainty about the expected cash flows resulting from these activities. When a common man selects a particular avenue for investing his funds, there is a risk involved in it as the return can vary. If a person invests in equity shares, he takes a risk of uncertain dividend and also capital gain. On the other hand, if he decides not to take risk at all, he will have to be satisfied with a comparatively lesser rate of return. For example, if he decides that he will invest only in nationalized bank fixed deposits or post office deposits, there will not be any risk but at the same time the returns will be quite less as compared to other avenues like investment in shares and so on.

Risk is divided into diversifiable and non diversifiable risk. Risk can be reduced by diversifying the portfolio in more than one type of securities. For example, rather than investing in only one company's shares, an investor can choose more than one companies from various sectors and thus reduce the risk considerably. Thus instead of investing into only one company, diversification will reduce the risk. This will ensure that if there is a loss from one sector, there will be profit from other sectors and thus overall risk can be reduced. There cannot be losses from all the sectors at one time. However it should be remembered that even though diversification will reduce the risk, it will not eliminate the risk. After a certain limit, the diversification will not reduce the risk. This is due to the reason that certain types of risks are non diversifiable. For example, even if an investor spreads his investments in several companies, if the economy of the country is not doing well, all sectors will suffer and hence this risk always remains. Thus it should be remembered that risk can be reduced but cannot be eliminated.

Measurement of Risk

The risks arising out of investments in financial assets are measured in terms of the riskiness of the cash flows. Thus variability of cash flows is the major criteria for measuring the risk arising from a financial asset. The risk measurement and its relation to the return is done in the following manner.

Risk and Return of a Single Asset

If an Investor invests in equity shares of a company, he will get certain returns. These returns may fluctuate from year to year. The risk is measured after taking into consideration these variations. This means that risk is measured by measuring the deviations in the returns from the average rate of return. In other words, standard deviation or variance are used as measures for such dispersion. Standard deviation is the square root of the variance. The calculation of standard deviation is illustrated in the following example.

Illustration:

Mr. A has invested ₹ 10000 in the equity shares of company X. His rate of return during the last five years were respectively, .10, .15,.05, .12 and .07. The standard deviation and variance will be calculated as follows.

Sr. No.	Rate of return	Deviation from average	Square of the deviations
1	0.10	0.002	0.000004
2	0.15	0.052	0.002704
3	0.05	– 0.048	0.002304
4	0.12	0.022	0.000484
5	0.07	– 0.028	0.000784
Average	49/5 = 0.098		0.00628

The standard deviation will be = $\sqrt{0.00628}$
= 0.00792

The variance will be 0.00628.

The standard deviation of this security will be compared with the standard deviation of returns from another security to find out the comparative risk of the two securities.

The standard deviation can be calculated from the historical data as well as from the expected returns, i.e. from the forecast of the returns in the future period.

1.9 Capital Asset Pricing Model

The capital asset pricing model [CAPM] is a model that provides a framework to determine the required rate of return on an asset and indicates the relationship between the return and risk of the asset. [Sharpe]This model indicates the relationship between risk and the expected rate of return on a risky security. According to this model, risk and return are related in a linear function and is indicated by the following equation.

$$E(R_j) = R_j + \beta_j [E(R_m) - R_f]$$

Where,
- $E(R_j)$ = Expected return on security j
- R_f = Risk free return
- β_j = Beta of security j
- $E(R_m)$ = Expected return on the market portfolio

The assumptions of this model are as follows:
1. Individuals are not keen on taking risk, i.e. they are risk averse.
2. Individual investors want to maximise their expected return on their portfolio over a single period planning horizon.
3. Expectations of the investors are similar to each other as regards to the risk, variations and returns.
4. The capital market is efficient which means that the share price reflect all available information. As happens in perfect competition, individual investors are not able to influence the share prices.
5. The interest rate is risk free which means that all investors can either borrow or lend at an interest rate which is risk free.

Points to Remember

- Management is an activity which is concerned with planning and controlling of different activities, in order to achieve a specific objective.
- The term 'financial management' can be defined as the management of flow of funds and it deals with financial decision-making.
- The traditional concept of financial management was mainly concerned with raising of funds for various requirements like diversification, expansion etc. with a focus on long-term funds.

- Financial management is concerned with the following activities:
  - Raising of funds
  - Investing of funds
  - Dividend decisions
- Goals of Financial Management are maximisation of profits and wealth.
- Functions of a finance manager can be classified as executive finance functions and incidental finance functions.
- Financial Management is thus influenced heavily by other disciplines like Accounting, Taxation, Economics, Marketing, Manufacturing and materials and so on.
- Effective and efficient Management implies use of the scarce resources in an efficient manner.
- Strategic planning is a formal process for establishing goals and objectives over the long run.

Questions for Discussion

1. What is Financial Management? Explain its Goals.
2. Explain the functions of Finance Manager.
3. Explain the Relationship between Financial Management and Other Disciplines.
4. What is Financial Planning? Explain its Importance.
5. Describe the various Elements of Financial Planning.
6. Write short notes on:
   (a) Financial Forecasting
   (b) Modern Concept of Financial Management.

Questions from Previous Pune University Examinations

1. Describe the Scope and Importance of the Finance Function in the Management of a Corporation. **[M.B.A. April 2006]**
2. Explain the Role of Finance Executive. **[M.B.A. Dec. 2007]**
3. Describe the Scope and Importance of the Financial Management. **[M.B.A. April 2006]**
4. Discuss in detail the Functions and Duties of Finance. **[M.B.A. Dec. 2009]**
5. Primary goal of financial management is said to be maximisation of shareholder's wealth. Whether this objectives is realistic in a world where corporate ownership and control are often separate. Discuss. **[M.B.A. Dec. 2011]**

■■■

Chapter 2...
Techniques of Financial Analysis

Contents ...
2.1 Introduction
2.2 Meaning, Nature, Objectives and Limitations of Financial Analysis
2.3 Ratio Analysis
2.4 Fund Flow Analysis
2.5 Cash Flow Statement
- Solved Problems
- Points to Remember
- Questions for Discussion
- Case Study
- Suggested Activity
- Questions from Previous Pune University Examinations

Learning Objectives ...
After studying this topic, you should be able to,
1. Know the meaning, goals and limitations of financial statements
2. Understand the need for financial analysis
3. Learn the tools and techniques used for financial analysis
4. Learn the meaning, types, formulae and interpretation of 'Ratio Analysis', a tool used for financial analysis
5. Get acquainted with the preparation and interpretation of Funds Flow Statements
6. Understand the method of preparation of Cash Flow Statements

2.1 Introduction

The primary uses of financial statements are evaluating past performance and predicting future performance, both of which are facilitated by comparisons. Therefore, the focus of financial analysis is always on the crucial information contained in the financial statements and depends on the objectives and purpose of such an analysis.

2.2 Meaning, Nature, Objectives and Limitations of Financial Analysis

The purpose of evaluating such financial statements is different for different people and depends on its need for that person. In other words, even though the business unit itself, its shareholders, debenture holders, investors and so on all undertake financial analysis, the purpose, means and the extent of such an analysis differs. For example:

(i) Trade creditors may be interested primarily in the liquidity of a firm because the ability of the business unit to pay their claims is best judged by means of a thorough analysis of its liquidity.

(ii) The shareholders and the potential investors may be interested in the present and future earnings per share, the stability of such earnings and comparison of these earnings with other units in the industry.

(iii) The debenture holders and financial institutions lending long-term loans may be concerned with the cash flow ability of the business unit to pay back the debts in the long-run.

The management of the business unit looks to the financial statements from various angles. These statements are required for

- the management's own evaluation and decision-making
- internal control
- overall performance of the firm

Thus, the scope, extent and means of any financial analysis will vary as per the specific needs of the analyst. Financial statement analysis is a part of the large information processing system, which forms the very basis of any 'decision–making'.

Advantages of 'Analysis of Financial Statements'

(i) **Knowing the Exact Position:** Everybody who is interested in knowing the exact financial position of the organisation is benefited by this 'analysis'. An interested party gets the information about the exact facts and figures of the organisation by analysing the financial statements by various methods theoretical, statistical and so on. For example, interested parties like debtors, creditors, outsiders, shareholders etc.

(ii) **Decision-making:** Every interested party is in a position to assess the exact financial condition of the organisation when it analyses financial statements of that organisation, by reliable methods. Thus, such an analysis ultimately helps that party in taking various types of decisions such as investment, sale, purchase etc.

(iii) **Forecasting:** After analysing the financial statements, one is in a position to forecast whether it would be profitable or not to invest in or to deal with the organisation.

Various tools and techniques are used for the interpretation of financial statements. One of the important techniques used for this purpose is 'Ratio Analysis'. Various aspects of these techniques are discussed in this chapter.

2.3 Ratio Analysis

(A) Meaning and Importance

Ratio can be defined as numerical or an arithmetical relationship between two figures. It is expressed when one figure is divided by the other.

For example, if 4000 is divided by 10, 000, the ratio can be expressed as 0.4 or 2:5 or 40%.

Absolute figures are no doubt, valuable but standing alone, they do not convey any meaning unless they are compared with each other. Accounting ratios show an inter-relationship that exists among various figures shown in the financial statements.

The importance of ratio analysis can be highlighted in the following manner:

(i) Accounting ratios reveal the financial position of a business firm. This helps banks, insurance companies as well as other financial institutions in assessing a firm before sanctioning any loan to them. Similarly, the ratios are also helpful to investors for finding the profitability of a firm.

(ii) The ratios are very useful in inter-firm and intra-firm comparisons. Inter-firm comparison is necessary to find out the exact position of a firm as compared to other firms in the same industry. Intra-firm comparison is also necessary to compare the performance of a firm of current year with that of previous years.

(iii) If accounting ratios are calculated for a number of years, a trend can be established. This trend helps in setting future plans and forecasting, for e.g. Net Profit as expressed as a percentage of sales can be forecasted on the basis of the past percentage of the same.

(iv) Accounting ratios are of great assistance in locating the weak spots in the business. This weakness may exist in a business in spite of a satisfactory performance otherwise. For example, if a firm finds that increase in selling and distribution expenses is more than proportionate to the results expected or achieved, remedial steps can be taken to overcome this situation.

(B) Classification and Calculation

For the sake of facilitation of calculations and interpretation, ratios may be classified according to different basis. One of the ways of classification is according to the financial statements. In this method, ratios are calculated on the following basis.

(i) Trading A/c ratios
(ii) Profit and Loss A/c ratios
(iii) Balance sheet ratios.

However, the classification according to the following basis will be more effective for analysing and interpreting the financial statements.

(i) Profitability Ratios
(ii) Turnover Ratios
(iii) Financial Ratios
(iv) Leverage Ratios

These ratios are explained in detail as follows:

(I) Profitability Ratios

These ratios give an idea about the profitability of a business firm. Profit and profitability differ from each other as profit is the difference between income and expenditure while profitability is measured by comparing the profit with some other parameter like sales, capital employed, total assets etc. The ratios falling under this category are usually expressed in percentage. The following are the ratios under this category:

(i) Gross Profit Ratio: Gross profit is the difference between the net sales [sales less sales returns] and the cost of goods sold. This ratio is calculated with the help of the following formula:

Gross Profit Ratio: Gross Profit / Net Sales × 100

For example, if the net sales are ₹ 50,0,000 and the gross profit is ₹ 5,00,000, the gross profit ratio will be,

₹ 5,00,000 / ₹ 50,00,000 × 100 = 10%

This ratio shows the margin left after meeting the purchases and manufacturing costs. It measures the efficiency of production as well as pricing. A high gross profit ratio means a high margin for covering other expenses like administrative, selling and distribution expenses, i.e. other than the cost of goods sold. Therefore, higher the ratio, the better it is. A high gross profit ratio is a sign of good management. It is also important for a business to maintain this ratio on a higher side; otherwise it will be difficult to cover other expenses. A gross profit ratio may increase due to any of the factors such as higher sales price while cost of goods remains the same or variations in sales price and cost of goods sold or an increase in the proportionate volume of higher margin items. The analysis of these factors will reveal to the management how a depressed gross profit margin can be improved. A firm should compare its gross profit ratio with the industry average to find out where it stands. A firm can also compare its own ratio of the past with the current year's ratio to find out its performance. This is known as intra-firm comparison.

(ii) Net Profit Ratio: This ratio shows the earnings left for shareholders [equity and preference] as a percentage of net sales. It measures overall efficiency of all the functions of a business firm like production, administration, selling, financing, pricing, tax management etc. This ratio is very useful for prospective investors because it reveals the overall profitability of the firm. Higher the ratio, the better it is because it gives an idea of overall efficiency of the firm. This ratio is calculated as follows:

Net Profit Ratio = Net Profit after Income Tax / Net Sales × 100

For example,

Net profit after income tax: ₹ 6,00,000
Net sales: ₹ 60,00,000
Net profit ratio will be: ₹ 6,00,000 / ₹ 60,00,000 × 100 = 10%

Net profit ratio shows the relationship between net profits and sales and shows the efficiency of management in performing various functions such as manufacturing, selling, and administration.

A firm with a consistently higher net profit ratio will become financially sound in the course of time and thus will be in a better position to face any adverse situation arising in the future. On the other hand, a firm with a consistently lower net profit ratio will remain financially weak and thus will find it difficult to survive in adverse conditions.

Similar to the gross profit ratio, for the interpretation of the net profit ratio, an inter firm and intra firm comparison will be required.

(iii) Operating Net Profit Ratio: This ratio establishes the relationship between the net sales and the operating net profit. The concept of operating net profit is different from the concept of net profit. Operating net profit is the profit arising out of business operations only. This is calculated as follows:

Operating net profit = Net profit + Non-operating expenses − non-operating income. Alternatively, this profit can also be calculated by deducting only operating expenses from gross profit. This ratio is calculated with the help of the following formula.

Operating Net Profit Ratio = Operating Net Profit / Sales × 100

Example: Calculation of operating net profit is shown in the following example.

Dr. Profit and Loss A/c for the year ended 31/3/2013 Cr.

Particulars	Amount ₹	Particulars	Amount ₹
To Administrative, Selling and Distribution Expenses	6,50,000	By Gross Profit	15,00,000
To loss of sale of fixed assets	2,50,000	By Profit on Sale of Shares	2,00,000
To equity dividend			
To provision for taxation	4,00,000		
To Net Profit	1,00,000		
	3,00,000		
Total	17,00,000	Total	17,00,000

The working of operating net profit is shown below.

Particulars	Amount ₹
Net Profit	3,00,000
Add: Loss On Sale of Fixed Assets	2,50,000
Add: Equity Dividend	4,00,000
Add: Taxation Provision	1,00,000
	10,50,000
	2,00,000
Less: Profit on Sale of Shares Operating Net Profit	**8,50,000**

Operating Net Profit Ratio = ₹ 8,50,000/₹ 15,00,000 × 100 = 20%.

(iv) Operating Ratio: This ratio is reciprocal to the operating net profit to sales to ratio. The cost of goods sold + operating expenses are compared to net sales. Non- operating expenses and non-operating incomes are excluded from this ratio. The calculation of this ratio is as follows.

Operating Ratio = Cost of goods sold + Operating expenses / Net sales × 100

Example: In the example given above, suppose the sales are ₹ 42,50,000 and the gross profit is ₹ 15,00,000. Therefore, the cost of goods sold is ₹ 27,50,000. Operating expenses are ₹ 6,50,000 [Administration, selling and distribution].

The operating ratio is calculated as follows:

Operating Ratio = ₹ 27,50,000 + ₹ 6,50,000 / ₹ 42,50,000 × 100 = 80%

Thus, higher this ratio, the lower is the margin of operating profit. This ratio can be further analysed to find out the percentage of each type of expenses to sales.

(v) Return On Capital Employed: This ratio indicates the percentage of net profits before interest and tax to total capital employed. The capital employed is calculated as follows.

Capital employed = Equity Capital + Preference Capital + Reserves and Surplus + Long Term Debt – Fictitious Assets

This ratio is calculated as follows,

Return on Capital Employed = Net Profit Before Interest And Tax / Capital Employed × 100

This ratio is considered to be a very important one because it reflects the overall efficiency with which capital is used. The ratio of a particular business should be compared with other business firms in the same industry to find out the exact position of the business. An intra firm comparison may also be conducted by comparing ratios of a firm at least of the previous 3 to 5 years.

(vi) Return On Equity: This ratio, also known as return on shareholders' funds or return on proprietor's funds or return on net worth, indicates the percentage of net profit available for equity shareholders to equity shareholders' funds. In other words, this ratio measures the return only on equity shareholders' funds and not on total capital employed like ratio number (v). The formula for calculation is as follows:

Return on equity = Net profit after interest, income tax and preference dividend if any / Equity shareholders' funds × 100

Note: Equity shareholders' funds = Equity capital + Reserves and surplus

This ratio indicates the productivity of the owned funds employed in the firm. However, in judging the profitability of a firm, it should not be overlooked that during inflationary periods, the ratio may show an upward trend because the numerator of the ratio represents current values whereas the denominator represents historical values.

Note: Depreciation policy of a firm may change over the years. Similarly firms in the same industry may follow different depreciation policies. Both these things will create distortion in the intrafirm and interfirm comparison. Hence the formula can be modified as EBITDA/Equity Shareholders' funds X 100 where EBITDA means earnings before interest, income tax and depreciation and amortisation. Of course, if there is preference share capital in the capital structure, the preference dividend will also be deducted as shown in the original formula.

(vii) Return on Total Assets: This ratio compares the net profit after tax with the total assets. The formula for calculation of this ratio is as follows:

Return on Total Assets = Net Profit After Tax / Total Assets × 100

This ratio shows the return achieved by a firm on the total investments made in the assets. Investments in fixed assets are made in order to improve the earning capacity in the long run while investment in current assets is required for the working capital purpose. It is necessary for a firm to find out whether the investments made in these assets are profitable or not. Hence this ratio becomes very important for any firm. The interpretation of this ratio should be made after comparing this ratio of similar firms and also ascertaining the trend of the firm's ratios shown in the past.

(viii) Earnings per Share: This is one of the important indicators of performance of a company. Earnings per share indicate the amount of profit available for distribution amongst the equity shareholders. This ratio is calculated as shown below:

Earnings Per Share: Net Profit After Interest, Income tax and Preference Dividend / Number of Equity Share

As mentioned above, EPS is one of the important criteria for measuring the performance of a company. If EPS increases, the possibility of a higher dividend per share also increases. However, the dividend payment depends on the policy of the company. Market price of shares of a company may also show an upward trend if the EPS is showing a rising trend. However, it should be remembered that EPS of different companies may vary from company to company due to the following different practices by different companies regarding stock in trade, depreciation, source of raising finance, tax-planning measures etc.

The EPS of a company should be compared with the industry average and also with other firms in the same industry. Similarly there should be intra firm comparison also. It should be remembered that the EPS shows the amount of profit available for distribution as dividend and not the actual dividend paid.

(ix) Price Earnings Ratio: This ratio is calculated with the help of the following formula:

Price Earnings Ratio = Market Price Per Equity Share / EPS

For example, if the share price of a company is ₹ 240 and EPS is ₹ 40, the P/E ratio will be ₹ 240 / ₹ 40 = 6 times. It indicates that the market value of every rupee of earnings is four times.

(x) Dividend Payout Ratio: EPS described above indicates the amount of profit available for equity shareholders. Dividend Payout Ratio indicates the percentage of profit distributed as dividends to the shareholders. A higher ratio indicates that the organisation is following a liberal policy regarding the dividend while a lower ratio indicates a conservative approach of the management towards the dividend. The ratio is calculated as shown below:

Dividend Payout Ratio = Dividend Per Share / EPS × 100

(xi) Dividend Yield Ratio: This ratio compares the dividend per share with the market price of the share. The formula for calculation is as follows:

Dividend Yield Ratio = Dividend Per Share / Market Price Per Share × 100

This ratio is very important for investors who purchase their shares in the open market. They will evaluate their return against their investment, i.e. the market price paid by them. The higher the ratio, the more attractive are their investments.

(xii) Market value to book value [MV/BV] Ratio: This is the ratio of share price to book value per share. The formula is as follows:

MV/BV Ratio = Market value per share / Book value per share

The book value of share is the net worth divided by the number of shares outstanding. Suppose if the market value per share is ₹ 95 and book value per share is ₹ 100, the ratio will be 0.95. This means that the company is worth 5% less than the amount invested by shareholders.

[II] Turnover Ratios

These ratios are also known as activity ratios or asset management ratios. These ratios are very important for a business organisation to find out how well the facilities at the disposal of the organisation are being used. These ratios are usually calculated on the basis of sales or cost of goods sold. High turnover ratios indicate better utilisation of resources. The important turnover ratios are discussed below.

(i) Working Capital Turnover Ratio: This ratio compares the net sales with net working capital of the business firm. The indication given by this ratio is the number of times working capital is turned around in a particular period. The ratio is calculated with the help of the following formula:

Working Capital Turnover Ratio = Net Sales / Net Working Capital *

* Net Working Capital = Current Assets – Current Liabilities.

The higher this ratio, the better is the utilisation of the working capital and also indication of lower working capital. However, a very high working capital turnover ratio is a sign of over trading and a firm may face shortage of working capital. A firm should compare this ratio with the ratio of other firms in the same industry and also with the industry average to find out its position as compared to other firms. Similarly, an intra-firm comparison will also help to find out the comparative performance of the firm.

(ii) Debtors Turnover Ratio: One of the important decisions regarding financial management is about the credit to be granted to the customers. There should be a well-defined credit policy, which should be followed carefully by a firm. The credit policy followed by a firm is indicated by this ratio. This ratio is calculated with the help of the following formula:

Debtors Turnover Ratio = Credit Sales / Average Accounts Receivables.*

* Average Accounts Receivables = Opening Balance of Debtors + Closing Balance of Debtors / 2 and Opening Balance of Bills Receivables + Closing Balance of Bills Receivables / 2

For example:　　　　　Credit Sales　　　　　=　₹ 12,00,000
　　　　　　Average Accounts Receivables　　=　₹ 3,00,000
　　　　　　　Debtors Turnover Ratio　　　=　₹ 12,00,000 / ₹ 3,00,000 = 4 times

As per the above calculations, this ratio is 4 times, which indicates that debtors have made payment 4 times during that period. From this, the average collection period can be calculated, which will be 12 months / 4 times = 3 months. This indicates that on an average, the collection period from debtors is 3 months.

The higher this ratio, lower is the collection period. On the other hand, a lower ratio indicates higher collection period. The average collection period as shown by this ratio should be compared with the credit period planned by the firm. If it is more than the credit period planned by the firm, it should be analysed carefully. It may mean efficient credit management or excessive conservatism in credit granting, which may result in some loss of sales. On the other hand, if the average collection period as indicated by this ratio is less than the credit planned by the firm, it indicates that the credit policy by the firm is not that efficient and hence, the firm may face liquidity crunch and therefore it needs to be tightened.

(iii) Creditors Turnover Ratio: Debtors turnover ratio as described above indicates the credit period allowed by the firm to its customers. Creditors Turnover Ratio indicates the credit period allowed by the creditors to the firm. In other words, it is exactly opposite the above ratio. The formula for calculation is as follows:

Creditors Turnover Ratio: Credit Purchases / Average Accounts Payable *

* Average Accounts Payable: Opening Balance of Creditors + Closing Balance of Creditors / 2 and Opening Balance of Bills Payable + Closing Balance of Bills Payable / 2

A high turnover ratio indicates that the payment to creditors is quite prompt but it also implies that the firm is not taking full advantage of the credit allowed by the creditors. A lower ratio indicates that there is not much promptness in the payment made to creditors and needs to be improved.

(iv) Inventory / Stock Turnover Ratio: This ratio establishes a relationship between the cost of goods sold during a given period and the average amount of inventory held during that period. The indication given by this ratio is the number of times the finished stock is turned over during a given accounting period. The ratio is calculated in the manner given below:

Inventory / Stock Turnover Ratio = Cost of Goods Sold / Average Inventory during that period *

* Average Inventory = Opening Inventory + Closing Inventory / 2

Higher this ratio, the better it is because it shows rapid turnover of stock and consequently shorter holding period. On the other hand, if this ratio is lower, it will indicate that stock is slow moving and there is a longer holding period.

(v) Fixed Assets Turnover Ratio: This ratio indicates the amount of sales realised per rupee of investment in fixed assets. Fixed assets are those assets, which are not acquired for re-sale. In other words, they are meant for utilisation in the business for the purpose of improving its earning capacity. Whether this purpose is being fulfilled or not is indicated by this ratio. The formula for calculation of this ratio is as follows:

Fixed Assets Turnover Ratio = Net Sales * / Net Fixed Assets **

* Cost of goods sold may be taken in place of sales

** Net Fixed Assets = Cost – Depreciation

This ratio is more important for manufacturing organisations as it indicates the utilisation of fixed assets. As mentioned earlier, fixed assets are acquired basically for improving the earning capacity of the business. However, it is important to find out whether this purpose is fulfilled or not. This ratio is one of the indicators of the same. A high ratio indicates higher amount of sales generated per rupee of investment in fixed assets. A lower ratio indicates lower sales per rupee of fixed assets and hence the investments in fixed assets are not justified.

(vi) Sales to Capital Employed: This ratio is also known as Capital Turnover Ratio and indicates sales per rupee of capital employed. The formula for this ratio is as given below:

Sales to Capital Employed = Net Sales / Capital Employed *

* Capital Employed = Shareholders' Funds + Long Term Liabilities.

Higher the ratio, the better it is, as it will indicate better utilisation of capital employed, which will result in higher amount of turnover. However, a low turnover ratio will indicate lower utilisation of capital employed in making sales.

[III] Financial Ratios

As the name suggests, these ratios are calculated to judge the financial position of a business firm from the long-term as well as the short- term angle. The following ratios are included in this category.

(i) Current Ratio: This ratio is calculated by dividing current assets by current liabilities. Current ratio is also known as 'solvency ratio' as it indicates how the expected current claims are covered by current assets. This ratio is calculated with the help of the following formula:

Current Ratio = Current Assets* / Current Liabilities*

* Current Assets mean assets, which have been purchased in order to convert them into cash or into other current assets within a period of normally one year. These assets include cash and bank balance, short-term investments, bills receivable, debtors, short- term loans, inventories and pre-paid expenses.

** Current Liabilities means liabilities with a short- term duration, which is normally up to one year from date of creation and are paid out of existing current assets or by creating a new current liability. These liabilities include bank overdraft, bills payable, creditors, provision for taxation, outstanding expenses, unclaimed dividends, short-term loans, outstanding interest, advance payment received and portion of a debt expected to mature within a period of one year.

Interpretation: This ratio indicates the coverage of current assets to the current liabilities. In other words, it indicates the proportion of current assets available for meeting the current liabilities. Normally it is expected that the current ratio should be 2:1, which indicates that current assets should be twice as compared to the current liabilities. However, for proper inference, the composition of current assets should not be overlooked. If a majority of current assets are in the form of inventories, which is the least liquid current asset, even a 2:1 ratio will not indicate the favourable position. Similarly, a very high current ratio will not indicate a favourable position as it means that there is an excessive investment in current assets is made. This will result in decrease in profitability due to blocking of large funds in working capital.

(ii) Liquid / Quick / Acid Test Ratio: This ratio is a better tool to measure the ability to honor day-to-day commitments. It is the ratio between the liquid assets and liquid liabilities. From the Balance Sheet, liquid assets are calculated by deducting inventories and prepaid expenses from current assets. Liquid liabilities are current liabilities less bank overdraft. The formula for calculation of this ratio is as follows:

Liquid Ratio = Liquid Current Assets / Liquid Liabilities

The ideal liquid ratio is considered to be 1:1, which means that liquid current assets should be equal to the liquid current liabilities. This ratio indicates whether the firm has the ability to pay its short- term liabilities or not.

(iii) Debt-Equity Ratio: This ratio is calculated to measure the comparative proportion of borrowed funds and shareholders' funds invested in the firm. A firm raises funds through owned funds, which are also called as shareholders' funds or proprietors' funds as well as borrowed funds. The proportion between these two sources should be properly balanced; otherwise the firm may face problems. This ratio indicates this proportion and is calculated as shown below:

Debt-Equity Ratio = Long Term Debt / Shareholders' Funds *

* Shareholders' funds = Share capital + Reserves and Surplus

This ratio can also be computed by taking total debt and dividing the same by shareholders' funds.

Interpretation: Ideally this ratio should be 2:1, which means that debt can be twice as compared to the owned funds. A ratio less than 2:1 will indicate that the firm is not taking any risk and is mainly using shareholders' funds for financing its requirements. However, if this ratio is above 2:1, it will indicate that the firm is using mainly borrowed funds to finance its requirements. This may prove to be more risky in the future and hence a firm should keep a constant watch on this ratio.

(iv) Proprietary Ratio: It is primarily the ratio between the proprietor's funds and total assets. This ratio is calculated with the help of the following formula:

Proprietary Ratio: Proprietor's Funds / Total Assets

Interpretation: This ratio indicates the proportion of proprietor's funds used for financing the total assets. As a very rough measure, it is suggested that 2/3rd to 3/4th of the total assets should be financed through the proprietor's funds while the balance may be financed through borrowings. A high ratio will indicate high financial strength but a very high ratio will indicate that the firm is not using external funds adequately.

(v) Current Assets to Fixed Assets: This ratio shows the proportion of current assets to fixed assets. As described in current ratio, current assets are held for converting them into cash in a short period of time while fixed assets are held for long- term purposes, i.e. to enhance the earning capacity of the firm. This ratio indicates the proportion between the two and is calculated with the help of the following formula:

Current Assets to Fixed Assets = Current Assets / Fixed Assets

[IV] Leverage Ratios

In this category, the following ratio is significant.

Capital Gearing Ratio: The ratio indicates the proportion between fixed charge bearing securities and equity capital. A firm raises finance through owned funds and borrowed funds. Owned funds include equity capital, preference capital and retained earnings while borrowed funds include term loans and debentures. In case of equity capital, it is not compulsory to pay dividend as it depends on the profits position and also on the discretion of the Board of Directors. In case of preference capital, it is mandatory to pay a fixed rate of dividends and in case of cumulative preference shares, if dividend for a particular year is not paid; the arrears are to be paid in the next year. This means that it becomes a fixed obligation on the part of the firm to pay preference dividend. In case of borrowings, it need not be stated that payment of interest is a fixed obligation. Thus, it can be seen that while equity capital and retained earnings do not have any fixed obligations, preference capital and borrowings have a fixed obligation. This ratio indicates the proportion between the two types of securities and is calculated with the help of the following formula:

Capital Gearing Ratio: Fixed Charges Bearing Securities / Equity Shareholders' Funds

Interpretation: A firm will be considered to be highly geared, if the major portion of the total capital is raised through fixed charges bearing securities. On the other hand, it will be called a low geared company if majority of the funds are raised through equity.

(C) Utility of Ratio Analysis

Ratio analysis is a powerful tool of financial analysis. As discussed in the beginning of this chapter, ratio analysis helps a business firm to find out its position regarding liquidity, solvency and profitability. The utility of ratio analysis can be explained as given below.

(i) **Measurement of Performance:** Financial Statements like Profit and Loss Account and Balance Sheet are indicators of the performance of a business firm. However, they do not disclose certain things due to their inherent limitations. Ratio analysis helps in the measurement of performance or in other words performance analysis of a firm. Thus, it is possible to find out the profitability of a firm by comparing the net profit with various parameters like sales, capital employed, total assets and so on. Similarly, the liquidity position can be found out by computing ratios like current ratio and liquid ratio. Solvency can be measured by computing ratio like the debt equity ratio. This analysis of performance is useful for various stakeholders like creditors, shareholders, Government authorities, as well as general public.

(ii) **Trend Analysis:** Another important utility of ratio analysis is that, with the help of this technique, it is possible to establish a trend. Thus, when various ratios are computed for a period of say, 10 years, a trend can be established. For example, Earnings Per Share for the previous 10 years shows a definite trend of either moving up or moving down. In some cases, it may also show a fluctuating trend. Thus, it becomes possible to compare the trend shown by the firm's ratios with the trend shown by the industry. This comparison can be an eye opener as it may reveal some important things. For example, if the trend in the net profit ratio of a firm is declining in the previous 10 years and during the same period the trend shown by the industry ratio is also declining, it can be concluded that the reason behind the declining trend in the firm's ratio is due to the overall declining trend in the industry. Thus, ratio analysis facilitates the trend analysis.

(iii) **Ratio analysis is a very good tool for predicting the Sickness of a Business Unit:** Based on certain key ratios, a multivariate model has been developed by Altman a financial expert, who advocates that rather than depending on a single ratio, if certain combination of key ratios is developed, it will have a power to predict the sickness of the unit. Prevention is always better than cure and hence, if the sickness of a unit can be predicted reasonably accurately, preventive measures can be taken to ensure that the sickness is averted. Since this model is based on more than one key ratio, it is called as a multivariate model. **The model is given below.**

$Z = 1.2$ [Working capital / Total Assets] + 1.4 [Retained earnings / Total Assets] + 3.3 [Earnings before interest and taxes / Total Assets] + .06 [Market value of equity / Book value of debt] + 1.0 [Sales / Total Assets]

Altman found that those firms, which have a Z score of less than 1.81 almost, went bankrupt, firms which had a Z score above 2.99 remained healthy and firms which had a Z score between 1.81 and 2.99 fell in a grey area.

(iv) **With the help of Ratio Analysis, Conclusions can be drawn regarding the Liquidity Position of a Firm.** The liquidity position of a firm would be satisfactory if it is able to meet its obligations when they become due. Liquidity rations like current ratio, quick ratio as well as the debt service coverage ratio help a firm to understand the liquidity position in a better manner.

(v) **Long Term Solvency:** A firm has to constantly examine its long term solvency. Solvency depends upon several things but the most important factor is the combination between the owned funds and the borrowed funds. If the proportion of borrowed funds is too high as compared to the owned funds, there is every possibility that the firm's solvency is in danger. The reason is that it may become difficult to service the debt and if the interest as well as the principal repayment obligations is not met, the firm will be caught in a debt trap. Therefore, the solvency position should be constantly watched. Debt-equity ratio will be extremely useful in this connection.

(vi) **Overall Profitability:** A firm has to verify its overall profitability. Outsiders as well as insiders like the shareholders are interested in the overall profitability of the firm. The performance of the firm depends on its profitability. Ratios like the gross profit ratio, net profit ratio, return on capital employed, return on shareholders' funds, return of total assets are some of the important ratios, that show the overall profitability of the firm. This is one of the important advantages of ratio analysis.

(D) Limitations of Ratio Analysis

Though ratio analysis is a very important and effective technique, there are certain limitations of the same. These limitations are as follows:

(i) One of the serious limitations of ratio analysis is that there are difficulties in the comparison between various firms through ratios. This difficulty is due to the following reasons.

- There may be a difference between inventory valuation methods followed by various firms.
- Firms follow various methods for providing depreciation.
- There may be a difference in the capital structures of firms.

Due to these variations, the financial statements of various firms are not comparable and hence comparison through ratios becomes difficult.

(ii) Another objection to ratio analysis is that ratios show position only on a particular day and not the picture of the entire year. For example, current ratio which is calculated by dividing current assets by the current liabilities takes into account the figures of current assets and current liabilities on a particular day. It does not take into account the position, which was there throughout the year.

(iii) Window dressing, which means artificially improving the financial statements, is another major drawback of ratio analysis. Many times there is a temptation for a firm to show higher profitability or better liquidity by manipulating the figures. If this is done, the basic purpose of ratio analysis will be defeated.

(iv) Several concepts like capital employed, net worth, shareholders' funds are not defined clearly and hence there may be differences in the practices followed across business firms. This will make the comparison impossible and conclusions cannot be drawn.

(v) Inflationary factors are not taken into account in computing ratio analysis. Thus when past performance is analysed, the figures may have become outdated or lose their significance as they are not adjusted to the inflationary trends. To remove this limitation, it is recommended that the ratios should be computed only when the financial statements are adjusted to the inflationary factors.

(E) DuPont Analysis

The DuPont Company of the USA has pioneered a system of financial analysis, which has received very good recognition and acceptance worldwide. This system makes use of the important interlink of information found in financial statements.

At the top of the DuPont chart, there is a ratio showing the return on total assets, which is defined as the product of net profit margin and the total assets turnover ratio. This relationship can be explained as below.

Net Profit / Average Total Assets = Net Profit / Net Sales x Net Sales / Average Total Assets

In other words,   ROA = NPM x TATR,

Where,   ROA = Return on Total Assets, NPM
= Net Profit Margin, TATR
= Total Assets Turnover Ratio

Such relationship helps to understand as to how the Return on Total Assets is affected by the Net Profit Margin and Total Assets Turnover Ratio.

The DuPont Chart also explains the details about the Net Profit Margin Ratio.

The lower side of the DuPont Chart explains the determinants of the Total Assets Turnover ratio. Thus, the basic DuPont Analysis may be extended to explore the determinants of the return on equity. [ROE]

Net Profit / Equity = Net Profit / Sales X Sales / Total Assets X Average Total Assets / Equity

ROE = NPM X TATR X 1/ (1- DAR)

The chart is shown below.

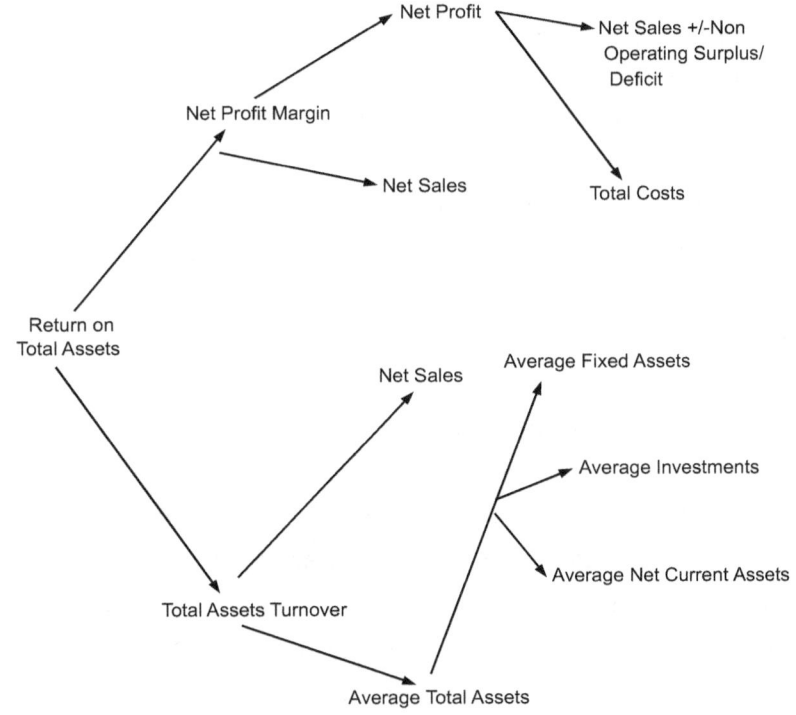

Fig 2.1

2.4 Fund Flow Analysis

(A) Introduction

The financial statements of a business organisation include: (i) Trading A/c. (ii) Profit and Loss A/c. and (iii) Balance–sheet. While the Trading A/c. and Profit and Loss A/c. disclose the gross profit and net profit respectively, the Balance–sheet discloses the position regarding assets and liabilities on a particular day. However, these financial statements do not provide information about sources of raising funds as well as the applications of these funds.

A funds flow statement or a statement showing sources and applications of funds helps to solve this problem. In this statement, the sources of raising funds and their applications are shown clearly and, therefore, the answering of the following questions is possible.

How much funds have been generated through the business operations?

Whether capital investments have been financed by long-term financing or short-term financing?

How was the company able to pay dividend inspite of debit balance of Profit and Loss A/c.?

How was the liquidity position of the company improved?

(B) Meaning of Funds

How can the funds be defined? In a broader sense it includes all resources i.e. total resources, used in the business whether in the form of men, materials, money, machinery, methods etc. However, in the narrow sense funds means only cash resources of the business. Funds are also taken as synonymous to working capital which is the excess of current assets over current liabilities.

(C) Funds Flow Statement

The funds flow statement is a statement which shows on one hand the sources from where the funds have been generated and where they have been applied on the other hand. If these statements are analysed over a period of time, they clearly show the sources from where the past activities were financed and also highlight the uses of the funds. The objectives of a funds flow statement can be summarised as follows:

(i) To help to understand the changes in assets as well as asset sources which are not revealed by the income statement or Balance-sheet.

(ii) To find out the uses of loans raised by the business.

(iii) To indicate the financial strength and weakness of the business.

(D) Preparation of Funds Flow Statements

The funds flow statements can be prepared on a monthly basis, six monthly or annual basis. The proforma of this statement can be given as follows:

Funds Flow Statement or Statement showing Sources and Application of Funds

	Sources	₹		Applications	₹
I.	Issue of shares		I.	Redemption of Pref. shares	
II.	Issue of debentures		II.	Redemption of debentures	
III.	Raising of term loans		III.	Repayment of term loans	
IV.	Sale of fixed assets		IV.	Purchase of fixed assets	
V.	Funds from operations		V.	Losses from operations	
VI.	Sale of other assets		VI.	Purchase of other assets (investments)	
VII.	Net decrease in Working Capital		VII.	Net increase in working capital	
VIII.	Receipt of interest on non–trade investments, dividend, refund of tax etc.		VIII.	Payments like tax paid, dividends paid	
	Total			**Total**	

In the preparation of the funds flow statements, the following working notes will have to be prepared in order to find out the hidden information.

(a) Changes in working capital: In the funds flow statement, net increase in working capital is shown on the application side, while net decrease in working capital is shown on the sources side. In order to find out this figure, the following statement is prepared.

Statement showing changes in Working Capital

	Particulars	Previous year	Current year	Increase/ Decrease in Working Capital
I.	Current Assets : Cash Debtors Bills Receivable Stocks Prepaid expenses Income outstanding Short-term investments.			
II.	Current liabilities : Creditors Bills payable Bank overdraft Expenses outstanding Short-term loans			
	Total			

Net increase / decrease in working capital:

Note: Any increase in current asset results in increase in working capital while increase in current liabilities results in decrease in working capital.

(b) Funds from operations: The concept of funds from operations is extremely important. In calculating funds from operations, non-business expenses like dividends paid etc. as well as non-cash expenses like depreciation etc. are added back in the net profits shown by the Profit and Loss A/c. Similarly, non–cash as well as non–business income is deducted from net profits. The method of finding out funds from operations is as follows:

Dr.   **Adjusted Profit & Loss A/c.**   Cr.

Particulars	₹	Particulars	₹
To non–cash items : (i) Depreciation on fixed assets (ii) Preliminary expenses written off (iii) Goodwill written off (iv) Discount on issue of shares & debentures written off (v) Transfer to Reserve (vi) Proposed dividend (vii) Loss on sale of assets (viii) Provision for taxation To Dividend paid To Income–tax paid To Balance c/d. (Closing balance).		By Balance b/d. (opening balance) **By non-operating income** (i) Interest received (ii) Profit on sale of fixed assets (iii) Dividends received (iv) Refund of taxation (v) Other items By funds from operations (Balancing figure)	
Total		**Total**	

The funds from operations can also be calculated by preparing a statement. The items shown on the debit side of the adjusted Profit and Loss A/c. are added in the net profits while the items on the credit side are deducted from net profits.

(c) Purchase/Sale of fixed assets: Sometimes, there are certain adjustments like depreciation, sale or purchase of fixed assets.

In such cases, it is desirable to prepare an account of fixed assets. The account can be opened in the following manner.

Dr.   **Fixed Assets A/c.**   Cr.

Particulars	₹	Particulars	₹
To Balance b/d (opening) To *Bank – (purchases) To Adjusted P & L A/c. (Profit on sale)		By Adjusted P & L A/c. (Dep.) or Dep. Provision A/c. By *Bank (sale of asset) By Adjusted P & L A/c. (Loss on sale) By Balance c/d.	
Total		**Total**	

*Either Purchase/Sale may be balancing figure. There may be other balancing figures also depending on the information given in the example.

(d) Proposed dividend: This item may be treated as a current liability. However, it is advisable to treat it as a non-current liability. A proposed dividend account is to be prepared in the following manner to find out any missing figure in the account.

Dr.		Proposed dividend A/c.		Cr.
Particulars	₹	Particulars	₹	
To Bank (payment of dividend)		By Balance b/d.		
To Balance c/d. (closing)		By Adjusted P & L A/c.		
		(Provision made)		
		(Balancing figure)		
Total		Total		

If dividends paid are not given, it can be assumed that dividends paid are equal to the opening balance of the proposed dividend.

(e) Provision for Taxation A/c.: In this account, either tax paid or provision made for taxation can be the missing figure. A provision for taxation account can be prepared to find out the missing figure.

Dr.		Provision for Taxation A/c.		Cr.
Particulars	₹	Particulars	₹	
To Bank A/c. (Tax paid)		By Balance b/d. (opening)		
To Balance c/d. (closing)		By Adjusted P & L A/c.		
		(Provision made)		
		(Balancing figure)		
Total		Total		

(f) Undistributed Reserve and Funds: If there are any undistributed profits in the form of reserves and funds, the difference of these reserves and funds will be shown on the debit or credit side of Adjusted P & L A/c. The account is shown as under.

Dr.		Reserve A/c.		Cr.
Particulars	₹	Particulars	₹	
To Adjusted P & L A/c.		By Balance b/d.		
(Reserve utilised)		By Adj. P & L A/c. (New Reserve)		
To Balance b/d. (closing)		Created		
Total		Total		

2.5 CASH FLOW STATEMENT

Introduction

Cash is the basic input, which is required to keep the business operations going on a continuing basis. Important point is that, cash is also the expected output, which is expected to be realised by selling the product manufactured by the manufactured unit. In other words, cash is both, the beginning and also the end of the business operations. Due to such a great importance to 'cash', it becomes of paramount importance that the cash is managed properly. Sometimes it so happens that a business unit earns sufficient profits, but in spite of this, it is not able to pay its liabilities when they become due. This is because there is no liquidity though the profitability is quite high. Therefore it is essential for a business organisation to keep sufficient cash, neither more than requirement, nor less as the shortage of cash may result in embarrassing situation of not meeting the liabilities in time. Effective cash management ensures a proper balancing between the two conflicting objectives of liquidity and profitability.

One of the effective tools of cash management is 'Cash Flow Statement'. This statement shows the inflows of cash as well as outflows of cash. Though normally it is prepared at the end of a particular period, say one year, it can also be prepared on projected basis for the future period. Thus a 'Cash Flow Statement' can also be prepared for next year or even for next five years so that it becomes possible to predict the cash inflows and cash outflows and necessary steps can be taken accordingly. The meaning of this statement, objectives and method of preparation of the same is discussed in detail in the following paragraphs.

Meaning

As mentioned above, the cash flow statement is a statement which shown the cash inflows and cash outflows occurred or would be occurred in a particular period. It starts with the opening balance of cash and ends with the closing balance with cash. In other words, a cash flow statement can be defined as, *'a statement which summarises sources of cash inflows and uses of cash outflows of a firm during a particular period of time, say a month or a year'*. Cash flow statement can be prepared from the data made available from comparative Balance Sheets, Profit and Loss Account and additional information.

Difference between Cash Flow Statement and Funds Flow Statement

The following is the difference between the cash flow statement and funds flow statement.

(i) A Cash Flow Statement is concerned only with the changes is cash position while Funds Flow Statement is concerned with changes in working capital position between the two Balance Sheet dates. Cash is one of the current assets and hence one of the components of working capital out of several other components like debtors, inventories, bills receivables etc.

(ii) A Cash Flow Statement is merely a record of cash receipts and payments. Though it is valuable in its own way, it fails to bring to light many important changes involving the disposition of resources.

(iii) Cash Flow Analysis is more useful to the management as a tool of financial analysis in short periods as compared to the Funds Flow Analysis.

(iv) In Cash Flow Statement, the current assets and current liabilities are considered individually while in Funds Flow Statement, the combined effect of current assets and current liabilities is taken by measuring the effect on working capital.

Utility of Cash Flow Statement

As mentioned above, cash flow statement is extremely useful in overall cash management. The basic objective of cash management is to maintain proper cash balance by avoiding any excessive surplus of cash and shortage of cash. This is possible when cash flow projections are made and cash inflows and outflows are projected. These projections will help the management to find out whether there is going to be any huge surplus of cash or shortage of cash. If there is a possibility of a surplus, planning can be made in advance for investing the same while in case of anticipated shortage, necessary arrangements can be made for raising the required cash. Thus cash flow statement is an important tool in the hands of management to watch the movement of cash and take appropriate decisions about the same.

Preparation of Cash Flow Statement

The Cash Flow Statement can be prepared on the same pattern on which a Funds Flow Statement is prepared. Sources, which generate cash, are termed as inflows of cash while the applications of the same are termed as outflows of cash. The sources of cash inflows and cash outflows are described below.

[I] Sources of Cash

The following are the sources of cash:

[A] Internal Sources or Cash From Operations:

Cash generated from operations is the internal source of generating cash inflows. The net profit as shown by the Profit and Loss Account is the starting point for the computation of the cash from operations. The net profit as shown by the Profit and Loss Account is not equal to the cash from operations as several non- cash items are taken into consideration while computing the same. Therefore the net profit will have to be adjusted for non-cash items to find out the cash from operations. Some of these items are as follows.

1. **Depreciation:** Depreciation is a non- cash item, which reduces the net profit but does not result in any cash outflows. Hence the amount of depreciation will have to be added back in the amount of profit.

2. **Loss on sale of fixed assets:** Sometimes fixed assets like land and building, plant and machinery, furniture etc. and so on are sold out and the loss on sale is debited to the Profit and Loss Account. The amount of loss does not result into cash outflows and therefore is added back in the amount of net profit.

3. **Creation of reserves:** If profits for the year have been arrived at after charging transfers to reserves, such transfers should be added back to the profits.

4. **Writing off the intangible assets:** Intangible assets like goodwill, preliminary expenses etc. are normally written off against profits. Such writing off these assets reduces the net profits but do not result in cash outflows. Therefore this item should be added back in the amount of net profits.

5. **Profit on sale of fixed assets:** Fixed assets may have been sold at a profit. Such item should be deducted from the net profit, as it is a non-cash item.

Thus it can be seen that the 'Cash From Operations' is worked out in the same fashion like 'Funds From Operations' worked out in the 'Funds Flow Statement'. However one important difference between 'Cash From Operations' and 'Funds From Operations' is that items of Current Assets and Current Liabilities are also taken into consideration while computing the 'Cash From Operations'. In Funds Flow Statement the total effect of the current assets and current liabilities is taken as 'Changes in working capital' while in Cash Flow Statement, individual items of current assets and current liabilities are considered for computing Cash From Operations. This is explained below.

(i) **Current Assets:** These assets include Debtors, Inventories, Cash and Bank Balance, Bills Receivables, Prepaid Expenses and Short term investments. Out of these, cash and bank balances at the beginning and at the end of the year are already taken into consideration while preparing the Cash Flow Statement. For other current assets, any increase as compared to the previous year is taken as cash outflow, while any decrease as compared to the previous year is taken as cash inflows. Thus if Debtors in the beginning of the year are ₹ 25,00,000 and at the end of the year are ₹ 27,00,000, the difference of ₹ 2,00,000 is taken as cash outflow. On the other hand if inventories at the beginning of the year are ₹ 10,00,000 and at the end are ₹ 9,00,000, the difference of ₹ 1,00,000 is taken as cash inflow. The reason behind the same is that if any current asset increase, more amounts are blocked in the same as compared to the previous year and hence it is cash outflow. However if it decreases as compared to the previous year, lesser amount is blocked in the same and so it is cash inflow.

(ii) **Current Liabilities:** These liabilities include bank overdraft, creditors, bills payable, expenses outstanding and other short-term loans. The treatment given to the current liabilities is exactly opposite to the current assets. If any current liability increases as compared to the previous year, it is treated as cash inflows because to that extent cash is made available to the business unit. On the other hand if there is any decrease in the current liability as compared to the previous year, it is treated as cash outflow.

(iii) The above discussion can be summarised in the following manner:

Increase in current assets and decrease in current liabilities result in cash outflows.

Decrease in current assets and increase in current liabilities result in cash inflows.

[B] External Sources:

We have discussed the internal sources of cash generation in the above paragraphs. Now we will discuss the external sources from which cash is generated or which are the sources of cash inflows.

(i) **Issue of new shares:** If new shares are issued for cash, the net proceeds i.e. after deducting the issue expenses will be treated as cash inflows.

(ii) **Raising of term loans:** If new term loans are raised through debentures or otherwise, such term loans are the sources of cash inflows.

(iii) **Purchase of fixed assets**: If fixed assets are purchased, it will be an outflow of cash. However if they are purchased on deferred payment system, it should be shown as a separate source of cash to the extent of deferred credit. However, the cost of machinery purchased will be shown as an application of cash.

(iv) **Short term borrowings:** Short-term borrowings etc. from banks increase cash available and they have to be shown separately under this head.

(v) **Sale of Fixed Assets, Investments etc:** Such sale results in generation of cash and therefore is a source of cash generation.

[II] Application Of Cash

The following items result in applications of cash or cash outflows.

(i) **Purchase of Fixed Assets:** Such purchases will result in application of cash and will be shown as cash outflows.

(ii) **Payment of Long Term Loans:** The payments of term loans, debentures etc. will be treated as cash outflows as the available cash is reduced.

(iii) **Redemption of Preference Shares and Buy Back of Equity Shares:** Such redemption of Preference Shares and Buy Back of Equity Shares result in reduction in availability of cash and hence is an outflow.

(iv) **Payment of Income Tax:** This is also an application of cash.

(v) Payment of Dividend: This will also reduce the availability of cash and hence is an outflow.

(vi) Decrease in Unsecured Loans, Deposits etc: The decrease in these liabilities indicates the repayment of these liabilities and hence it is an outflow of cash.

(vii) Loss from Operations: Cash generated from operations is a source of cash while any loss from operations is an outflow of cash as the available cash is reduced.

Format of Cash Flow Statement

The following is the format of Cash Flow Statement.

Cash Flow Statement
For The Year Ended On ------------

Particulars	Amount ₹
Opening Balance: Cash	
Bank	
Add: Sources of Cash:	
• Issue of Shares	
• Raising of Long Term Loans	
• Sale of Fixed Assets	
• Short Term Borrowings	
• Cash From Operations *	
Total Cash Available [1]	
Less: Applications Of Cash:	
• Redemption of Preference Shares	
• Buy Back of Equity Shares	
• Redemption of Long Term Loans	
• Purchase of Fixed Assets	
• Decrease in Deferred Payment Liabilities	
• Loss From Operations	
• Income Tax Paid	
• Dividends Paid	
• Decrease in unsecured Loans, Deposits etc	
Total Applications [2]	
Closing Balance: Cash	
Bank	

* Can be worked out by preparing working note.

Note: Working notes for finding out various missing figures can be prepared on the same lines of Funds Flow Statement as shown earlier.

FINANCIAL MANAGEMENT — TECHNIQUES OF FINANCIAL ANALYSIS

Format of Cash Flow Statement as per Accounting Standard-3.

Cash Flow Statement

Particulars	Amount [₹]
Cash flow from Operating Activities	
Cash receipts from customers	
Cash paid to suppliers and employees	
Cash generated from operations	
Income tax	
Cash flow before extra ordinary items	
Proceeds from earthquake disaster settlement	
Net cash from operating activities	
Cash flow from Investing Activities	
Purchase of fixed assets	
Proceeds from sale of equipments	
Interest received	
Dividends received	
Net Cash from investing activities	

contd. ...

Particulars	Amount
Cash flow from investing activities	
Proceeds from issuance of share capital	
Proceeds from long- term borrowings	
Repayment of long – term borrowings	
Interest paid	
Dividends paid	
Net cash used in financing activities	
Net Increase in Cash and Cash-equivalents*	
Cash and cash-equivalents at the beginning of the a period	
Cash and cash-equivalents at the end of a period	

*Consists of cash on hand and balance with banks, investments in money market [short term] investments and effect of exchange rate changes.

FINANCIAL MANAGEMENT   TECHNIQUES OF FINANCIAL ANALYSIS

Solved Problems

RATIO ANALYSIS

Problem 1

From the following Balance-sheet of XYZ Ltd., calculate the following ratios.
(i)   Current ratio,
(ii)   Liquid ratio,
(iii) Absolute liquidity ratio,
(iv)   Current assets to Fixed assets ratio,
(v)   Debt to equity ratio,
(vi)   Proprietary ratio,
(vii) Capital gearing ratio; and
(viii) Fixed assets ratio.

Balance–sheet as on 31st March, 2013

Liabilities	₹	Assets	₹
Equity Capital	10,00,000	Goodwill [At cost]	5,00,000
6% Pref. Capital	5,00,000	Plant & Machinery	6,00,000
General reserve	1,00,000	Land & Building	7,00,000
Profit & Loss A/c.	4,00,000	Furniture	1,00,000
Prov. for taxation	1,76,000	Inventories	6,00,000
Bills payable	1,24,000	Bills Receivable	30,000
Bank overdraft	20,000	Debtors	1,50,000
Creditors	80,000	Bank	2,00,000
12% Debentures	5,00,000	Investments (short-term)	20,000
	29,00,000		**29,00,000**

Solution :

(i) Current ratio $= \dfrac{\text{Current assets}}{\text{Current liabilities}} = \dfrac{10,00,000}{4,00,000} = 2.5 : 1$

Note: Current assets include inventories, debtors, bills receivable, bank balance and short-term investments.

Current liabilities include creditors, bills payable, bank overdraft, taxation provision.

(ii) Liquid ratio $= \dfrac{\text{Liquid assets}}{\text{Liquid liabilities}} = \dfrac{10,00,000 - 6,00,000}{4,00,000 - 20,000}$

Liquid assets = Current assets – Stock
Liquid liabilities = Current liabilities – Bank overdraft.

o/d $= \dfrac{4,00,000}{3,80,000} = 1.05 : 1$

2.27

FINANCIAL MANAGEMENT   TECHNIQUES OF FINANCIAL ANALYSIS

(iii) Absolute liquidity ratio $= \dfrac{\text{Cash at bank + Short term investments}}{\text{Current liabilities}}$

$= \dfrac{2,20,000}{4,00,000} = 0.55 : 1$

(iv) Current assets to fixed assets $= \dfrac{\text{Current assets}}{\text{Fixed assets}} = \dfrac{10,00,000}{19,00,000} = 0.526 : 1$

Note: Fixed assets include Goodwill, Plant & Machinery, Furniture and Land and Building.

(v) Debt to equity ratio =

(a) $\dfrac{\text{Long term debt}}{\text{Shareholders funds}}$

$= \dfrac{5,00,000}{\underset{\text{Equity Capital}}{10,00,000} + \underset{\text{Pref. Capital}}{5,00,000} + \underset{\text{General Reserve}}{1,00,000} + \underset{\text{Profit & Loss A/c.}}{4,00,000}}$

$= \dfrac{5,00,000}{20,00,000}$

$= .25 : 1$

(b) $\dfrac{\text{Long term debt}}{\text{Long term debt + Shareholders funds}}$

$= \dfrac{5,00,000}{5,00,000 + 20,00,000}$

$= \dfrac{5,00,000}{25,00,000}$

$= .20 : 1$

(vi) Proprietary ratio $= \dfrac{\text{Shareholders funds}}{\text{Total assets}}$

$= \dfrac{20,00,000}{29,00,000}$

$= .69 : 1$

(vii) Capital gearing ratio $= \dfrac{\text{Fixed interest bearing securities}}{\text{Equity capital + Reserves & Surplus}}$

$= \dfrac{10,00,000 \;[5,00,000 \text{ Pref.} + 5,00,000 \text{ Deb.}]}{10,00,000 + 5,00,000}$

$= \dfrac{10,00,000}{15,00,000}$

$= .66 : 1$

(viii) Fixed assets ratio $= \dfrac{\text{Fixed assets}}{\text{Capital employed}}$

$= \dfrac{19,00,000}{25,00,000}$

[shareholders funds + long term debt]

$= .76 : 1$

Problem 2

Betal Manufacturing Company submits the following Profit and Loss Account for the year ended 31st March 2013.

Dr. Profit & Loss A/c. **Cr.**

Particulars	₹	Particulars	₹
To opening stock	52,000	By Sales	3,20,000
To Purchase	1,60,000	By Closing stock	76,000
To Wages	48,000		
To Manu. expenses	32,000		
To Gross profit c/d.	1,04,000		
	3,96,000		**3,96,000**
To Selling & Dist. exps.	8,000	By Gross profit b/d.	1,04,000
To Admin. exps.	45,600	By Profit on sale of Shares	9,600
To Loss by fire	2,400		
To Loss on sale of furniture	1,600		
To Net profit	56,000		
	1,13,600		**1,13,600**

Calculate: (i) Gross profit ratio, (ii) Net profit ratio, (iii) Operating profit ratio, (iv) Operating net profit ratio.

Solution:

(i) Gross profit ratio $= \dfrac{\text{Gross profit}}{\text{Sales}} \times 100$

$= \dfrac{1,04,000}{3,20,000} \times 100$

$= 32.5\%$

(ii) Net profit ratio $= \dfrac{\text{Net profit}}{\text{Sales}} \times 100$

$= \dfrac{56,000}{3,20,000} \times 100$

$= 17.5\%$

(iii) Operating ratio = $\dfrac{\text{Cost of goods sold + Operating expenes}}{\text{Sales}} \times 100$

= $\dfrac{2,16,000 + 53,600}{3,20,000} \times 100$

= 84.25%

(iv) Operating profit ratio = $\dfrac{\text{Operating net profit}}{\text{Sales}} \times 100$

= $\dfrac{56,000 + 1,600 - 9,600}{3,20,000} \times 100 = 15\%$

Problem 3

The following is a summarised Profit and Loss A/c. for the year ending 31st March 2013 and the Balance-sheet as on that date of ABC Ltd.

Dr.   Profit & Loss A/c.   Cr.

Particulars	₹	Particulars	₹
To Opening stock	10,000	By Sales	1,00,000
To Purchases	55,000	By Closing stock	15,000
To Gross profit	50,000		
	1,15,000		1,15,000
To Adm. expenses	15,000	By Gross profit	50,000
To Interest	3,000		
To Selling expenses	12,000		
To Net profit	20,000		
	50,000		50,000

Balance-sheet as on 31.3.2013

Liabilities	₹	Assets	₹
Share Capital		Land & Building	50,000
[₹ 10 each]	1,00,000	Plant & Machinery	30,000
Profit & Loss A/c.	20,000	Stock	15,000
Creditors	25,000	Debtors	15,000
Bills payable	15,000	Bills receivable	12,500
		Cash & Bank	17,500
		Furniture	20,000
	1,60,000		1,60,000

Additional information:
Average debtors   ₹ 12,500
Credit purchases   ₹ 40,000
Credit sales   ₹ 80,000

Calculate : (i) Stock turnover ratio, (ii) Debtors turnover ratio, (ii) Creditors turnover ratio, (iv) Working capital turnover ratio, (v) Sales to capital employed, (vi) Return on shareholders' funds, (vii) Gross profit ratio, (viii) Net profit ratio, (ix) EPS, (x) Operating ratio.

Solution:

(i) Stock turnover ratio $= \dfrac{\text{Cost of goods sold}}{\text{Average stock}} = \dfrac{50{,}000 \ [\text{Sales} - \text{G.P.}]}{10{,}000 + 15{,}000 / 2}$

$= \dfrac{50{,}000}{12{,}500}$

$= 4 \text{ times}$

(ii) Debtors turnover ratio $= \dfrac{\text{Credit sales}}{\text{Average debtors}} = \dfrac{80{,}000}{12{,}500}$

$= 6.4 \text{ times}$

(iii) Creditors turnover ratio $= \dfrac{\text{Credit purchases}}{\text{Average A/c's payable}} = \dfrac{40{,}000}{40{,}000 \ [\text{Crs.} + \text{B/P}]}$

$= 1 \text{ time}$

(iv) Working capital turnover $= \dfrac{\text{Sales}}{(\text{Working Capital})}$

[Current assets − Current liabilities]

$= \dfrac{1{,}00{,}000}{20{,}000} = 5 \text{ times}$

(v) Sales to Capital employed $= \dfrac{\text{Sales}}{\text{Capital employed}} \times 100 = \dfrac{1{,}00{,}000}{1{,}00{,}000 \ \text{Equity} + 20{,}000 \ \text{P \& L A/c.}}$

$= \dfrac{1{,}00{,}000}{1{,}20{,}000} = .83 : 1$

(vi) Returns on shareholders funds $= \dfrac{\text{Net profit}}{\text{Shareholders funds}} \times 100$

$= \dfrac{20{,}000}{1{,}20{,}000} \times 100 = 16.67\%$

(vii) Gross profit ratio $= \dfrac{\text{Gross profit}}{\text{Sales}} \times 100 = \dfrac{50{,}000}{1{,}00{,}000} \times 100 = 50\%$

(viii) Net profit ratio $= \dfrac{\text{Net profit}}{\text{Sales}} \times 100$

$= \dfrac{20{,}000}{1{,}00{,}000} \times 100 = 20\%$

(ix) EPS : $\dfrac{\text{Net profit}}{\text{No. of equity shares}} = \dfrac{20{,}000}{10{,}000} = ₹ 2$

(x) Operating ratio : $\dfrac{\text{Cost of goods sold} + \text{Operation expenses}}{\text{Sales}} \times 100$

$= \dfrac{50{,}000 + 27{,}000}{1{,}00{,}000} \times 100 = 77\%$

FINANCIAL MANAGEMENT   TECHNIQUES OF FINANCIAL ANALYSIS

Problem 4

The summarised Balance-sheets of Ashwin Ltd. as on 31st March 2006, 2007 and 2008 are given below:

Balance-sheet as on 31st March

Liabilities	[₹ in lakhs]		
	2006	2007	2008
Paid–up capital	194	194	194
Long term borrowings			
(i) From banks	68	97	127
(ii) From others	281	343	376
Current liabilities	52	54	99
Total	**595**	**688**	**796**
Assets :			
Net Block	286	261	239
Current assets	143	199	234
P & L A/c.	166	228	323
	595	688	796

Calculate the following ratios for the three years:

(i) Debt equity ratio
(ii) Current ratio
(iii) Fixed assets ratio
(iv) Proprietary ratio.

Solution:

	2006	2007	2008
1. Debt-equity ratio = $\dfrac{\text{Long term debt}}{\text{Shareholders equity funds}}$	$\dfrac{349}{194-166}$ $= \dfrac{349}{28}$ $= 12.46$	Negative	Negative
2. Current ratio = $\dfrac{\text{Current assets}}{\text{Current liabilities}}$	$\dfrac{143}{52}$ $= 2.75 : 1$	$\dfrac{199}{54}$ $= 3.685 : 1$	$\dfrac{234}{99}$ $= 2.36 : 1$
3. Fixed assets ratio = $\dfrac{\text{Fixed assets}}{\text{*Capital employed}}$ =	$\dfrac{286}{377}$ $= .76 : 1$	$\dfrac{261}{406}$ $= .64 : 1$	$\dfrac{239}{374}$ $= .64 : 1$
4. Proprietary ratio = $\dfrac{\text{Shareholders funds}}{\text{Total assets}}$ =	$\dfrac{28}{429}$ $= 0.65 : 1$	Negative	Negative

* Capital employed = Paid-up capital + Long term borrowings – Profit & Loss A/c – debit balance.

FINANCIAL MANAGEMENT TECHNIQUES OF FINANCIAL ANALYSIS

Problem 5

Selected statistical information for X Ltd. for three years is given below:

	Year ended		
	31-3-2009	31-3-2010	31-3-2011
Gross profit	36%	$33\frac{1}{3}$%	30%
Stock turnover	20 times	25 times	14 times
Average stock	₹ 38,400	₹ 36,000	₹ 70,000
Average debtors	87,500	1,68,750	2,00,000
Income-tax rate	50%	50%	50%
Net income after tax as % of sales	6%	7%	12%
Maximum credit period allowed to customers	60 days	60 days	30 days

Required:
1. A statement of profits in comparative form for all the three years.
2. Evaluate the position of the company regarding profitability and liquidity on the basis of information available.
3. What additional information will you require to evaluate the position of company on the liquidity front fully?

Solution:

1. Income statements

	Year ended		
Particulars	31-3-2009 [₹]	31-3-2010 [₹]	31-3-2011 [₹]
Sales	12,00,000	13,50,000	14,00,000
Less: Cost of goods sold.	7,68,000	9,00,000	9,80,000
Gross profit	4,32,000	4,50,000	4,20,000
Less: Operating expenses.	2,88,000	2,61,000	84,000
Profit before tax	1,44,000	1,89,000	3,36,000
Less: Taxes	72,000	94,500	1,68,000
Profit after tax	72,000	94,500	1,68,000
Working notes:			
Cost of goods sold :	20 × 38,400	25 × 36,000	14 × 70,000
Stock turnover × Average Stock	= 7,68,000	= 9,00,000	= 9,80,000
Cost of goods sold as % of Sales	64%	66 2/3%	70%
Sales	12,00,000	13,50,000	14,00,000
Net income as % to sales [given]	6%	7%	12%
Net income / PAT	72,000	94,500	1,68,000
Profit before tax	1,44,000	1,89,000	3,36,000
Operating expenses [Gross profit − Profit before tax]	2,88,000	2,61,000	84,000

2. From the above statements and ratios, it is quite clear that the profitability of the company is increasing quite consistently. From 6% in the year 2008-09, it has gone up to 7% in the year 2009-10 and upto 12% in the year 2010-11. However, stock turnover ratio which was 20 times in the year 2008-09 has slumped to 14 times in the year 2010-11 after showing improvement to 25 times in the year 2009-10. This ratio needs improvement in order to improve the liquidity position. The debtor's turnover ratio was 13.7 times in the first year and 8 and 7 times respectively in the second and third year. This means that this ratio is also going down consistently and needs to be improved. It should be noted that debtor's turnover ratio is decreasing in spite of reducing credit allowed to debtors in the third year, i.e. 2010-11. This suggests that the collection policy should be tightened.
3. In order to evaluate the position of the company regarding liquidity fully, current liabilities and current assets should also be available.

Problem 6

From the following information, prepare the Balance-sheet of A Ltd. as on 31st March 2013 with as many details as possible.

(i) Current ratio = 2.5 to 1
(ii) Liquid ratio = 1.5 to 1
(iii) Working capital = ₹ 60,000.
(iv) Reserves and surplus = ₹ 20,000.
(v) Bank overdraft = ₹ 10,000.
(vi) Fixed assets to Proprietor's funds = .75.
(vii) There are no long term liabilities or fictitious assets.

Solution:

The Balance-sheet can be prepared with the help of the following working notes:

(i) Working Capital = ₹ 60,000 which is current assets – Current liabilities
Therefore, C.A – C.L. = 60,000
or 2.5 – 1 = 60,000
[Current ratio is 2.5 which means current assets are 2.5 times of current liabilities]
or 1.5 = 60,000
so, 1 = 40,000
Therefore, current liabilities = ₹ 40,000.
Current assets are 2.5 × ₹ 40,000 = ₹ 1,00,000.

(ii) To find out liquid current assets, the following calculations can be made.

$$\text{Liquid ratio} = 1.5 = \frac{\text{Liquid current assets}}{\text{Current liabilities} - \text{Bank O/D}}$$

$$1.5 = \frac{\text{LCA}}{40{,}000 - 10{,}000}$$

LCA = ₹ 45,000
Therefore, stock = ₹ 55,000

(iii) Fixed assets to proprietor's funds = .75 which means that out of proprietor's funds, 75% amount is invested in fixed assets. This suggests that remaining 25% of proprietor's funds are invested in working capital.

$$25\% = 60,000 \text{ [working capital]}$$
$$100\% = ₹ 2,40,000 - \text{Proprietor's funds}$$
$$\text{Fixed assets} = 75\% = ₹ 1,80,000$$
$$\text{Proprietor's funds} = \text{Share Capital} + \text{Reserves}$$
$$= ₹ 2,00,000 + ₹ 40,000 = ₹ 2,40,000$$

Balance Sheet of A Ltd. As on 31st March 2013

Liabilities	₹	Assets		₹
Share Capital	2,00,000	Fixed assets		1,80,000
Reserves & Surplus	40,000	Current assets		
Current liabilities		Stock	55,000	
Creditors	30,000	Other Current Assets	+ 45,000	1,00,000
Bank overdraft	10,000			
	2,80,000			2,80,000

Problem 7

Using the following data, complete the Balance sheet given below:

	₹
Gross profit: 20% of sales	60,000
Shareholders funds	50,000
Credit sales	80% of total sales
Total assets turnover	3 times
Inventory turnover [to cost of sales]	8 times
Average collection period [360 days a year] (to cost of sales)	18 days
Current ratio	1.6
Long term debt to equity	40%

Balance Sheet

Liabilities	₹	Assets	₹
Creditors	......	Cash	......
Long term debt	......	Debtors	......
Shareholders' equity	......	Inventory	......
		Fixed assets	......
Total	......	**Total**	......

Solution:

1. Gross profit 20% of sales = ₹ 60,000.

 Therefore, Sales = ₹ 3,00,000 $\left(₹ 60,000 \times \dfrac{100}{20}\right)$

 Cost of sales = 3,00,000 − 60,000 = 2,40,000

2. Inventory turnover ratio = 8 times

$$8 = \frac{\text{Cost of goods sold}}{\text{Av. inventory}}$$

$$8 = \frac{2,40,000}{\text{Av. inventory}}$$

∴ Av. inventory = ₹ 30,000

Since, opening stock is not given, ₹ 30,000 is taken as the closing stock.

3. Total assets turnover = 3 times = $\frac{\text{Sales}}{\text{Total assets}}$

∴ $3 = \frac{3,00,000}{\text{Total assets}}$

∴ Total assets = 1,00,000
∴ Total liabilities = ₹ 1,00,000

4. Average collection period = 18 days

∴ Debtors turnover ratio = $\frac{360 \text{ days}}{18 \text{ days}}$

= 20 times

Debtors = $\frac{2,40,000}{20}$ Cost of sales

= ₹ 12,000

5. Debt – equity ratio [Long term] = 40%
Shareholders' funds = ₹ 50,000
Debt 40% of ₹ 50,000 = ₹ 20,000.

6. Creditors: Total liabilities – Equity – Long term debt
= 1,00,000 – 50,000 – 20,000
= ₹ 30,000

7. Current ratio = $\frac{\text{Current assets}}{\text{Current liabilities [Crs.]}}$

$1.6 = \frac{\text{C.A.}}{30,000}$

∴ Current assets = ₹ 48,000

8. Fixed Assets = ₹ 1,00,000 – ₹ 48,000 = ₹ 52,000

Balance-sheet

Liabilities	₹	Assets	₹
Creditors	30,000	Cash [Bal. Figure]	6,000
Long term debt	20,000	Debtors	12,000
Shareholders' equity	50,000	Inventory	30,000
		Fixed assets	52,000
Total	**1,00,000**		**1,00,000**

Problem 8

The following is the Balance-sheet of a limited company as on 31st March 2013.

Balance-sheet as on 31.03.2013

Liabilities	₹	Assets	₹
Share Capital	2,00,000	Land and Building	1,40,000
Profit & Loss A/c	30,000	Plant and Machinery	3,50,000
General Reserve	40,000	Stock-in-trade	2,00,000
12% Debentures	4,20,000	Debtors	1,00,000
Creditors	1,00,000	Bills Receivable	10,000
Bills Payable	50,000	Bank Balance	40,000
Total	**8,40,000**	**Total**	**8,40,000**

Calculate:

(i) Current Ratio, (ii) Quick Ratio, (iii) Inventory to Working Capital, (iv) Debt to Equity, (v) Proprietary Ratio, (vi) Capital Gearing Ratio, (vii) Current Assets to Fixed Assets.

Solution:

1. Current Ratio = $\dfrac{\text{Current Assets}}{\text{Current Liabilities}}$

    = $\dfrac{3,50,000}{1,50,000}$

    = 2.33 : 1

Note:

(i) Current Assets = Stock + Debtors + Bills Receivable + Bank balance

Current Liabilities = Creditors + Bills payable

(ii) Quick Ratio = $\dfrac{\text{Liquid Current Assets}}{\text{Current Liabilities}}$

    = $\dfrac{1,50,000}{1,50,000}$

    = 1 : 1

Note:

Liquid Current Assets = Debtors + Bills Receivable + Bank Balance

(iii) Inventory to Working Capital = $\dfrac{\text{Inventory}}{\text{Working capital}}$

    = $\dfrac{2,00,000}{2,00,000}$

    = 1 : 1

Working Capital = Current Assets – Current Liabilities

(iv) Debt to Equity Ratio = $\dfrac{\text{Long term debt}}{\text{Shareholder's funds}}$

= $\dfrac{4,20,000}{2,70,000}$

= 1.55 : 1

Note: Long term debt = 12% Debentures

Shareholder's funds = Share Capital + Reserves + Profit & Loss A/c

(v) Proprietary Ratio = $\dfrac{\text{Proprietor's Funds}}{\text{Total Assets}}$

= $\dfrac{2,70,000}{8,40,000}$ = .32 : 1

Proprietor's funds = Share Capital + Reserve + Profit & Loss A/c

(vi) Capital Gearing Ratio = *Fixed income bearing Securities / Equity Shareholders Funds

= $\dfrac{4,20,000}{2,00,000}$ = 2.1 : 1

* 12% Debentures

(vii) Current Assets to Fixed Assets = $\dfrac{\text{Current Assets}}{\text{Fixed Assets}} = \dfrac{3,50,000}{4,90,000}$ = .71 : 1

Problem 9

The following figures are extracted from the books of ABC Ltd. as on 31st March 2013.

Balance-sheet as on 31.03.2013

Particulars	Amount (₹)
Sales	24,00,000
Less : Operating expenses	18,00,000
Gross Profit	**6,00,000**
Less : Non operating expenses	2,40,000
Net Profits	**3,60,000**
Current Assets :	7,60,000
Inventories	8,00,000
Fixed Assets	**14,40,000**
TOTAL ASSETS	**30,00,000**
Net Worth	15,00,000
Debt	9,00,000
Current liabilities	6,00,000
Total liabilities	**30,00,000**
Working Capital	9,60,000

Calculate:
(i) Gross profit Ratio,
(ii) Net profit Ratio,
(iii) Return on Assets,
(iv) Inventory Turnover,
(v) Working Capital Turnover,
(vi) Net Worth to Debt.

Solution:

(i) Gross Profit Ratio $= \dfrac{\text{Gross Profit}}{\text{Sales}} \times 100$

$= \dfrac{6,00,000}{24,00,000} \times 100 = 25\%$

(ii) Net Profit Ratio $= \dfrac{\text{Net Profit}}{\text{Sales}} \times 100$

$= \dfrac{3,60,000}{24,00,000} \times 100 = 15\%$

(iii) Return on Assets $= \dfrac{\text{Net Profit}}{\text{Total Assets}} \times 100$

$= \dfrac{3,60,000}{30,00,000} \times 100 = 12\%$

(iv) Inventory turnover : $\dfrac{\text{Sales}}{\text{Average Inventory}}$

$= \dfrac{24,00,000}{8,00,000} = 3 \text{ times}$

Note:
1. In the absence of 'Cost of goods sold', Sales are taken for calculation of inventory turnover ratio.
2. Opening stock is not given in the example and therefore, closing stock is taken as Average inventory.

(v) Working Capital Turnover $= \dfrac{\text{Sales}}{\text{Net Working Capital}}$

$= \dfrac{24,00,000}{9,60,000}$

$= 2.5 \text{ times}$

Net Working Capital = Current Assets – Current Liabilities

(vi) Net Worth to Debt $= \dfrac{\text{Net worth}}{\text{Debt}}$

$= \dfrac{15,00,000}{9,00,000}$

$= 1.66 : 1$

FINANCIAL MANAGEMENT	TECHNIQUES OF FINANCIAL ANALYSIS

Problem 10

The following are the summarised Profit and Loss A/c and Balance-sheet of Z Ltd. for the year ended 31st March 2013 and a Balance-sheet as on 31St March 2013.

Dr.   **Profit & Loss A/c**   **Cr.**

Particulars	₹	Particulars	₹
To Opening stock	99,500	By Sales	9,50,000
To Purchases	5,45,000	By Closing Stock	1,50,000
To Carriage inwards	15,500		
To Gross profits	4,40,000		
	11,00,000		**11,00,000**
To Opening expenses	2,00,000	By Gross Profits	4,40,000
To Non-operating expense	40,000	By Non-operating income	60,000
To Net Profit	2,60,000		
	5,00,000		**5,00,000**

Balance-sheet as on 31St March 2013

Liabilities	₹	Assets	₹
Capital	2,00,000	Land and Building	1,50,000
(Equity Shares of ₹ 10 each]		Plant and Machinery	80,000
Reserves	2,00,000	Stock-in-trade	1,50,000
Profit & Loss A/c	60,000	Debtors	45,000
Other current liabilities	90,000	Cash and Bank	60,000
Bills Payable	40,000	Bills Receivable	1,05,000
Total	**5,90,000**	**Total**	**5,90,000**

Calculate:
- (i) Gross Profit Ratio
- (ii) Net Profit Ratio
- (iii) Operating Profit Ratio
- (iv) Operating Ratio
- (v) Return on Capital employed
- (vi) Net Profit to Fixed Assets
- (vii) Stock Turnover Ratio
- (viii) Debtors Turnover Ratio
- (ix) Creditors Turnover Ratio
- (x) Sales to Working Capital
- (xi) Sales to Fixed Assets
- (xii) Sales to Capital Employed
- (xiii) Return on Total Resources
- (xiv) Turnover of Total Assets

Solution:

(i) Gross Profit Ratio $= \dfrac{\text{Gross Profit}}{\text{Sales}} \times 100$

$= \dfrac{4,40,000}{9,50,000} \times 100$

$= 46.31\%$

(ii) Net Profit Ratio $= \dfrac{\text{Net Profit}}{\text{Sales}} \times 100$

$= \dfrac{2,60,000}{9,50,000} \times 100$

$= 27.36\%$

(iii) Operating Profit Ratio $= \dfrac{\text{Operating Profit}}{\text{Sales}} \times 100$

$= \dfrac{2,40,000}{9,50,000} \times 100$

$= 25.26\%$

Note: Operating Profit = Net Profit + Non-Operating Expenses − Non Operating Income

$= 2,60,000 + 40,000 - 60,000$

$= 2,40,000$

(iv) Operating Ratio $= \dfrac{\text{Cost of goods sold + Operating expenses}}{\text{Sales}} \times 100$

$= \dfrac{5,10,000 + 2,00,000}{9,50,000} \times 100 = 74.74\%$

(v) Return on Capital Employed $= \dfrac{\text{Net Profit}}{\text{Capital employed}} \times 100$

$= \dfrac{2,60,000}{*4,60,000} \times 100 = 56.52\%$

* Share capital + Reserves + P & L A/c.

(vi) Net Profits to Fixed Assets $= \dfrac{\text{Net Profits}}{\text{Fixed Assets}} \times 100$

$= \dfrac{2,30,000}{3,30,000} \times 100$

$= 69.69\%$

(vii) Stock Turnover Ratio $= \dfrac{\text{Cost of goods sold}}{\text{Average stock*}}$

$= \dfrac{5,10,000}{1,24,750}$

$= 4.088$ times

FINANCIAL MANAGEMENT TECHNIQUES OF FINANCIAL ANALYSIS

$$* \text{ Average stock} = \frac{\text{Opening stock + Closing stock}}{2}$$

$$= \frac{99{,}500 + 1{,}50{,}000}{2}$$

$$= 1{,}24{,}750$$

(viii) Debtors Turnover Ratio $= \dfrac{\text{Credit Sales}}{\text{Average Debtors + Average Bills Receivable}}$

$$= \frac{9{,}50{,}000}{45{,}000 + 1{,}05{,}000}$$

$$= 6.33$$

Note:
1. It is assumed that all sales are on credit.
2. In the absence of information closing Debtors and Bills Receivable are assumed to be average Debtors and Bills Receivable.

(ix) Creditors turnover ratio $= \dfrac{\text{Credit Purchases}}{\text{Average creditors + Average Bills Payable}}$

$$= \frac{5{,}45{,}000}{50{,}000 + 40{,}000}$$

$$= 6.05 \text{ times}$$

Note:
1. All purchases are assumed to be on credit.
2. Creditors are not given clearly in the example and therefore, they are assumed to be ₹ 50,000 out of other current liabilities.
3. Closing balances of Bills Payable and Creditors are assumed to be average balances.

(x) Sales to Working capital $= \dfrac{\text{Sales}}{\text{Working capital}}$

$$= \frac{9{,}50{,}000}{1{,}30{,}000}$$

$$= 7.31 \text{ times}$$

Working Capital = Stock + Debtors + Cash and Bank + B/R − [Other current liabilities + Bills payable]

$$= 50{,}000 + 45{,}000 + 60{,}000 + 1{,}05{,}000 - [90{,}000 + 40{,}000]$$

$$= 2{,}60{,}000 - 1{,}30{,}000$$

$$= 1{,}30{,}000$$

(xi) Sales to Fixed Assets $= \dfrac{\text{Sales}}{\text{Fixed Assets}}$

$$= \frac{9{,}50{,}000}{3{,}30{,}000} = 2.87 \text{ times}$$

(xii) Sales to Capital employed $= \dfrac{\text{Sales}}{\text{Capital employed}}$

$= \dfrac{9,50,000}{4,60,000}$

$= 2.06$

Capital employed as per Ratio No. V

(xiii) Return on Total Resources $= \dfrac{\text{Net Profit}}{\text{Total Assets}} \times 100$

$= \dfrac{2,60,000}{5,90,000} \times 100$

$= 44.06\%$

(xiv) Turnover of Total Assets $= \dfrac{\text{Sales}}{\text{Total Assets}}$

$= \dfrac{9,50,000}{5,90,000}$

$= 1.61 \text{ times}$

Problem 11

The following is the condensed Balance-sheet of XYZ Ltd. for 3 years ended on 31st March 2010, 31st March 2011 and 31st March 2012.

Balance-sheet of XYZ Ltd.

Particulars	[₹ in Lakhs]		
	31.3.2010 [₹]	31.3.2011 [₹]	31.3.2012 [₹]
Current Assets :			
Stock : Raw materials	12	18	20
Finished goods	30	35	25
Stores & Spares	3	4	5
Debtors	40	50	50
Cash and Bank	5	10	20
Fixed Assets	90	110	120
	180	227	240
Current Liabilities :	20	32	30
Debentures – Secured	60	60	60
Unsecured Loans - Bank	15	40	45
Reserves & Surplus	30	32.5	38.75
Profit & Loss A/c before providing for taxation and dividends	15	22.5	26.25
Equity Shares [₹ 100 each]	20	20	20
10% Preference Shares [₹ 100 each]	20	20	20
	180	227	240
Sales	300	360	400
Gross profit	15%	18%	20%

FINANCIAL MANAGEMENT   TECHNIQUES OF FINANCIAL ANALYSIS

The company earned the net profits before providing for income-tax @50%. Equity shareholders to get dividends 50% more than Preference Shareholders. Show the Appropriation A/c and work out the following ratios after reworking the Balance-sheet.

- (i) Acid-test ratio
- (ii) Stock turnover ratio
- (iii) Earning per share
- (iv) Ratio of fixed assets to shareholder's funds
- (v) Return on capital employed.

Solution:

Profit and Loss Appropriation Account of XYZ Ltd.

Particulars	31.3.2010 [₹]	31.3.2011 [₹]	31.3.2012 [₹]
Profit before tax and dividend	15,00,000	22,50,000	26,25,000
Less : Income-tax @ 50%	7,50,000	11,25,000	13,12,500
Profit after tax	7,50,000	11,25,000	13,12,500
Less : Pref. Dividends [10%]	2,00,000	2,00,000	2,00,000
Earnings for Equity shareholders	5,50,000	9,25,000	11,12,500
Less : Equity dividends [15%]	3,00,000	3,00,000	3,00,000
Balance of profits	2,50,000	6,25,000	8,12,500

Balance-sheet of XYZ Ltd.

Particulars	31.3.2010 [₹]	31.3.2011 [₹]	31.3.2012 [₹]
Current Liabilities :	20,00,000	32,00,000	30,00,000
Add : Provision for tax	7,50,000	11,25,000	13,12,500
Total current Liabilities	27,50,000	43,25,000	43,12,500
Current Assets*	90,00,000	1,17,00,000	12,00,000
Working Capital [CA – CL]	62,50,000	73,75,000	76,87,500
Add : Fixed Assets	90,00,000	1,100,00,000	12,00,000
Capital employed	1,52,50,000	1,83,75,000	1,96,87,500
Shareholder's funds – Equity	20,00,000	20,00,000	20,00,000
Share Capital-Preference	20,00,000	20,00,000	20,00,000
Reserves & Surplus	30,00,000	32,50,000	38,75,000
Profit and Loss Appropriation A/c. Bal.	2,50,000	6,25,000	8,12,500
Shareholder's funds	72,50,000	87,75,000	86,87,500

*   Current Assets = Total Assets – Fixed Assets

FINANCIAL MANAGEMENT — TECHNIQUES OF FINANCIAL ANALYSIS

Calculation of Ratios:

	31.3.2010 [₹]	31.3.2011 [₹]	31.3.2012 [₹]
(i) Acid Test Ratio = $\frac{\text{Liquid Current Assets}}{\text{Current Liabilities}}$ =	$\frac{45,00,000}{27,50,000}$ = 1.64 : 1	$\frac{60,00,000}{43,25,000}$ = 1.39 : 1	$\frac{70,00,000}{43,12,500}$ = 1.62 : 1
(ii) Stock Turnover Ratio = $\frac{\text{Cost of Goods Sold}}{\text{Average stock}}$	$\frac{2,55,00,000}{45,00,000}$ = 5.67 times	= $\frac{2,95,20,000}{51,00,000}$ = 5.78 times	= $\frac{3,20,00,000}{53,50,000}$ = 5.98 times
(iii) Earnings per share = Earnings for $\frac{\text{Equity shareholders}}{\text{Number of equity shares}}$	= $\frac{5,50,000}{20,000}$ = ₹ 27.5	= $\frac{9,25,000}{20,000}$ = ₹ 46.25	= $\frac{11,12,500}{20,000}$ = ₹ 55.62
(iv) Fixed Assets to Shareholder's funds = $\frac{\text{Fixed Assets}}{\text{Shareholder's funds}}$	$\frac{90,00,000}{72,50,000}$ = 1.24 times	$\frac{1,10,00,000}{78,75,000}$ = 1.4 times	$\frac{1,20,00,000}{86,87,500}$ = 1.38 times
(v) Return on Capital employed = $\frac{\text{Profit after tax}}{\text{Capital employed}}$	= $\frac{7,50,000}{1,52,50,000} \times 100$ = 4.92%	= $\frac{11,25,000}{1,83,75,000} \times 100$ = 6.12%	= $\frac{13,12,500}{1,96,87,500} \times 100$ = 6.67%

Problem 12

From the following annual accounts of ABC Ltd. for the year ended on 31st March 2012 and 31st March 2013, you are requested to calculate important ratios which will help the management in assessing overall performance of the company.

Balance-sheet of ABC Ltd.

Particulars	31.3.2012 (₹)	31.3.2013 (₹)
Sales	12,00,000	14,96,000
Cost of Sales	9,44,000	11,92,000
Gross profits	**2,56,000**	**3,04,000**
Expenses :		
Warehousing & Transport	76,000	96,000
Administration	76,000	76,000
Selling	44,000	56,000
Debenture interest	—	8,000
Net Profits	**60,000**	**68,000**
Fixed Assets less depreciation	1,20,000	1,60,000
Stock	2,40,000	3,76,000
Debtors	2,00,000	3,28,000
Cash	40,000	28,000
Total	**6,00,000**	**8,92,000**
Share Capital	3,00,000	3,00,000
Reserves	60,000	1,20,000
Profit and Loss A/c	40,000	48,000
Debentures	—	1,20,000
Current Liabilities	2,00,000	3,04,000
Total	**6,00,000**	**8,92,000**

FINANCIAL MANAGEMENT TECHNIQUES OF FINANCIAL ANALYSIS

Solution:

In order to comment on overall performance of the company, it is necessary to calculate the following ratios:

1. Profitability Ratios:

Particulars	31.3.2012 (₹)	31.3.2013 (₹)
(a) Gross Profit Ratio $= \dfrac{\text{Gross Profit}}{\text{Sales}} \times 100$	$= \dfrac{2,56,000}{12,00,000} \times 100$ = 21.33%	$= \dfrac{3,04,000}{14,96,000} \times 100$ = 20.32%
(b) Net Profit Ratio: $= \dfrac{\text{Net Profit}}{\text{Sales}} \times 100$	$= \dfrac{60,000}{12,00,000} \times 10$ = 5%	$= \dfrac{68,000}{14,96,000} \times 100$ = 4.54%
(c) Operating Net Profit: Ratio $= \dfrac{\text{Operating N/P}}{\text{Sales}} \times 100$	$= \dfrac{60,000}{12,00,000} \times 100$ = 5%	$= \dfrac{68,000 + 8,000^*}{14,96,000} \times 100$ = 5.08%
* ₹ 8,000 = Interest on Debentures		
(d) Operating Ratio: $\dfrac{\text{Cost of goods sold} + \text{Operating expenses}}{\text{Sales}} \times 100$	$= \dfrac{9,44,000 + 1,96,000}{12,00,000} \times 100$ = 95%	$= \dfrac{11,92,000 + 2,28,000}{14,96,000} \times 100$ = 94.92%
Note: Operating expenses are the expenses excluding interest on debentures.		
(e) Return on Capital employed $= \dfrac{\text{Net Profit}}{\text{Capital employed}} \times 100$	$= \dfrac{60,000}{4,00,000} \times 100$ = 15%	$= \dfrac{76,000}{5,88,000} \times 100$ = 12.93%

Note: Capital employed = Share Capital + Reserves + Profit and Loss A/c + Debentures

2. Financial Position:

Particulars	31.3.2012 (₹)	31.3.2013 (₹)
(a) Current Ratio $= \dfrac{\text{Current Assets}}{\text{Current Liabilities}}$	$= \dfrac{4,80,000}{2,00,000}$ = 2.4 : 1	$= \dfrac{7,32,000}{3,04,000}$ h = 2.40 : 1
(b) Quick Ratio $= \dfrac{\text{Quick Assets}}{\text{Current Liabilities}}$ *Stock	$= \dfrac{4,80,000 - 2,40,000}{2,00,000}$ = 1.2 : 1	$= \dfrac{7,32,000 - 3,66,000}{3,04,000}$ = 1.17 : 1
(c) Debt-Equity Ratio $= \dfrac{\text{Long-term debt}}{\text{Proprietor's funds}}$ [Share Capital + P & L A/c + Reserves]	Nil	$= \dfrac{1,20,000}{4,68,000}$ = .256 : 1
(d) Proprietary Ratio $= \dfrac{\text{Total Assets}}{\text{Proprietor's funds}}$	$= \dfrac{6,00,000}{4,00,000}$ = 1.5 : 1	$= \dfrac{8,92,000}{4,68,000}$ = 1.90 : 1

3. Turnover Ratios:

Particulars		31.3.2012 (₹)		31.3.2013 (₹)
(a) Fixed Assets Turnover = $\dfrac{\text{Sales}}{\text{Fixed Assets}}$	=	$\dfrac{12,00,000}{1,20,000}$	=	$\dfrac{14,96,000}{1,60,000}$
	=	10 times	=	9.35 times
(b) Working Capital Turnover = $\dfrac{\text{Sales}}{\text{*Working Capital}}$ * Current Assets – Current Liabilities	= =	4.28 times $\dfrac{12,00,000}{2,80,000}$	= =	3.49 times $\dfrac{14,96,000}{4,28,000}$
(c) Debtors turnover = $\dfrac{\text{Credit Sales}}{\text{Average Debtors}}$ [Closing Debtors]	= =	$\dfrac{12,00,000}{2,00,000}$ 6 times	= =	$\dfrac{14,96,000}{3,28,000}$ 4.56 times
(d) Stock Turnover Ratio = $\dfrac{\text{Cost of goods sold}}{\text{Average Stock}}$ [Closing Stock]	= =	$\dfrac{9,44,000}{2,40,000}$ 3.93 times	= =	$\dfrac{11,92,000}{3,76,000}$ 3.17 times

Conclusion:

If we look at the above-mentioned ratios, it is clear that most of the ratios in the profitability group are declining in 2010-11 as compared to 2009-10. The only exception to this is the ratio of operating net profit to sales, which has increased marginally from 5% to 5.08% in the year 2010-11.

The turnover ratios also show a declining trend. There is an increase in fixed assets as well as working capital in the year 2010-11 but this increase has not resulted in increase in sales. As a result of this, the various turnover ratios have declined in 2010-11 as compared to 2009-10.

Financial ratios are more or less stable in both the years. However, debt-equity ratio in 2010-11 is 256: 1, against a nil ratio in 2009-10. This is because the company has issued debentures in the year 2010-11.

In conclusion, it can be said that the overall position of the company seems to be on the decline and therefore, an urgent action is required to rectify the situation.

Problem 13

The capital of Kapil Ltd. is as follows:

	₹
Equity shares of ₹ 100 each	= 10,00,000
12% Preference shares of ₹ 10 each	5,00,000
Profit after tax	4,00,000
Equity dividend paid	20%
Market price of equity share	₹ 120

FINANCIAL MANAGEMENT   TECHNIQUES OF FINANCIAL ANALYSIS

Calculate the following ratios :
(i) Dividend yield on equity shares.
(ii) Cover for preference and equity dividend.
(iii) Earnings per equity shares.
(iv) Price-earnings ratio.

Solution:

	₹
Profit after tax	= 4,00,000
Less : Preference dividend 12% on ₹ 5,00,000	= 60,000
Profit available for equity shareholders	3,40,000
Equity dividend 20% on ₹ 10,00,000 = ₹ 2,00,000	

$$\text{Dividend per equity share} = \frac{2,00,000}{10,000} = ₹ 20$$

Ratios:

(i) $\text{Dividend yield on equity shares} = \frac{\text{Dividend per equity share}}{\text{Market price per equity}} \times 100$

$= \frac{20}{120} \times 100 = 16.67\%$

(ii) Cover for preference and equity dividend

$= \frac{\text{Profit available for dividend}}{\text{Dividend}}$

$= \frac{4,00,000}{2,60,000}$

$= 1.53 \text{ times}$

(iii) $\text{Earnings per equity share} = \frac{\text{Profits for equity shareholders}}{\text{No. of equity shares}}$

$= \frac{3,40,000}{10,000} = ₹ 34$

(iv) $\text{Price earnings ratio} = \frac{\text{Market price of an equity}}{\text{Earnings per share}}$

$= \frac{120}{34} = 3.52 \text{ times}$

Problem 14

Assume that a firm has owner's equity of ₹ 1,00,000. The ratios for the firm are,

Short-term debt to total debt = 0.4
Total debt to owner's equity = 0.6
Fixed assets to owner's equity = 0.6
Total assets turnover = 2 times
Inventory turnover = 8 times

Complete the following Balance-sheet, with the help of the information given above:

Balance - Sheet

Liabilities	₹	Assets	₹
Short-term debt	–	Cash	–
Long-term debt	–	Inventory	–
Total Debt	–	Total current assets	–
Owner's equity	–	Fixed assets	–
Total Capital and Liabilities	–	Total assets	–
	–		–

Solution:

$$\text{Owner's Equity} = ₹\,1,00,000$$
$$\text{Total debt to owner's equity} = .6$$

Therefore, Total debt = ₹ 60,000

Short-term debt is .4 of ₹ 60,000

∴ Short-term debt = ₹ 24,000

Therefore, Long-term debt = ₹ 60,000 – ₹ 24,000
$$= ₹\,36,000$$

Fixed assets are 6 of owner's equity

∴ Fixed assets = ₹ 60,000

Total assets = Total of liabilities side of Balance-sheet
= 1,00,000 + 36,000 + 24,000
  Equity   Long term debt + Short term debt
= ₹ 1,60,000

$$\text{Total assets turnover} = \frac{\text{Cost of goods sold}}{\text{Total assets}} = 2$$

$$= \frac{\text{Cost of goods sold}}{1,60,000} = 2$$

∴ Cost of goods sold = ₹ 3,20,000

Note: The numerator for the above ratio is taken as cost of goods sold instead of sales in the absence of information.

$$\text{Inventory turnover ratio} = \frac{\text{Cost of goods sold}}{\text{Average inventory}}$$

$$8 = \frac{3,20,000}{\text{Average inventory}}$$

Therefore, Average inventory i.e.

Closing inventory = ₹ 40,000

Cash = Total assets – Fixed assets – Inventory
= 1,60,000 – 60,000 – 40,000 = ₹ 60,000

Balance Sheet

Liabilities	₹	Assets	₹
Short-term debt	24,000	Cash	60,000
Long-term debt	36,000	Inventory	40,000
Owner's equity	1,00,000	Fixed assets	60,000
	1,60,000		1,60,000

Problem 15

From the following figures and ratios, make out the Balance Sheet in the following format.

Balance Sheet of PQR Ltd.

Liabilities	₹	Assets	₹
Equity Capital	3,00,000	Fixed Assets	6,00,000
Retained Earnings	2,00,000	Inventory	–
Debentures	1,25,000	Debtors	–
Other long-term loans	–	Cash	–
Accounts payable	1,00,000		

Gross profit margin = 20%
Quick ratio = 1.5 : 1
Stock turnover ratio = 12 times
Average collection period = 30 days
Total asset turnover = 3 times
Other Long-term debts [excluding debentures] to proprietor's funds = .75 : 1

Solution:

(a) Long-term debt to Proprietor's funds = $\dfrac{\text{Other long-term debt}}{\text{Proprietor's funds}}$

$$.75 = \dfrac{\text{Long-term debt}}{\underset{\substack{\text{Share} \quad \text{Retained} \\ \text{capital} \quad \text{earnings}}}{3,00,000 + 2,00,000}}$$

Other Long-term debt = ₹ 3,75,000

(b) Sales:

Total assets turnover ratio = $\dfrac{\text{Sales}}{\text{Total assets}}$

$3 = \dfrac{\text{Sales}}{11,00,000}$

Sales = ₹ 33,00,000

Note: Total assets = Total Liabilities

Total liabilities = Share Capital + Retained earnings
+ Debentures + Other long-term debt
+ Accounts payable
= 3,00,000 + 2,00,000 + 1,25,000 + 3,75,000 + 1,00,000
= ₹ 11,00,000

(c) Debtors:

$$\text{Average collection period} = 30 \text{ days}$$
$$\text{Sales} = ₹ 33,00,000$$
$$\text{Debtors' turnover} = \frac{360 \text{ days}}{30 \text{ days}}$$
$$= 12 \text{ times}$$
$$\text{Debtors' turnover} = \frac{\text{Credit Sales}}{\text{Average Debtors [Closing balance]}}$$
$$12 = \frac{33,00,000}{\text{Debtors}}$$

Therefore, Debtors = ₹ 2,75,000

Note:
1. It is assumed that there are 360 days in a year.
2. All sales are assumed to be on credit in the absence of information.

(d) Inventory:

$$\text{Inventory turnover ratio} = \frac{\text{Cost of goods sold}}{\text{Average inventory}}$$
$$12 = \frac{26,40,000}{\text{Average inventory}}$$

Therefore, Average inventory [Closing] = ₹ 2,20,000

Note:
1. Cost of goods sold = Sales – Gross profit
2. In the absence of information, closing inventory is taken as average inventory.

Cash:
Total Assets	= ₹ 11,00,000
Fixed Assets	= ₹ 6,00,000
Debtors [As per c]	= ₹ 2,75,000
Inventory [As per d]	= ₹ 2,20,000
Cash [Balancing figure]	= ₹ 5,000
Total	**₹ 11,00,000**

Balance Sheet of PQR Ltd.

Liabilities	₹	Assets	₹
Equity Capital	3,00,000	Fixed Assets	6,00,000
Retained Earnings	2,00,000	Debtors	2,75,000
Debentures	1,25,000	Inventory	2,20,000
Long-term loans	3,75,000	Cash	5,000
Accounts payable	1,00,000		
Total	**11,00,000**		**11,00,000**

FINANCIAL MANAGEMENT   TECHNIQUES OF FINANCIAL ANALYSIS

Problem 16

The following data represents the ratios pertaining to X Ltd. for the year ending on 31st March 2013.

	₹
Annual Sales	40,00,000
Sales to net worth	4 times
Current Liabilities to Net Worth	50%
Total Debt to Net Worth	80%
Current Ratio	2.2 times
Sales to Inventory	8 times
Average collection period	40 days
Fixed Assets to Net Worth	70%

From the above information, prepare the Balance-sheet with as many details as possible. Assume all sales on credit.

Solution:

(i) Sales to Net worth = 4 times
Sales = ₹ 40,00,000

Therefore, $4 = \dfrac{40,00,000}{\text{Net worth}}$

Net worth = ₹ 10,00,000

(ii) Current Liabilities to net worth = 50%
This means that current liabilities are 50% of net worth.
Therefore, Current liabilities = ₹ 5,00,000

(iii) Total Debt to Net Worth = 80%
This means that total debt is 80% of the Net worth.
Therefore, Total Debt = ₹ 8,00,000

(iv) Current ratio = $\dfrac{\text{Current Assets}}{\text{Current liabilities}} = 2.2$

Therefore, $\dfrac{\text{Current Assets}}{5,00,000} = 2.2$

Current Assets = ₹ 11,00,000

(v) Sales to Inventory = 8 times
Sales = ₹ 40,00,000

Inventory = $\dfrac{₹ 40,00,000}{8}$ = ₹ 5,00,000

(vi) Average collection period = 40 days
Sales = ₹ 40,00,000

Debtors turnover = $\dfrac{360 \text{ days}}{40 \text{ days}}$ = 9 times

Therefore, Debtors = $\dfrac{40,00,000}{9}$ = ₹ 4,44,444

(vii) Fixed Assets to Net Worth = 70%
Therefore, Fixed Assets = 70% of ₹ 10,00,000 = ₹ 7,00,000

Balance Sheet of X Ltd. as on 31st March 2013

Liabilities	₹	Assets		₹
Net Worth	10,00,000	Fixed Assets		7,00,000
Long-term Debt	3,00,000	Current Assets		
Current Liabilities	5,00,000	Stock	5,00,000	
		Debtors	4,44,444	
		Cash	1,55,556	11,00,000
Total	**18,00,000**	**Total**		**18,00,000**

Note:

1. Total Debt is ₹ 8,00,000 and Current Liabilities are ₹ 5,00,000.

   Therefore, Long-term debt = ₹ 3,00,000

2. Total current assets = ₹ 11,00,000

   Out of these stock and debtors together are ₹ 9,44,444. Therefore, cash ₹ 1.55,556 is the balancing figure.

Problem 17

The standard ratios for the industry and the ratios of a company are given below. Determine the efficiency of the working of the company.

Balance-sheet

Particulars	31.3.2013 (₹) Industry Average	31.3.2013 (₹) Company Position
Current Ratio	2.50	1.90
Gross Profit Ratio	.30	.35
Fixed Expenses to Sales	.15	.20
Variable Expenses to Sales	.10	.08
Sales/Capital	3.00	4.00
Fixed Assets/Long-term funds	1.00	.90
Rate of Return on Capital	15%	22%

Solution:

(a) The profitability of Company is better than the industry standard. The gross profit ratio as well as variable expenses to sales and rate of return on capital is better for Company than industry standard. However, the fixed expenses to sales ratio is not satisfactory for the company as compared to the industry average. Sales to capital ratio for the company is better than the industry average.

(b) Current ratio for company is, however, not satisfactory as compared to industry standard. There is a scope for improvement for company X in this respect.

FUNDS FLOW ANALYSIS

Problem 1

From the following Balance-sheets of XYZ Ltd. prepare a statement showing sources and application of funds for the year ended 31st March, 2013

Balance-Sheet of XYZ Ltd. as on 31.3.2012 and 31.3.2013

Liabilities	Amounts ₹ 31.3.12	Amounts ₹ 31.3.13	Assets	Amounts ₹ 31.3.12	Amounts ₹ 31.3.13
Equity Capital	3,00,000	4,00,000	Goodwill	1,15,000	90,000
8% Redeemable			Land & Building	2,00,000	1,70,000
Pref. Capital.	1,50,000	1,00,000	Plant	80,000	2,00,000
General Reserve	40,000	70,000	Debtors	1,60,000	2,00,000
Profit & Loss A/c.	30,000	48,000	Stock	77,000	1,09,000
Proposed dividend	42,000	50,000	Bills Receivable	20,000	30,000
Creditors	55,000	83,000	Cash in hand	15,000	10,000
Bills payable	20,000	16,000	Cash at bank	10,000	8,000
Taxation provision	40,000	50,000			
Total	**6,77,000**	**8,17,000**	**Total**	**6,77,000**	**8,17,000**

Additional Information:

1. Depreciation has been charged on Plant and Land and Building ₹ 10,000 and ₹ 20,000 respectively, in 2012-13.
2. Interim dividend of ₹ 20,000 has been paid in 2012-13.
3. Income-tax paid during 2012-13 ₹ 35,000.

Solution:

Working notes:

1. Statement showing changes in working capital

	Particulars	31.3.12 ₹	31.3.13 ₹	Increase in working Capital ₹	Decrease in working Capital ₹
[A]	**Current Assets:**				
(i)	Debtors	1,60,000	2,00,000	40,000	—
(ii)	Stock	77,000	1,09,000	32,000	—
(iii)	Bills Receivable	20,000	30,000	10,000	—
(iv)	Cash in hand	15,000	10,000	—	5,000
(v)	Cash at bank	10,000	8,000	—	2,000
	Total	**2,82,000**	**3,57,000**		
[B]	**Current liabilities:**				
(i)	Creditors	55,000	83,000	—	28,000
(ii)	Bills payable	20,000	16,000	4,000	—
	Total	**75,000**	**99,000**	**86,000**	**35,000**

Net increase in working capital = ₹ 86,000 – ₹ 35,000 = ₹ 51,000.

2.

Dr.   Land & Building A/c.   **Cr.**

Particulars	₹	Particulars	₹
To Balance b/d.	2,00,000	By Adjust. P & L A/c. (Dep.)	20,000
		By Bank A/c. sale (Bal. figure)	10,000
		By Balance c/d.	1,70,000
Total	**2,00,000**	**Total**	**2,00,000**

3.

Dr.   Plant A/c.   **Cr.**

Particulars	₹	Particulars	₹
To Balance b/d.	80,000	By Adjust. P & L A/c. (Dep.)	10,000
To Bank A/c. (purchases) (Balancing figure)	1,30,000	By Balance c/d.	2,00,000
Total	**2,10,000**	**Total**	**2,10,000**

4.

Dr.   Proposed Dividend A/c.   **Cr.**

Particulars	₹	Particulars	₹
To Bank A/c.* (Dividends paid)	42,000	By Bal. b/d.	42,000
		By Adjust. P & L A/c.	
To Balance c/d.	50,000	(Dividend proposed)	50,000
Total	**92,000**	**Total**	**92,000**

* Dividends paid are not given and so it is assumed.

5.

Dr.   Provision for Taxation A/c.   **Cr.**

Particulars	₹	Particulars	₹
To Bank A/c. [I/T paid]	35,000	By Balance b/d.	40,000
To Balance c/d.	50,000	By Adjust. P & L A/c. (Prov. made)	45,000
Total	**85,000**	**Total**	**85,000**

6. Funds from operations

Dr.   Adjusted Profit & Loss A/c.   **Cr.**

Particulars	₹	Particulars	₹
To Depreciation on :		By Balance b/d.	30,000
Plant 10,000		By funds from	
Land & Bldg. 20,000	30,000	Operation	
To Proposed dividend	50,000	[Balancing figure]	2,18,000
To Taxation provision	45,000		
To Transfer to Reserve			
(₹ 70,000 – ₹ 40,000)	30,000		
To Interim dividend	20,000		
To Goodwill written off	25,000		
To Balance c/d.	48,000		
Total	**2,48,000**	**Total**	**2,48,000**

Funds Flow Statement

	Sources	₹		Applications	₹
I.	Issue of equity	1,00,000	I.	Redemption of Pref.	50,000
II.	Sale of Land & Bldg. [working note 2]	10,000		Capital	1,30,000
III.	Funds from Operations [working note 6]	2,18,000	II.	Purchase of plant (working note 3)	20,000
			III.	Interim dividends paid	42,000
			IV.	Final dividends paid	35,000
			V.	Income-tax paid	
			VI.	Net increase in working capital (working note 1)	51,000
	Total	**3,28,000**		**Total**	**3,28,000**

Problem 2

Following Balance-sheets have been extracted from the records of Zenith Ltd.

Balance–Sheet of Zenith Ltd.

Liabilities	31.3.12 (₹)	31.3.13 (₹)	Assets	31.3.12 (₹)	31.3.13 (₹)
Share Capital	1,00,000	1,10,000	Building	40,000	38,000
General reserve	14,000	18,000	Plant & Machinery	37,000	36,000
P & A/c.	16,000	13,000	Investment	10,000	21,000
Creditors	8,000	5,400	Stock	30,000	23,400
Bills payable	1,200	800	Bills Receivable	2,000	3,200
Provision for tax	16,000	18,000	Debtors	18,000	19,000
Provision for doubtful Debts	400	600	Bank Balance	6,600	15,200
			Preliminary exp.	12,000	10,000
Total	**1,55,600**	**1,65,800**	**Total**	**1,55,600**	**1,65,800**

Additional information:
1. Depreciation charged on Plant ₹ 4,000.
2. Provision for taxation made ₹ 19,000 during 2012-13
3. Interim dividend ₹ 8,000 was paid during 2012-13
4. A piece of machinery was sold for ₹ 8,000 during 2012-13. It had costed ₹ 12,000. Depreciation of ₹ 7,000 was provided on that.

Prepare a funds flow statement.

FINANCIAL MANAGEMENT   TECHNIQUES OF FINANCIAL ANALYSIS

Solution:

Working notes:

1. **Statement showing changes in working capital**

Particulars	31.3.12 ₹	31.3.13 ₹	Increase in working Capital ₹	Decrease in working Capital ₹
[A] Current Assets:				
(i) Stock	30,000	23,400	–	6,600
(ii) Debtors*	17,600	18,400	800	–
(iii) Bills receivable	2,000	3,200	1,200	–
(iv) Bank balance	6,600	15,200	8,600	–
Total	56,200	60,200		
[B] Current liabilities:				
(i) Creditors	8,000	5,400	2,600	–
(ii) Bills payable	1,200	800	400	–
Total	9,200	6,200	13,600	6,600

* Debtors less provision for doubtful debts.

Net increase in working capital = ₹ 13,600 – 6,600 = ₹ 7,000.

2.

Dr.   **Plant and Machinery A/c**   **Cr.**

Particulars	₹	Particulars	₹
To Balance b/d.	37,000	By Adjust. P & L A/c. (Dep.)	4,000
To Adjusted P & L A/c.		By Bank A/c. (Sale)	8,000
(Profit on sale)		By Balance c/d.	36,000
[₹ 12,000 – ₹ 7,000 – ₹ 8,000]	3,000		
To Bank A/c. (Purchases)			
Balancing Figure.	8,000		
Total	48,000	Total	48,000

3.

Dr.   **Building A/c**   **Cr.**

Particulars	₹	Particulars	₹
To Balance b/d.	40,000	By Adjust. P & L A/c. (Dep.) (Balancing figure)	2,000
		By Balance c/d.	38,000
Total	40,000	Total	40,000

4.

Dr.	Provision for Taxation A/c		Cr.
Particulars	₹	**Particulars**	₹
To Bank A/c. (Tax paid) (Balancing figure)	17,000	By Balance c/d.	16,000
To Balance c/d.	18,000	By Adjust. P & L A/c. (Provision made)	19,000
Total	**35,000**	**Total**	**35,000**

5. Funds from operations:

Dr.		Adjusted Profit & Loss A/c.		Cr.
Particulars		₹	**Particulars**	₹
To Depreciation on : Building	2,000		By Balance b/d.	16,000
Plant & Mach.	4,000	6,000	By Profit on sale of (Machinery)	3,000
To General reserve		4,000	By Funds from oper.	
To Prov. for taxation		19,000	(Balancing figure)	33,000
To Preliminary exps.		2,000		
To Interim dividend		8,000		
To Balance c/d.		13,000		
Total		**52,000**	**Total**	**52,000**

Funds Flow Statement

Sources	₹	**Applications**	₹
I. Issue of share capital	10,000	I. Purchase of Plant & Mach. [working note 2]	8,000
II. Sale of Machinery	8,000	II. Income-tax paid	17,000
III. Funds from operations [working note 5]	33,000	III. Interim dividend paid	8,000
		IV. Purchase of Invests.	11,000
		V. Increase in working capital	7,000
Total	**51,000**	**Total**	**51,000**

Problem 3

From the following Balance-sheet of A Ltd., prepare a statement showing sources and application of funds.

Balance-Sheet of A Ltd.

Liabilities	31.3.12 (₹)	31.3.13 (₹)	Assets	31.3.12 (₹)	31.3.13 (₹)
Share Capital	10,00,000	11,00,000	Goodwill	50,000	40,000
Debentures	5,00,000	3,00,000	Land & Building	4,20,000	6,60,000
General reserve	2,00,000	2,00,000	Plant & Machinery	6,00,000	8,00,000
Profit & Loss A/c.	1,10,000	1,90,000	Stocks	2,50,000	2,10,000
Income-tax provision	40,000	1,10,000	Debtors	3,00,000	2,40,000
Creditors	50,000	40,000	Cash	3,00,000	24,000
Bills Payable	20,000	30,000	Preliminary exps.	30,000	20,000
Provision for Doubtful debts	30,000	24,000			
Total	**19,50,000**	**19,94,000**	**Total**	**19,50,000**	**19,94,000**

Additional Information:

1. During the year 2012-13, a part of machinery costing ₹ 7,500 [accumulated depreciation on that ₹ 2,500] was sold for ₹ 3,000.
2. Dividend of ₹ 1,00,000 was paid during 2012-13
3. Income-tax paid during the year 2012-13 ₹ 50,000.
4. Depreciation for the year 2012-13 was provided as under:
   Land and Building ₹ 10,000.
   Plant and Machinery ₹ 50,000.

Prepare a funds flow statement.

Solution:

Working notes:

1. Statement showing changes in working capital:

	Particulars	31.3.12 ₹	31.3.13 ₹	Increase in working Capital ₹	Decrease in working Capital ₹
[A]	**Current Assets:**				
(i)	Stock	2,50,000	2,10,000		40,000
(ii)	Debtors*	2,70,000	2,16,000		54,000
(iii)	Cash	3,00,000	24,000		2,76,000
	Total Current Assets	8,50,000	2,50,000		3,70,000
[B]	**Current liabilities:**				
(i)	Creditors	50,000	40,000	10,000	–
(ii)	Bills payable	20,000	30,000	–	10,000
	Total Liabilities			10,000	3,80,000

*Debtors less provision for doubtful debts. Net decrease in working capital = ₹ 3,70,000.

2.

Dr.		Land & Building A/c.			Cr.
Particulars		₹	**Particulars**		₹
To Balance b/d.		4,20,000	By Adjus. P & L A/c. Depre.		10,000
To Bank A/c. (Additions)			By Balance c/d.		6,60,000
(Balancing figure)		2,50,000			
Total		**6,70,000**	**Total**		**6,70,000**

3.

Dr.		Plant and Machinery A/c.			Cr.
Particulars		₹	**Particulars**		₹
To Balance b/d.		6,00,000	By Bank A/c. (sale)		3,000
To Bank A/c. (Additions)			By Adj. P & L A/c. (loss)		2,000
Balancing figure		2,55,000	By Adj. P & L A/c. (Depre.)		50,000
			By Balance c/d.		8,00,000
Total		**8,55,000**	**Total**		**8,55,000**

4.

Dr.   Income-tax provision A/c.   Cr.

Particulars	₹	Particulars	₹
To Bank A/c. (Tax paid)	50,000	By Balance b/d.	40,000
To Balance c/d.	1,10,000	By Adj. P & L A/c. (Prov. made) (Balancing figure)	1,20,000
Total	**1,60,000**	**Total**	**1,60,000**

5. **Funds from operations:**

Dr.   Adjusted Profit and Loss A/c.   Cr.

Particulars		₹	Particulars	₹
To Depreciation on:			By Balance b/d.	1,10,000
Land & Bldg.	10,000		By Funds from operations	
Plant & Mach.	50,000	60,000	(Balancing figure)	3,82,000
To Loss on sale of				
Machinery (W.N.B.)		2,000		
To I/T provision		1,20,000		
To Goodwill written off		10,000		
To Prel. exp. written off		10,000		
To Dividends		1,00,000		
To Balance c/d.		1,90,000		
Total		**4,92,000**	**Total**	**4,92,000**

Funds Flow Statement

Sources	₹	Applications	₹
1. Issue of share capital	1,00,000	1. Redemption of Debs.	2,00,000
2. Sale of Machinery	3,000	2. Purchase of Land & Building (W.N.2)	2,50,000
3. Funds from operations [working note 5]	3,82,000	3. Purchase of Plant & Machinery (W.N.3)	2,55,000
4. Net decrease in Working Capital (W.N.1)	3,70,000	4. Dividends paid	1,00,000
		5. Tax paid	50,000
Total	**8,55,000**	**Total**	**8,55,000**

FINANCIAL MANAGEMENT   TECHNIQUES OF FINANCIAL ANALYSIS

Problem 4

From the following Balance-sheet of AO Ltd., prepare a funds flow statement for the year ended 31st March, 2013.

Balance–Sheet of AO Ltd. as on 31st March, 2012 and 2013

Liabilities	31.3.12 (₹)	31.3.13 (₹)	Assets	31.3.12 (₹)	31.3.13 (₹)
Equity Capital	3,00,000	4,00,000	Goodwill	1,00,000	80,000
8% Redeemable			Land & Building	2,00,000	1,70,000
Pref. Capital	1,50,000	1,00,000	Plant	80,000	2,00,000
Capital Reserve	–	20,000	Investments	20,000	30,000
General Reserve	40,000	50,000	Debtors	1,40,000	1,70,000
Profit & Loss A/c.	30,000	48,000	Stock	77,000	1,09,000
Proposed Dividend	42,000	50,000	Bills Receivable	20,000	30,000
Creditors	25,000	47,000	Cash in hand	15,000	10,000
Bills payable	20,000	16,000	Cash at bank	10,000	8,000
Expenses outstanding	30,000	36,000	Preliminary exps.	15,000	10,000
Taxation Provision	40,000	50,000			
Total	**6,77,000**	**8,17,000**	**Total**	**6,77,000**	**8,17,000**

Additional information:
1. A piece of land has been sold out in the year 2012-13 and the profit on sale has been carried to capital reserve.
2. A machine has been sold for ₹ 10,000. The written down value of the machine was ₹ 12,000. Depreciation of ₹ 10,000 is charged in the Plant A/c. for the year 2007-08.
3. The investments are trade investments, ₹ 3,000 by way of dividend are received including ₹ 1,000 from pre-acquisition profit which has been credited to investment A/c.
4. An interim dividend of ₹ 20,000 has been paid in year 2012-13.

Solution:

Working notes:

1. **Statement showing cheques in working capital**

Particulars		31.3.12 ₹	31.3.13 ₹	Increase in working Capital ₹	Decrease in working Capital ₹
[A]	**Current Assets:**				
(i)	Debtors	1,40,000	1,70,000	30,000	–
(ii)	Stock	77,000	1,09,000	32,000	–
(iii)	Bills receivable	20,000	30,000	10,000	–
(iv)	Cash in hand	15,000	10,000	–	5,000
(v)	Cash at bank	10,000	8,000	–	2,000
	Total	2,62,000	3,27,000	–	–

contd. ...

[B]	Current liabilities:				
(i)	Creditors	25,000	47,000	–	22,000
(ii)	Bills payable	20,000	16,000	4,000	–
(iii)	Expenses O/s.	30,000	36,000	–	6,000
	Total	75,000	99,000	76,000	35,000

Net increase in working capital ₹ 41,000.

2.

Dr.		Land & Building A/c.		Cr.
Particulars	₹	Particulars	₹
To Balance b/d.	2,00,000	By Bank A/c. [sale]	50,000
To Capital reserve	20,000	(Balancing figure)	
		By Balance c/d.	1,70,000
Total	2,20,000	Total	2,20,000

3.

Dr.		Plant and Machinery A/c.		Cr.
Particulars	₹	Particulars	₹
To Balance b/d.	80,000	By Bank A/c. (Sale)	10,000
To Bank A/c.		By Adj. P & L A/c. (Loss on sale)	
(Purchases) (Balancing figure)	1,42,000	By Adj. P & L A/c. (Dep.)	2,000
		By Balance c/d.	10,000
			2,00,000
Total	2,22,000	Total	2,22,000

4.

Dr.		Investments A/c.		Cr.
Particulars	₹	Particulars	₹
To Balance b/d.	20,000	By Dividend	1,000
To Bank A/c. (Purchases)	11,000	(out of Pre-acq. profit)	
(Balancing figure)		By Balance c/d.	30,000
Total	31,000	Total	31,000

5.

Dr.		Proposed Dividend A/c.		Cr.
Particulars	₹	Particulars	₹
To Bank A/c. (Dividend paid)	42,000	By Balance b/d.	42,000
To Balance c/d.	50,000	By Adj. P & L A/c.	50,000
		(Prov. made) (Balancing figure)	
Total	92,000	Total	92,000

6.

Dr.		Provision for Taxation A/c.		Cr.
Particulars	₹	Particulars	₹
To Bank A/c. Tax paid	40,000	By Balance b/d.	40,000
To Balance c/d.	50,000	By P & L A/c. Balancing figure	50,000
Total	90,000	Total	90,000

7. Funds from Operations:

Dr.		Adjusted Profit & Loss A/c.		Cr.
Particulars	₹	Particulars	₹
To Depreciation on: Plant & Machinery	10,000	By Balance b/d.	30,000
To loss on sale of: Plant & Machinery	2,000	By Dividends from Investments	2,000
To Prov. for taxation [working note 6]	50,000	By funds from operation [Balancing figure]	1,83,000
To Proposed dividend [working note 5]	50,000		
To Goodwill written off	20,000		
To General reserve	10,000		
To Prel. Exp. written off	5,000		
To Interim dividend	20,000		
To Balance c/d.	48,000		
Total	2,15,000	Total	2,15,000

Funds Flow Statement

Sources	₹	Applications	₹
1. Issue of shares	1,00,000	1. Redemption of Pref. Shares	50,000
2. Sale of land [working note 2]	50,000	2. Purchase of Plant & Mach. [working note 3]	1,42,000
3. Sale of Machinery	10,000		
4. Funds from operations [working note 7]	1,83,000	3. Purchase of Invest. [working note 4]	11,000
5. Receipt of dividend	3,000	4. Payment of interim dividend	20,000
		5. Payment of Tax [working note 6]	40,000
		6. Payment of dividend [working note 6]	42,000
		7. Net increase in working capital [working note 1]	41,000
Total	3,46,000	Total	3,46,000

FINANCIAL MANAGEMENT

TECHNIQUES OF FINANCIAL ANALYSIS

Problem 5

The following are the summarised Balance-sheets of Star Ltd. as on 31st March, 2012 and 31st March, 2013.

Balance-sheet of Star Ltd. as on 31st March, 2012 and 2013

Liabilities	31.3.12 (₹)	31.3.13 (₹)	Assets	31.3.12 (₹)	31.3.13 (₹)
Share Capital	2,00,000	2,60,000	Goodwill	–	20,000
Profit & Loss A/c.	39,690	41,220	Plant & Machinery	1,12,950	1,16,200
Reserves	50,000	50,000	Land & Building	1,48,500	1,44,250
Prov. for taxation	40,000	50,000	Stock	1,11,040	97,370
Bank overdraft	59,510	–	Sundry Advances	2,315	735
Bills payable	33,780	11,525	Sundry Debtors	85,175	72,625
Creditors	39,500	41,135	Bank	2,500	2,700
Total	**4,62,480**	**4,53,880**	**Total**	**4,62,480**	**4,53,880**

Additional information:

1. During the year 2012-13, an interim dividend of ₹ 26,000 was paid.
2. The assets of another company were purchased for ₹ 60,000 payable in fully paid shares of the company. The assets consisted of Stock ₹ 21,640, Machinery ₹ 18,360 and Goodwill ₹ 20,000. In addition, Sundry purchases of plant of ₹ 5,650 were made.
3. Income-tax paid during the year amounted ₹ 25,000.
4. Net profit for the year 2012-13 before tax ₹ 62,350.

Prepare funds flow statement.

Solution:

Working notes:

1. **Statement showing changes in working capital:**

Particulars	31.3.12 ₹	31.3.13 ₹	Increase in working Capital ₹	Decrease in working Capital ₹
[A] Current Assets:				
(i) Stock	1,11,040	97,370	–	13,670
(ii) Sundry Advances	2,315	735	–	1,580
(iii) Sundry Debtors	85,175	72,625	–	12,550
(iv) Bank Balance	2,500	2,700	200	–
Total	**2,01,030**	**1,73,430**	**–**	**–**
[B] Current Liabilities:				
(i) Bank overdraft	59,510	–	59,510	–
(ii) Bills payable	33,780	11,525	22,255	–
(iii) Creditors	39,500	41,135	–	1,635
Total	**1,32,790**	**52,660**	**81,965**	**29,435**

Net increase in the working capital = ₹ 81,965 – ₹ 29,435 = ₹ 52,530.

2.

Dr.		Land and Building A/c.		Cr.
Particulars	₹	Particulars		₹
To Balance c/d.	1,48,500	By Adj. P & L A/c. (Depreciation) (Balancing figure)		4,250
		By Balance c/d.		1,44,250
Total	1,48,500	Total		1,48,500

3.

Dr.		Plant and Machinery A/c.	Cr.
Particulars	₹	Particulars	₹
To Balance c/d.	1,12,950	By Adj. P & L A/c.	20,760
To Share Capital		(Dep. - bal. fig.)	
(Purchase for shares)	18,360	By Balance c/d.	1,16,200
To Bank A/c. (Purchases)	5,650		
Total	1,36,960	Total	1,36,960

4.

Dr.		Provision for Taxation A/c.	Cr.
Particulars	₹	Particulars	₹
To Bank A/c.	25,000	By Balance b/d.	40,000
(Income-tax paid)		By Adj. P & L A/c.	
To Balance c/d.	50,000	(Prov. made) (Balancing figure)	35,000
Total	75,000	Total	75,000

5. Funds from operations:

Dr.			Adjusted Profit & Loss A/c.	Cr.
Particulars		₹	Particulars	₹
To Depreciation on :			By Balance b/d.	39,690
Land & Bldg.	4,250		By Funds from Operations	
Plant & Mach.	20,760	25,010	Balancing figure	87,540
To Prov. for taxation				
[working note 4]		35,000		
To interim dividend		26,000		
To Balance c/d.		41,220		
Total		1,27,230	Total	1,27,230

FINANCIAL MANAGEMENT   TECHNIQUES OF FINANCIAL ANALYSIS

Funds Flow Statement

Sources	₹	Applications		₹
1. Issue of share capital	60,000	1. Purchase of machinery		
2. Funds from operations		For shares	18,360	
[working note 3]	87,540	For cash	5,650	24,010
		2. Purchase of goodwill		20,000
		3. Payment of interim dividend		26,000
		4. Payment of income-tax		25,000
		5. Increase in working capital		
		[working note 1]		52,530
Total	**1,47,540**	**Total**		**1,47,540**

Problem 6

The comparative Balance-sheets of Mr. Abhijit Roy for two years were as follows:

Balance-Sheet of Mr. Abhijit Roy

Liabilities	31.3.12 (₹)	31.3.13 (₹)	Assets	31.3.12 (₹)	31.3.13 (₹)
Capital	1,50,000	1,75,000	Land & Building	1,10,000	1,50,000
Loan from Bank			Machinery	2,00,000	1,40,000
(long term)	1,60,000	1,00,000	Stock	50,000	45,000
Creditors	90,000	1,00,000	Debtors	70,000	80,000
Bills payable	50,000	40,000	Cash	20,000	25,000
Loan (long term)	–	25,000			
Total	**4,50,000**	**4,40,000**	**Total**	**4,50,000**	**4,40,000**

Additional information:

1. Net profit for the year 2012-13 was ₹ 60,000.
2. During the year a machine costing ₹ 25,000.
   [Accumulated depreciation ₹ 10,000] was sold for ₹ 13,000. The provision for depreciation against machinery as on 31.3.2012 was ₹ 50,000 and as on 31.3.2013 was ₹ 85,000.

   Prepare a funds flow statement.

FINANCIAL MANAGEMENT   TECHNIQUES OF FINANCIAL ANALYSIS

Solution:

Working notes:

1. **Statement showing changes in working capital**

Particulars	31.3.12 ₹	31.3.13 ₹	Increase in working Capital ₹	Decrease in working Capital ₹
[A] Current Assets:				
(i) Stock	50,000	45,000	–	5,000
(ii) Debtors	70,000	80,000	10,000	–
(iii) Cash	20,000	25,000	5,000	–
Total	1,40,000	1,50,000	–	–
[B] Current liabilities:				
(i) Creditors	90,000	1,00,000	–	10,000
(ii) Bills payable	50,000	40,000	10,000	–
Total	1,40,000	1,40,000	25,000	15,000

Net increase in working capital ₹ 10,000.

2.

Dr.		Provision for Taxation A/c.		Cr.
Particulars	₹	Particulars		₹
To Machinery A/c. [Accum. Dep. on Machinery sold]	10,000	By Balance b/d.		50,000
To Balance c/d.	85,000	By Profit & Loss A/c. (Depreciation for 2012-13) (Balancing figure)		45,000
Total	95,000	Total		95,000

3.

Dr.		Plant and Machinery A/c.	Cr.
Particulars	₹	Particulars	₹
To Balance b/d. (₹ 2,00,000 + ₹ 50,000) Acc. Dep.	2,50,000	By Bank A/c. (Sale)	13,000
		By Provision for Dep. A/c. (Accu. Dep. on sale)	10,000
		By P & L A/c. (Loss on sale of machine)	2,000
		By Balance c/d. ₹ 1,40,000 + ₹ 85,000 (Accu. depreciation)	2,25,000
Total	2,50,000	Total	2,50,000

4. **Funds from operations**

Particulars	₹
Net profit for the year	60,000
Add, Non-cash items:	
(i) Loss on sale of machine	2,000
(ii) Depreciation 45,000	47,000
	₹ 1,07,000

Funds Flow Statement

Sources	₹	Applications	₹
1. Sale of Machinery	13,000	1. Purchase of land & building	40,000
2. Realising of term loan	25,000	2. Repayment of loan from bank	60,000
3. Funds from operations [working note 4]	1,07,000	3. Drawings*	35,000
		4. Net increase in working capital	10,000
Total	**1,45,000**	**Total**	**1,45,000**

* Drawings:	₹
Capital 31.3.2012	1,50,000
Add: Net profit	60,000
	2,10,000
Less: Capital 31.3.2013	1,75,000
Drawings	**35,000**

Problem 7

From the following information, prepare funds flow statement for the year ended 31st March, 2013

Balance–Sheet as on 31st March, 2012 and 31st March 2013

Liabilities	31.3.12 (₹)	31.3.13 (₹)	Assets	31.3.12 (₹)	31.3.13 (₹)
Equity Capital	3,00,000	3,50,000	Fixed Assets [Net]	5,10,000	6,20,000
Pref. Capital	2,00,000	1,00,000	Investments	30,000	80,000
Debentures	1,00,000	2,00,000	Current Assets	2,40,000	3,75,000
Reserves	1,10,000	2,70,000	Discount on Debs.	10,000	5,000
Provision for doubtful debts	10,000	15,000			
Current liabilities	70,000	1,45,000			
Total	**7,90,000**	**10,80,000**	**Total**	**7,90,000**	**10,80,000**

Additional information:
1. A machine costing ₹ 70,000 with a book value ₹ 40,000 was disposed-off for ₹ 25,000.
2. Preference share redemption was carried out at a premium of 5%.

FINANCIAL MANAGEMENT TECHNIQUES OF FINANCIAL ANALYSIS

3. Dividend at 15% was paid on equity shares for the year 2012-13.
4. Provision for depreciation was ₹ 1,50,000 on 31.3.2012 and ₹ 1,90,000 as on 31.3.2013.
5. Stock which was valued at ₹ 90,000 as on 31.3.2012 was written upto its cost ₹ 1,00,000 for preparing P & L A/c. for 2012-13.

Solution:

Working notes:

1. Statement showing changes in working capital

Particulars	31.3.2012 ₹	31.3.2013 ₹	Increase in working Capital ₹	Decrease in working Capital ₹
[A] Current Assets : Less provision for doubtful debts	2,40,000*	3,60,000	1,20,000	–
Total	2,40,000	3,60,000	–	–
[B] Current liabilities :	70,000	1,45,000		75,000
Total	70,000	1,45,000	1,20,000	75,000

Net increase in working capital – ₹ 45,000.

*2,40,000 – 10,000 + 10,000 (Stock valuation)

2.

Dr. Fixed Assets A/c. Cr.

Particulars	₹	Particulars	₹
To Balance b/d. (₹ 5,10,000 + ₹ 1,50,000 Bal.) (Accu. Dep.)	6,60,000	By Bank A/c. By Prov. for Dep. By Adjusted	25,000 30,000
To Bank A/c. (Purchases) (Balancing figure)	2,20,000	P & L A/c. Loss on sale By Bal. c/d. (₹ 6,20,000 + ₹ 1,90,000 Bal.) (Accu. dep.)	15,000 8,10,000
Total	8,80,000	Total	8,80,000

3.

Dr. Provision for Depreciation A/c. Cr.

Particulars	₹	Particulars	₹
To Fixed Assets A/c. (Dep. prov. on sale)	30,000	By Bal. b/d. By Adj. P & L A/c.	1,50,000
To Balance c/d.	1,90,000	Pro. made (Bal. Fig.)	70,000
Total	2,20,000	Total	2,20,000

4. Funds from operations

Dr.   Reserves A/c.   **Cr.**

Particulars	₹	Particulars	₹
To Provision for Dep. A/c. [working note 3]	70,000	By Balance b/d.	1,10,000
To Fixed Assets A/c. Loss on sale	15,000	By Stock written up	10,000
To Discount on debs. written off	5,000	By Funds from Operations By Balancing figure	2,95,000
To Prem. on Red. of Pref. shares	10,000		
To Dividend on equity	45,000		
To Balance c/d.	2,70,000		
Total	**4,15,000**	**Total**	**4,15,000**

Funds Flow Statement

Sources	₹	Applications	₹
1. Issue of equity shares	50,000	1. Redemption of Pref. Capital	1,00,000
2. Sale of machine	25,000	2. Payment of Share Premium on Redemption.	10,000
3. Funds from operations [W.N. 4]	2,95,000	3. Payment of dividend	45,000
4. Issue of debentures	1,00,000	4. Purchase of Machinery [W.N.1]	2,20,000
		5. Purchase of invests.	50,000
		6. Increase in working Capital (W.N. 1)	45,000
Total	**4,70,000**	**Total**	**4,70,000**

Problem 8

Given below is the Balance-Sheet of X Ltd.

Particulars	As on 31st March 2012		As on 31st March 2013	
	₹	₹	₹	₹
Fixed Assets at Cost	62,000		70,000	
Additions during the year	8,000		17,000	
	70,000		87,000	
Depreciation		45,000	36,000	51,000
Current Assets :				
Investments			15,000	
Stock at cost	25,000		1,90,000	
Trade Debtors	10,000		1,38,700	
			3,43,700	
Less : Current Liabilities :				
Bank overdraft	1,81,500		55,000	
Trade creditors and provisions	1,31,500		1,19,200	
Proposed dividends		91,200	24,000	1,45,500
Represented by :		3,23,000 1,36,200		1,96,500
Ordinary share capital	1,16,000	75,000		1,00,000
General reserve	99,800	26,000		38,000
Profit & Loss A/c.	16,000	35,200		48,500
8% Debentures		—		10,000
Total		**1,36,200**		**1,96,500**

2.70

FINANCIAL MANAGEMENT

TECHNIQUES OF FINANCIAL ANALYSIS

(i) Prepare a funds flow statement for the year ended on 31st March 2013.

(ii) Highlight the areas of major achievement of the Management and mention the areas where the Management should re-examine from view point of the financing pattern.

Solution:

Working notes:

(a) Statement showing changes in working capital

Particulars	31.3.12 (₹)	31.3.13 (₹)	Increase in working Capital (₹)	Decrease in working Capital (₹)
(i) Current Assets:				
Stock	1,81,500	1,90,000	8,500	
Debtors	1,31,500	1,38,700	7,200	
	3,13,000	3,28,700		
(ii) Current liabilities:				
Bank overdraft	1,16,000	55,000	61,000	
Trade creditors and provisions	99,800	1,19,200		19,400
Total	**2,15,800**	**1,74,200**	**76,700**	**19,400**

Net increase in working capital = ₹ 76,700 – ₹ 19,400 = ₹ 57,300

(b)

Dr.		Proposed Dividend A/c.		Cr.
Particulars	₹	Particulars	₹
To Bank A/c*	16,000	By Balance b/d.	16,000
To Balance c/d	24,000	By Profit & Loss A/c. (Balancing figure)	24,000
Total	**40,000**	**Total**	**40,000**

* Dividends paid - assumed.

(c) Funds from operations:

Dr.		Adjusted Profit and Loss A/c.		Cr.
Particulars	₹	Particulars	₹
To General reserve	12,000	By Balance b/d.	35,200
[₹ 38,000 – ₹ 26,000]		By funds from operations	60,300
To Depreciation	11,000	[Balancing figure]	
To Proposed dividends	24,000		
To Balance c/d	48,500		
Total	**95,500**	**Total**	**95,500**

2.71

FINANCIAL MANAGEMENT

TECHNIQUES OF FINANCIAL ANALYSIS

Funds Flow Statement

Sources		Applications	
Particulars	**Amount ₹**	**Particulars**	**Amount ₹**
Increase in share capital	25,000	Additions in fixed assets	17,000
Funds from operations [W.N.C]	60,300	Purchase of investments	5,000
Issue of 8% Debentures	10,000	Net increase in working capital [W.N.A]	57,300
		Dividends paid	16,000
Total	**95,300**	**Total**	**95,300**

Major achievements of the management in the year 2012-13:

(i) There is a drastic reduction in the amount of bank overdraft. This means that there will be reduced interest burden on the company.

(ii) Proposed dividend for the year 2012-13 is ₹ 24,000. In the previous year, it was ₹ 16,000 which comes to 21%. This year it comes to 24% which is definitely an achievement.

The following areas should be looked into:

(i) Creditors have increased quite substantially and efforts should be made to reduce them, otherwise it may affect the future purchases.

(ii) Induction of more debt would be advantageous as it would give an advantage of trading on equity.

Problem 9

Two divisions of ABC Ltd. start the year 2013 with identical Balance-sheets but the position changed by the end of the year as shown below:

Balance-sheet of ABC Ltd.

	2013 Division A		2013 Division B	
Particulars	**January 1 (₹)**	**December 31 (₹)**	**January 1 (₹)**	**December 31 (₹)**
Current Assets	6,25,000	6,25,000	6,25,000	6,25,000
Current Liabilities	3,75,000	3,75,000	3,75,000	5,00,000
Working Capital	2,50,000	2,50,000	2,50,000	1,25,000
Fixed Assets (Net)	2,50,000	6,25,000	2,50,000	5,00,000
Capital Employed	5,00,000	8,75,000	5,00,000	6,25,000
Financed by :				
Long-term debt	—	2,50,000	—	—
Equity Capital & Reserve	5,00,000	6,25,000	5,00,000	6,25,000
Total	**5,00,000**	**8,75,000**	**5,00,000**	**6,25,000**

The following additional information is available:
(i) Both the divisions have identical earning power.
(ii) Each division earns a net profit of ₹ 60,000 after taxation @ 50%.
(iii) Depreciation amounts to ₹ 40,000.

Prepare funds flow statement and comment on policy and practices adopted by each as revealed by the funds flow analysis.

Solution:

(a) Working notes:

Dr.			Fixed Assets A/c			Cr.
	Division				Division	
	A	B			A	B
To Balance b/d	2,50,000	2,50,000	By Depreciation		40,000	40,000
To Bank A/c			By Balance c/d		6,25,000	5,00,000
[Pur. Bal. figure]	4,15,000	2,90,000				
	6,65,000	5,40,000			6,65,000	5,40,000

(b) Funds from operations:

Net profit ₹ 60,000 for each division
Add: Depreciation ₹ 40,000 for each division
Funds from operations ₹ 1,00,000 for each division

Funds flow statement

Sources	A	B	Applications	A	B
Long-term debt	2,50,000	–	Purchase of fixed assets	4,15,000	2,90,000
Equity *	65,000	65,000			
Funds from operations	1,00,000	1,00,000			
Decrease in working capital	–	1,25,000			
Total	4,15,000	2,90,000	Total	4,15,000	2,90,000

*Equity and Reserves 6,25,000
Less : Opening Balance 5,00,000
Profit for 2008 60,000

Therefore, issue of equity ₹ 65,000 in each division.

Comments: In case of division A, fixed assets have been financed by:
(i) Long-term debt
(ii) Issue of equity and
(iii) Funds from operations.

For division B, issue of equity, funds from operations and decrease in working capital has been used for financing fixed assets.

FINANCIAL MANAGEMENT

TECHNIQUES OF FINANCIAL ANALYSIS

Problem 10

From the following details relating to HV Ltd., prepare a statement showing sources and application of funds for the year ended on 31st March 2013.

Balance-sheet of HV Ltd. as on 31.3.2008

Liabilities	31.3.2013 (₹)	31.3.2012 (₹)
Share Capital	4,00,000	3,00,000
Reserve	1,00,000	80,000
Profit and Loss A/c.	50,000	30,000
Debentures	1,00,000	1,50,000
Income-tax provision	40,000	50,000
Trade creditors	70,000	90,000
Proposed dividends	40,000	30,000
Total	**8,00,000**	**7,30,000**
Assets	**31.3.2013 (₹)**	**31.3.2012 (₹)**
Goodwill	90,000	1,00,000
Plant and Machinery	4,29,250	2,98,000
Debenture discount	5,000	8,000
Prepaid expenses	5,750	4,000
Investments	60,000	1,00,000
Debtors	1,10,000	1,60,000
Stock	80,000	50,000
Cash & Bank	20,000	10,000
Total	**8,00,000**	**7,30,000**

Additional Information:

(i) 15% depreciation has been charged in the accounts on plant and machinery.

(ii) Old machines costing ₹ 50,000 [written down value ₹ 20,000] have been sold for ₹ 35,000.

(iii) A machine costing ₹ 10,000 [written down value ₹ 3,000] has been discarded.

(iv) ₹ 10,000 profit has been earned by sale of investments.

(v) Debentures have been redeemed at 5% premium.

(vi) ₹ 45,000 income-tax has been paid and adjusted against income-tax provision account.

FINANCIAL MANAGEMENT   TECHNIQUES OF FINANCIAL ANALYSIS

Solution:

Working notes:

(a) Statement showing changes in working capital

Particulars	31.3.12	31.3.13	Increase in working Capital	Decrease in working Capital
(i) **Current Assets :**				
Stock	50,000	80,000	30,000	–
Debtors	1,60,000	1,10,000	–	50,000
Prepaid expenses	4,000	5,750	1,750	
Cash & Bank	10,000	20,000	10,000	
	2,24,000	2,15,750		
(ii) **Current liabilities :**				
Creditors	90,000	70,000	20,000	
Total	90,000	70,000	61,750	50,000

Net increase in working capital = ₹ 11,750.

(b)

Dr.   Plant & Machinery A/c.   Cr.

Particulars	₹	Particulars	₹
To Balance b/d	2,98,000	By Bank A/c [Sale]	35,000
To Profit & Loss A/c	15,000	By Profit & Loss A/c	3,000
[Profit on sale]		Machine discarded	
To Bank A/c. *	2,30,000	By Depreciation	75,750
[Purchases during the year]		By Balance c/d	4,29,250
Total	5,43,000	**Total**	5,43,000

* The purchases of machinery are calculated in the following manner:

	Closing balance	=	₹ 4,29,250	
	Opening balance	=	₹ 2,98,000	
Less:	Sale & discarded machinery	=	₹ 23,000	
			₹ 2,75,000	
Less:	Depreciation @15%	=	41,250	
				₹ 2,33,750
				₹ 2,33,750

Written down value of
machinery added   ₹ 1,95,000

+   Depreciation charged on machinery
       15% on ₹ 2,30,000 = ₹ 34,500
       15% on ₹ 2,75,000 = ₹ 41,250
                              ₹ 75,750

FINANCIAL MANAGEMENT　　　　　　　　　　　　　　TECHNIQUES OF FINANCIAL ANALYSIS

(c) Funds from operations:

Dr.　　　　　　　　　　　Adjusted Profit & Loss A/c.　　　　　　　　　　　Cr.

Particulars	₹	Particulars	₹
To Reserve	20,000	By Balance b/d	30,000
To Provision for taxation	45,000	By Profit on sale of Machinery	15,000
To Proposed dividend	40,000	By Profit on sale of investments	10,000
To Depreciation	75,750	By Funds from operations	1,94,250
To Goodwill written-off	10,000	[Balancing figure]	
To Debenture discount written-off	3,000		
To Machinery discarded	3,000		
To Loss on debenture redeemed	2,500		
To Balance c/d	50,000		
Total	**2,49,250**	**Total**	**2,49,250**

(d)

Dr.　　　　　　　　　　　Provision for Taxation A/c.　　　　　　　　　　　Cr.

Particulars	₹	Particulars	₹
To Bank A/c. – tax paid	45,000	By Balance b/d	50,000
To Balance c/d	40,000	By P & L A/c.	
		Balancing figure	45,000
Total	**95,000**	**Total**	**95,000**

(e)

Dr.　　　　　　　　　　　Proposed Dividend A/c.　　　　　　　　　　　Cr.

Particulars	₹	Particulars	₹
To Bank A/c.	30,000	By Balance b/d	30,000
Dividends paid [assumed]		By P & L A/c	40,000
To Balance c/d	40,000	Balancing figure	
Total	**70,000**	**Total**	**70,000**

Statement of Sources and Application of Funds for the year ended on 31st March 2013

Sources	Amount (₹)	Applications	Amount (₹)
Issue of shares	1,00,000	Redemption of debentures	52,500
Sale of investments*	50,000	Payment of dividends	30,000
Sale of machine	35,000	Purchase of machinery	2,30,000
Funds from operations	1,49,250	Increase in working capital	21,750
Total	**3,34,250**	**Total**	**3,34,250**

*Sale of investments can be calculated by preparing the following working note:

Investment A/c.

Dr. Particulars	₹	Cr. Particulars	₹
To Balance b/d	1,00,000	By Bank A/c. (Sale)	50,000
To P & L A/c. profit on sale of investment	10,000	Balancing figure	
		By Balance c/d	60,000
Total	1,10,000	Total	1,10,000

Problem 11

The financial position of ABC Ltd. on 1st January 2012 and 31st December 2013 was as follows:

Balance-sheet of ABC Ltd.

	1st January (₹)	31st December (₹)
Cash	8,000	7,200
Debtors	70,000	76,800
Stock	50,000	44,000
Land	40,000	60,000
Building	1,00,000	1,10,000
Machinery	1,60,000	1,72,000
Total	4,28,000	4,70,000
Current Liabilities :	72,000	82,000
Loan from associate company	–	40,000
Loan from bank	60,000	50,000
Capital and Reserves	2,96,000	2,98,000
Total	4,28,000	4,70,000

During the year dividends paid were ₹ 52,000. The provision for depreciation against machinery as on 1st January 2008 was ₹ 54,000 and on 31st December 2008 was ₹ 72,000. Prepare a funds flow statement. Net profit after tax was ₹ 2,000.

Solution:

Working notes:

(i) Statement showing changes in working capital:

Particulars	1.1.2012 ₹	31.12.2013 ₹	Increase in working Capital ₹	Decrease in working Capital ₹
(A) Current Assets:				
Cash	8,000	7,200	–	800
Debtors	70,000	76,800	6,800	
Stock	50,000	44,000		6,000
	1,28,000	1,28,000		
(B) Current Liabilities:	72,000	82,000	–	10,000
	72,000	82,000	6,800	16,800

Net decrease in working capital = ₹ 10,000.

(ii)

Dr.		Building A/c.		Cr.
Particulars	₹	Particulars	₹
To Balance b/d	1,00,000	By Balance c/d	1,10,000
To Bank A/c. [Additions, Balancing figure]	10,000		
Total	1,10,000	Total	1,10,000

(iii)

Dr.		Machinery A/c.		Cr.
Particulars	₹	Particulars	₹
To Balance b/d [Op. bal. + Prov.]	2,14,000		
To Bank A/c. [Additions, balancing figure]	30,000	By Balance c/d [Op. balance + provision]	2,44,000
Total	2,44,000	Total	2,44,000

(iv)

Dr.		Provision for Depreciation A/c.		Cr.
Particulars	₹	Particulars	₹
To Balance c/d	72,000	By Balance b/d	54,000
		By Profit & Loss A/c. [Provision made, bal. figure]	18,000
Total	72,000	Total	72,000

(v)

Dr.		Funds from Operations A/c.		Cr.
Particulars	₹	Particulars	₹
To Depreciation provision	18,000	By Funds from operations [Balancing figure]	72,000
To Dividends paid	52,000		
To Balance c/d	2,000		
Total	72,000	Total	72,000

Funds Flow Statement

Sources	Amount ₹	Applications	Amount ₹
Loan from Associate company	40,000	Purchase of land	20,000
Funds from operations	72,000	Purchase of building	10,000
Net decrease in working capital	10,000	Purchase of machinery	30,000
		Repayment of bank loan	10,000
		Dividends paid	52,000
Total	1,22,000	Total	1,22,000

FINANCIAL MANAGEMENT — TECHNIQUES OF FINANCIAL ANALYSIS

Problem 12

From the following balance-sheet of ABC Ltd., as on 31st March 2012, prepare a projected funds flow statement for the year ending on 31st March 2013.

Balance-sheet of ABC Ltd. as on 31st March 2012

Liabilities		Assets	
Particulars	**Amount ₹**	**Particulars**	**Amount ₹**
Share Capital	8,00,000	Fixed Assets at cost less dep.	6,00,000
8% Debentures	1,00,000	Stock	4,00,000
Profit and Loss A/c.	2,00,000	Debtors	1,00,000
Creditors	2,00,000	Cash and Bank	2,00,000
Total	**13,00,000**	**Total**	**13,00,000**

Estimates for the year ended 31st March 2013.

	Upto January 2013 (₹)	Feb. & March 2013 (₹)
Purchases	15,00,000	2,00,000
Sales	26,00,000	4,00,000

(i) Rate of gross profit on sales is 33.33%.
(ii) Expected rate of net profit on sales is 20%.
[Excluding depreciation on fixed assets.]
(iii) Rate of depreciation is 10%.
(iv) Estimated purchase of fixed assets amounted ₹ 1,00,000.
(v) Credit allowed by creditors and credit allowed to debtors are two months respectively.
(vi) There may be an issue of shares of ₹ 1,00,000 and that of debentures ₹ 50,000.
(vii) Estimated further investments in gilt-edged securities amounted to ₹ 50,000.

Solution:

Working notes:

(i) Statement showing changes in working capital

Particulars	31.3.12 ₹	31.3.13 ₹	Increase in working Capital ₹	Decrease in working Capital ₹
(A) Current Assets:				
Stock*	4,00,000	1,00,000	—	3,00,000
Debtors+	1,00,000	4,00,000	3,00,000	—
Cash^H	2,00,000	8,00,000	6,00,000	
	7,00,000	13,00,000		
(B) Current Liabilities:				
Creditors (b)	2,00,000	2,00,000	—	—
Total	**2,00,000**	**2,00,000**	**9,00,000**	**3,00,000**

2.79

Net increase in working capital = ₹ 6,00,000.

* Stock is calculated as follows:

Gross profit is given as 33.33% of sales.

Sales are ₹ 30,00,000, so gross profit is ₹ 10,00,000.

∴ Cost of goods sold = ₹ 30,00,000 – ₹ 10,00,000
= ₹ 20,00,000

Cost of goods sold = Opening stock + Purchases – Closing stock
20,00,000 = ₹ 4,00,000 + ₹ 17,00,000 – Closing stock
Closing stock = 1,00,000

+ Calculation of debtors as on 31.3.2013

Sales = ₹ 30,00,000
Opening debtors = ₹ 1,00,000

By preparing debtors account, calculation of debtors as on 31st March 2013 can be done as follows:

Dr. Debtors A/c. **Cr.**

Particulars	Amount (₹)	Particulars	Amount (₹)
To Balance b/d	1,00,000	By Cash collections from debtors [Balancing figure]	27,00,000
To Sales	30,00,000	By Balance c/d [Last 2 months sales]	4,00,000
Total	**31,00,000**	**Total**	**31,00,000**

Cash and Bank Balance as on 31st March 2013

Dr. Cash and Bank A/c. **Cr.**

Particulars	Amount (₹)	Particulars	Amount (₹)
To Balance b/d	2,00,000	By Investments in securities	50,000
To Debtors	27,00,000	By Fixed assets	1,00,000
To Issue of shares	1,00,000	By Creditors	17,00,000
To Issue of debentures	50,000	By Expenses @	4,00,000
		By Balance c/d	8,00,000
Total	**30,50,000**	**Total**	**30,50,000**

Dr. Creditors A/c. **Cr.**

Particulars	Amount (₹)	Particulars	Amount (₹)
To Cash paid (Balancing figure)	17,00,000	By Balance b/d	2,00,000
To Balance c/d (Last 2 months purchases)	2,00,000	By Purchases	17,00,000
Total	**19,00,000**	**Total**	**19,00,000**

FINANCIAL MANAGEMENT   TECHNIQUES OF FINANCIAL ANALYSIS

@ Payment of expenses is calculated as follows:

Gross profit 33.33% of sales = ₹ 10,00,000
Net profit 20% of sales = ₹ 6,00,000

Therefore, the expenses will be ₹ 10,00,000 – ₹ 6,00,000 = ₹ 4,00,000.

Projected Funds Flow Statement

Sources		Applications	
Particulars	Amount (₹)	Particulars	Amount (₹)
Issue of shares	1,00,000	Purchase of investments	50,000
Issue of debentures	50,000	Purchase of fixed assets	1,00,000
Funds from operations [20% on sales]	6,00,000	Net increase in working capital	6,00,000
Total	7,50,000	Total	7,50,000

Problem 13

The following is the audited Balance-sheet of Mr. X as on 31st March 2012.

Balance-Sheet of Mr. X as on 31st March 2012

Liabilities		Assets	
Particulars	Amount (₹)	Particulars	Amount (₹)
Capital Account	1,62,000	Machinery	40,000
Creditors for purchases	30,000	Furniture	10,000
		Stock	35,000
		Debtors	90,000
		Cash in hand	6,000
		Cash at bank	11,000
Total	1,92,000	Total	1,92,000

A fire occurred on 31st March 2013, destroying the books of accounts and records. The cashier absconded with the available cash in the cash box. However, the following information is available:

(i) Sales are effected 20% for cash and the balance on credit. His total sales for the year ended on 31st March 2013 were 20% higher than the previous year. All sales and purchases of goods were evenly spread out in the year.

(ii) Credit allowed to debtors is 2 months and by creditors is 1 month.

(iii) Stock level was maintained at ₹ 35,000 throughout the year.

(iv) A steady gross profit rate of 33.33% on turnover was maintained throughout. Creditors are paid by through cheque only. There are no cash purchases.

FINANCIAL MANAGEMENT TECHNIQUES OF FINANCIAL ANALYSIS

(v) His private records and bank pass-book kept with him disclosed the following transactions for the year.
  (a) Miscellaneous expenses ₹ 1,80,000 [including ₹ 35,000 paid by cheque and ₹ 5,000 outstanding on 31st March 2013].
  (b) Repairs ₹ 2,500 paid by cash.
  (c) Additions to machinery ₹ 50,000 paid by cheque.
  (d) Private drawings ₹ 36,000 paid by cash.
  (e) Travelling expenses ₹ 12,000 paid by cash.
  (f) Collection from debtors [including ₹ 30,000 for cash] and payment to creditors were prompt all along.
  (g) Depreciation is to be provided on fixed assets @10% of the closing book value.
  (h) Cash stolen is to be charged to Profit and Loss A/c.

Prepare a statement showing sources and applications of funds.

Solution:
Working notes:
(i) Sales:

$$\begin{aligned}
\text{Credit to debtors} &= 2 \text{ months} \\
\text{Debtors as on } 31.3.2012 &= ₹ 90{,}000 \\
\text{Amount of credit sales for the year ended } 31.3.2012 &= ₹ 5{,}40{,}000 \\
\text{Credit sales are 80\% of the total sales} \\
\therefore \text{Total sales} &= ₹ 6{,}75{,}000 \\
\text{Sales for the year ended } 31.3.2013 &= ₹ 6{,}75{,}000 + 20\% \text{ of } ₹ 6{,}75{,}000 \\
\text{Total sales for } 1997 - 2012\text{-}13 &= ₹ 8{,}10{,}000 \\
\text{Cash sales} &= 20\% \text{ of } ₹ 8{,}10{,}000 = ₹ 1{,}62{,}000 \\
\text{Credit sales} &= 80\% \text{ of } ₹ 8{,}10{,}000 = ₹ 6{,}48{,}000
\end{aligned}$$

(ii) Cash collected from Debtors:

Dr. Debtors A/c. Cr.

Particulars	Amount (₹)	Particulars	Amount (₹)
To Balance b/d	90,000	By Cash A/c.	6,30,000
To Credit sales	6,48,000	[Collections from debtors – balancing figure]	
		By Balance c/d*	1,08,000
Total	**7,38,000**	**Total**	**7,38,000**

*Credit sales = ₹ 6,48,000
Credit period = 2 months
Debtors as on 31.3.2013 – ₹ 6,48,000 × $\frac{2}{12}$ = ₹ 1,08,000

(iii) Purchases for 2012-13:

$$\text{Sales} = ₹\,8,10,000$$
$$\text{Gross profit margin} = 33\tfrac{1}{3}\%\text{ of sales}$$
$$= ₹\,2,70,000$$
$$\text{Cost of goods sold} = ₹\,8,10,000 - ₹\,2,70,000$$
$$= ₹\,5,40,000$$
$$\text{Cost of goods sold} = \text{Opening stock} + \text{Purchases} - \text{Closing stock}$$
$$5,40,000 = 35,000 + P - 35,000$$
$$\therefore \text{Purchases} = ₹\,5,40,000$$
$$\text{Credit allowed by suppliers} = 1\text{ month}$$
$$\therefore \text{Creditors} = ₹\,45,000$$

(iv) Cash paid to Creditors:

Dr. Creditors A/c. Cr.

Particulars	Amount (₹)	Particulars	Amount (₹)
To Bank A/c. (Balancing figure)	5,25,000	By Balance b/d	30,000
To Balance c/d	45,000	By Purchases	5,40,000
Total	5,70,000	Total	5,70,000

(v) Cash Book:

Particulars	Receipts Cash (₹)	Receipts Bank (₹)	Particulars	Payment Cash (₹)	Payment Bank (₹)
To Balance b/d	6,000	11,000	By Repairs	2,500	–
To Cash sales	1,62,000	–	By Machinery	–	50,000
To Debtors	30,000	6,00,000	By Drawings	36,000	–
			By Trading expenses	12,000	–
			By Miscellaneous business expenses	1,40,000	35,000
			By Creditors	–	5,25,000
			By P & L A/c. (Balancing figure)	7,500	–
			By Balance c/d	–	1,000
Total	1,98,000	6,11,000	Total	1,98,000	6,11,000

(vi) Net profit for the year 2012-13:

Dr.   Profit and Loss A/c.   Cr.

Particulars	Amount (₹)	Particulars	Amount (₹)
To Dep. on fixed assets [10% on ₹ 50,000 + ₹ 50,000 add]	10,000	By Gross profit	2,70,000
To Repairs	2,500		
To Travelling expenses	12,000		
To Miscellaneous expenses [Including ₹ 5,000 outstanding]	1,80,000		
To Cash Stolen	7,500		
To Net Profit	58,000		
Total	**2,70,000**	**Total**	**2,70,000**

(viii) Statement showing changes in working capital:

Particulars	31.3.12 ₹	31.3.13 ₹	Increase in working Capital ₹	Decrease in working Capital ₹
Current Assets:				
(i) Stock	35,000	35,000	–	–
(ii) Debtors	90,000	1,08,000	18,000	–
(iii) Bank balance	11,000	1,000	–	10,000
(iv) Cash balance	6,000	–	–	6,000
	1,42,000	1,44,000		
Current Liabilities:				
(i) Creditors	30,000	45,000	–	15,000
(ii) Outstanding expenses	–	5,000	–	5,000
Total	**30,000**	**50,000**	**18,000**	**36,000**

Net decrease in working capital = ₹ 18,000

Statement showing Sources and Application of funds:

Sources	Amount (₹)	Applications	Amount (₹)
Funds from operations		Purchase of machinery	50,000
Net profit 58,000		Drawings	36,000
Add : Depreciation 10,000	68,000		
Decrease in working capital	18,000		
Total	**86,000**	**Total**	**86,000**

Problem 14

The following is the summarised Balance-sheet of Sneha Ltd. as on 31st March 2012 and 31st March 2013

Balance–sheet of Sneha Ltd.

Liabilities	31.3.12 (₹)	31.3.13 (₹)	Assets	31.3.12 (₹)	31.3.13 (₹)
Equity Capital			Fixed Assets	20,00,000	22,00,000
[₹ 10 each]	5,00,000	8,00,000	Less : Depreciation	7,00,000	7,50,000
8% Redeemable				13,00,000	14,50,000
Pref. Capital			Shares in		
[₹ 100 each]	6,00,000	4,00,000	Subsidiary Co.	4,00,000	5,50,000
Plant Replacement			Stock	2,00,000	2,50,000
Reserve	1,00,000	80,000	Debtors	1,00,000	80,000
Profit & Loss A/c.	6,00,000	7,00,000	Cash	1,10,000	70,000
6% Debentures	–	1,00,000	Prepaid expenses	40,000	80,000
Bank loan (long-term)	1,00,000	–			
Creditors	2,00,000	3,00,000			
Proposed Dividend					
(Equity)	50,000	1,00,000			
Total	**21,50,000**	**24,80,000**	**Total**	**21,50,000**	**24,80,000**

Additional information:

(i) ₹ 1,00,000 was appropriated from Profit and Loss A/c. and capitalised by issuing bonus shares, one share being issued for every 5 shares held.

(ii) 8% Redeemable Pref. shares are redeemed at the specific premium out of the proceeds of fresh issue of 20,000 equity shares at ₹ 10 each and the premium was adjusted against Profit and Loss Account.

(iii) The difference in the Plant Replacement Reserve represents transfer to Profit and Loss Account.

(iv) The Preference Dividend was paid in March 2012 and the proposed dividend for 2012-13 was paid in addition to interim dividends of ₹ 30,000.

(v) Adjustments regarding fixed assets:
    (a) Fixed assets were revalued by ₹ 50,000 in excess of book value and credited to Profit and Loss A/c.
    (b) Expenditure on fixed assets of ₹ 5,000 which was carried forward in Debtors Account on 31st December, 2012.

(c) A plant costing ₹ 50,000 [accumulated depreciation being ₹ 40,000] was sold at ₹ 5,000 loss, the loss being charged to Profit and Loss A/c.

(vi) Additional shares in subsidiary company were purchased during the year.

Prepare a statement of sources and application of funds.

Solution:

Working notes:

(i) **Statement showing Sources and Application of Funds:**

Particulars	31.3.12 ₹	31.3.13 ₹	Increase in working Capital ₹	Decrease in working Capital ₹
Current Assets :				
Stock	2,00,000	2,50,000	50,000	–
Debtors	1,00,000	80,000	–	20,000
Cash	1,10,000	70,000	–	40,000
Prepaid expenses	40,000	80,000	40,000	–
Total	**4,50,000**	**4,80,000**		
Current Liabilities :				
Creditors	2,00,000	3,00,000	–	1,00,000
Total	**2,00,000**	**3,00,000**	**90,000**	**1,60,000**

Net decrease in working capital = ₹ 70,000.

(ii)

Dr. **Equity Share Capital A/c.** Cr.

Particulars	Amount (₹)	Particulars	Amount (₹)
To Balance c/d	8,00,000	By Balance b/d	5,00,000
		By Profit and Loss (Bonus issue)	1,00,000
		By Bank (issue)	2,00,000
Total	8,00,000	Total	8,00,000

(iii)

Dr. **8% Redeemable Pref. Shares A/c.** Cr.

Particulars	Amount (₹)	Particulars	Amount (₹)
To Preference shareholders A/c.	2,00,000	By Balance b/d	6,00,000
To Balance c/d	4,00,000		
Total	6,00,000	Total	6,00,000

(iv)

Dr.   **Preference Shareholders A/c.**   **Cr.**

Particulars	Amount (₹)	Particulars	Amount (₹)
To Bank A/c.	2,20,000	By 8% Pref. Shares A/c.	2,00,000
		By Premium on Redemption of Preference shares	20,000
Total	2,20,000	Total	2,20,000

(v)

Dr.   **Plant Replacement Reserve A/c.**   **Cr.**

Particulars	Amount (₹)	Particulars	Amount (₹)
To Profit and Loss A/c. (Balancing figure)	20,000	By Balance b/d	1,00,000
To Balance c/d	80,000		
Total	1,00,000	Total	1,00,000

(vi)

Dr.   **Proposed Dividend A/c.**   **Cr.**

Particulars	Amount (₹)	Particulars	Amount (₹)
To Bank A/c. (Dividends paid)	50,000	By Balance b/d	50,000
To Balance c/d	1,00,000	By P & L A/c. (proposed dividend)	1,00,000
Total	1,50,000	Total	1,50,000

(vii)

Dr.   **Provision for Depreciation on Fixed Assets A/c.**   **Cr.**

Particulars	Amount (₹)	Particulars	Amount (₹)
To Fixed assets (Depreciation on plant sold)	40,000	By Balance b/d	7,00,000
To Balance c/d	7,50,000	By P & L A/c. (Depreciation for the year)	90,000
Total	7,90,000	Total	7,90,000

(viii)

Dr.		Fixed Assets A/c.		Cr.
Particulars	Amount (₹)	Particulars	Amount (₹)
---	---	---	---
To Balance b/d	20,00,000	By Provision for depreciation	40,000
To Profit & Loss A/c. (revaluation)	50,000	By Bank A/c. (sale)	5,000
To Transfer from debtors	5,000	By Profit and Loss (loss on sale)	5,000
To Bank A/c. [Purchases, balancing figure]	1,95,000	By Balance c/d	22,00,000
Total	**22,50,000**	**Total**	**22,50,000**

(ix)

Dr.		Adjusted Profit and Loss A/c.		Cr.
Particulars	Amount (₹)	Particulars	Amount (₹)
---	---	---	---
To Share Capital (bonus issue)	1,00,000	By Balance b/d	6,00,000
To Premium on Redemption of Preference shares	20,000	By Plant replacement reserve	20,000
To Preference dividend	48,000	By Profit on revaluation of fixed assets	50,000
To Interim dividend	30,000	By Funds from operations (Balancing figure)	4,23,000
To Proposed dividend	1,00,000		
To Loss on sale of fixed assets	5,000		
To Provision for depreciation	90,000		
To Balance c/d	7,00,000		
Total	**10,93,000**	**Total**	**10,93,000**

Statement of Sources and Application of Funds for the year ended 31st March 2013

Sources	Amount (₹)	Applications	Amount (₹)
Issue of shares	2,00,000	Redemption of Pref. Capital	2,20,000
Sale of fixed assets	5,000	Pref. dividend paid	48,000
Issue of debentures	1,00,000	Interim dividends paid	30,000
Funds from operations	4,23,000	Final dividend paid	50,000
Net decrease in working capital	70,000	Purchase of fixed assets	2,00,000
		Repayment of bank loan	1,00,000
		Purchase of shares	1,50,000
Total	**7,98,000**	**Total**	**7,98,000**

FINANCIAL MANAGEMENT   TECHNIQUES OF FINANCIAL ANALYSIS

CASH FLOW STATEMENTS

Problem 1

The following is the Statement of financial position of Mr. X

Liabilities	1/1/2012 ₹	31/12/2012 ₹	Assets	1/1/2012 ₹	31/12/2012 ₹
Accounts Payable	29,000	25,000	Cash	40,000	30,000
Capital	7,39,000	6,15,000	Debtors	20,000	17,000
			Stock	8,000	13,000
			Building	1,00,000	80,000
			Other Fixed Assets	6,00,000	5,00,000
Total	7,68,000	6,40,000	Total	7,68,000	6,40,000

Additional Information:

[I] There were no drawings

[II] There was no purchase or sales of either building or other fixed assets.

Prepare Cash Flow Statement

Solution:

The following working notes are prepared

W.N.1 Cash From Operations:

Particulars		Amount ₹
Net Profit For The Year		
Capital: 31/12/2012:	₹ 6,15,000	
Less:		
Capital: 1/1/2012:	₹ 7,39,000	(1,24,000)
Add: Non- cash Charges		
❖ Depreciation on Building:	₹ 20,000	
❖ Depreciation on other Fixed Assets:	₹ 1,00,000	1,20,000
Add: Decrease in Current Assets: Debtors		3,000
Less: Increase in Current Assets : Stock		(5,000)
Less: Decrease in Current Liabilities: Accounts Payable		(4,000)
Cash From Operations		**(10,000)**

Cash Flow Statement
For The Year Ended 31/12/2012

Particulars	Amount ₹
Cash Balance As On 1/1/2012	40,000
Add: Sources Of Cash	
❖ Cash From Operations	(30,000)
Cash Available	10,000
Applications Of Cash	Nil
Cash Balance As On 31/12/2012	**10,000**

Problem 2

The following are summarised Balance Sheets of XYZ Ltd. as on 31st March 2012 and 31st March 2013.

Liabilities	Amount ₹ 31/3/2012	Amount ₹ 31/3/2013	Assets	Amount ₹ 31/3/2012	Amount ₹ 31/3/2013
Share Capital	4,50,000	4,50,000	Fixed Assets	4,00,000	3,20,000
General Reserve	3,00,000	3,10,000	Investments	50,000	60,000
Profit & Loss A/c	56,000	68,000	Stock	2,40,000	2,10,000
Creditors	1,68,000	1,34,000	Debtors	2,10,000	4,55,000
Provision for Taxation	75,000	10,000	Bank	1,49,000	1,97,000
Mortgage Loan	-------	2,70,000			
Total	**10,49,000**	**12,42,000**	**Total**	**10,49,000**	**12,42,000**

Additional Information:
(i) Investments costing ₹ 8000 were sold during the year for ₹ 8500.
(ii) Provision for taxation made during the year was ₹ 9000.
(iii) During the year Fixed Assets costing ₹ 10000 were sold for ₹ 12000 and the profit was credited to Profit and Loss Account.
(iv) Dividends paid during the year ₹ 40,000.
    Prepare Cash Flow Statement

Solution:

Cash Flow Statement
For The Year Ended 31/12/2008

Particulars	Amount (₹)	Amount (₹)
[I] Opening Balance of Bank:		1,49,000
[II] **Add:** Sources of Cash		
• Raising of Mortgage Loan:	2,70,000	
• Sale of Fixed Assets:	12,000	
• Sale of Investments:	8,500	2,90,500
[III] Total Cash Available [I + II]		4,39,500
[IV] Applications Of Cash		
• Purchase of Investments: [W.N.2]	18,000	
• Payment Of Income Tax	74,000	
• Payment of Dividends	40,000	
• Loss From Operations [W.N.4]	1,10,500	2,42,500
• Total IV		
[V] Closing Balance of Bank		1,97,000

Working Notes:

W.N.1:

Dr.		Fixed Assets A/c	Cr.
Particulars	Amount (₹)	Particulars	Amount (₹)
To Balance b/d	4,00,000	By Bank A/c – Sale	12,000
To Profit and Loss A/c		By Depreciation [Balancing figure]	70,000
Profit on sale of Fixed Assets	2,000	By Balance c/d	3,20,000
Total	4,02,000	Total	4,02,000

W.N.2:

Dr.		Investments A/c	Cr.
Particulars	Amount (₹)	Particulars	Amount (₹)
To Balance b/d	50,000	By Bank A/c – Sale	8,500
To Profit and Loss A/c Profit on sale	500	By Balance c/d	60,000
To Bank A/c – Purchases [Balancing figure]	18,000		
Total	68,500	Total	68,500

W.N.3:

Dr.		Provision for Taxation A/c	Cr.
Particulars	Amount (₹)	Particulars	Amount (₹)
To Bank A/c – Income Tax Paid	74,000	By Balance b/d	75,000
[Balancing figure]	10,000	By Profit & Loss A/c [Provision made during the year]	9,000
To Balance c/d			
Total	84,000	Total	84,000

W.N.4] Cash From Operations: For finding out the Cash From Operations, Funds From Operations will be found out by preparing Adjusted Profit and Loss Account as shown below.

Dr.		Adjusted Profit and Loss A/c	Cr.
Particulars	Amount (₹)	Particulars	Amount (₹)
To Provision for taxation	9,000	By Balance b/d	56,000
To Dividends	40,000	By Profit on sale of Investments	500
To Transfer to General Reserve	10,000	By Profit on sale of Fixed Assets	2,000
To Depreciation	70,000	By Funds From Operations [Balancing figure]	1,38,500
To Balance c/d	68,000		
Total	1,97,000	Total	1,97,000

Cash From Operations

Particulars	Amount (₹)	Amount (₹)
Funds From Operations		1,38,500
Add: Decrease in Stock		
[₹ 240000 – ₹ 210000]		30,000
		1,68,500
Less:		
Increase in Debtors		
[₹ 4,55,000 – ₹ 2,10,000]	2,45,000	
Decrease in Creditors		
[₹ 1,68,000 – ₹ 1,34,000]	1,34,000	3,79,000
Cash From Operations		**(2,10,500)**

Problem 3

The Balance Sheets of Zenith Ltd. as on 31st March 2007 and 31st March 2008 were as follows.

Liabilities	Amount (₹) 31/3/2007	Amount (₹) 31/3/2008	Assets	Amount (₹) 31/3/2007	Amount (₹) 31/3/2008
Share Capital	5,00,000	7,00,000	Land & Building	80,000	1,20,000
Profit & Loss A/c	1,00,000	1,60,000	Plant & Machinery	5,00,000	8,00,000
General Reserve	50,000	70,000	Stock	1,00,000	75,000
Creditors	1,53,000	1,90,000	Debtors	1,50,000	1,60,000
Bills Payable	40,000	50,000	Cash	20,000	20,000
Expenses Outstanding	7,000	5,000			
Total	**8,50,000**	**11,75,000**	**Total**	**8,50,000**	**11,75,000**

Additional Information:

[I] Depreciation of ₹ 50,000 have been provided during the year.

[II] A piece of machinery was sold for ₹ 8000 during the year 2007-08. The cost of the machinery was ₹ 12,000 and depreciation of ₹ 7000 was provided on the same.

[III] Income tax paid during the year was ₹ 60,000.

[IV] Dividends paid during the year was ₹ 50,000.

Prepare Cash Flow Statement.

Solution:

Cash Flow Statement
For The Year Ended 31/3/2008

Particulars	Amount (₹)	Amount (₹)
[I] Cash Balance: 31/3/2007		20,000
[II] Sources Of Cash		
• Issue of Shares	2,00,000	
• Sale Of Machinery	8,000	
• Cash From Operations [W.N.3]	2,97,000	5,05,000
		5,25,000
[III] Cash Available [I + II]		
[IV] Applications Of Cash		
• Purchase of Machinery [W.N.1]	3,55,000	
• Purchase of Land & Building [W.N.2]	40,000	
• Income Tax paid	60,000	
• Dividends paid	50,000	5,05,000
[V] Total Applications of Cash		20,000
[VI] Closing Balance of Cash		

Working Notes:

W.N.1

Dr.   Plant & Machinery A/c   Cr.

Particulars	Amount (₹)	Particulars	Amount (₹)
To Balance b/d	5,00,000	By Depreciation	50,000
To Profit & Loss A/c		By Cash A/c – Sale	8,000
Profit on sale	3,000	By Balance c/d	8,00,000
To Bank A/c – Purchases Balancing figure	3,55,000		
	8,58,000		8,58,000

W.N.2

Dr.   Land & Building A/c   Cr.

Particulars	Amount (₹)	Particulars	Amount (₹)
To Balance b/d	80,000	By Balance c/d	1,20,000
To Cash A/c Purchases – Balancing figure	40,000		
Total	1,20,000	Total	1,20,000

W.N.3

Dr.	Adjusted Profit & Loss A/c			Cr.
Particulars	Amount (₹)	Particulars		Amount (₹)
To General Reserve	20,000	By Balance c/d		1,00,000
To Depreciation	50,000	By Profit on sale of Machinery		3,000
To Dividends	60,000			
To Income Tax	50,000	By Funds From Operations [Balancing figure]		2,37,000
To Balance c/d	1,60,000			
Total	**3,40,000**	**Total**		**3,40,000**

Cash From Operations

Particulars	Amount (₹)	Amount (₹)
Funds From Operations	25,000	2,37,000
Add:	37,000	
Decrease in Stock	10,000	
Increase in Creditors		
Increase in Bills Payable		72,000
Less:		3,09,000
Increase in Debtors	10,000	
Increase in Outstanding Expenses	2,000	12,000
Cash From Operations		2,97,000

Points to Remember

➢ The focus of financial analysis is always on the crucial information contained in the financial statements and depends on the objectives and purpose of such an analysis.
➢ The purpose of evaluating such financial statements is different for different people and depends on its need for that person.
➢ **Financial statement analysis** is a part of the large information processing system, which forms the very basis of any 'decision–making'.
➢ After analysing the financial statements, one is in a position to forecast whether it would be profitable or not to invest in or to deal with the organisation.
➢ One of the important techniques used for the interpretation of financial statements is 'Ratio Analysis'.
➢ **Accounting ratios** show an inter-relationship which exists among various figures shown in the financial statements.
➢ One of the serious limitations of ratio analysis is that there are difficulties in the comparison between various firms through ratios.
➢ **A funds flow statement** or a statement showing sources and applications of funds provides information about sources of raising funds as well as the applications of these funds.
➢ **The DuPont system** makes use of the important interlink of information found in financial statements.

Questions for Discussion

1. What is Ratio? Explain the various types of Ratios.
2. Explain the classification and utility of ratio analysis.
3. What are the limitations of ratio analysis?
4. Explain the preparation of Funds Flow Statement.
5. How will you interpret the funds flow statement?
6. Explain the concept of 'Funds from operations'.
7. Distinguish between funds flow statement and cash flow statement.
8. What is the utility of cash flow statement?
9. Write short notes on :
   (a) Utility of Ratio Analysis.
   (b) Funds Flow Analysis.
   (c) DuPont Analysis.

Case Study

Selected financial data for two companies in the same industry is as follows as on 31st March 2013.

₹ in lakhs

Particulars	ABC Ltd.	XYZ Ltd.
Cash and cash equivalents	630	960
Debtors	990	1890
Inventories	3,690	2850
Plant and Machinery	5,085	7200
Total Assets	10,395	12,900
Creditors	2,700	3,150
12% Debentures	1,500	3,000
Equity Capital	3,300	5,250
Retained Earnings	2,895	1,500
Total Liabilities	10,395	12,900
Sales	16,800	24,600
Cost of goods sold	12,000	19,440
Other operating expenses	2,400	2,580
Interest expenses	180	360
Income taxes	798	819
Dividends	300	540

As a financial consultant, you are required to comment on the financial position of the company by calculating various ratios and interpret them.

Suggested Activity

Collect the Balance Sheet and Profit and Loss Account of at least 10 companies, calculate various ratios and interpret them.

Questions from Previous Pune University Examinations

1. Discuss fully the Importance of Ratio Analysis as a Tool for Performance Analysis.
   [P.G.D.B.M. April 2006]
2. Write Short Notes on:
   (a) Utility of Funds Flow Statement. **[P.G.D.B.M. April 2006]**
   (b) Debt Equity Ratio. **[P.G.D.B.M. April 2006]**
   (c) Current Ratio. **[M.B.A. April 2007]**
3. What is the Significance of the following Ratios?
   (a) Net Profit Ratio,
   (b) Debt Ratio,
   (c) Current Ratio. **[M.B.A. Dec. 2006]**
4. Explain the Significance of Net Profit Ratio and Debt Equity Ratio. **[M.B.A. Dec. 2007]**
5. Discuss in detail the Merits and Limitations of Ratio Analysis. **[M.B.A. April 2009]**
6. Differentiate between : Funds Flow Statement and Cash Flow Statement.
   [M.B.A. Dec. 2010]
7. Differentiate between : Debt Equity Ratio and Return on Investment.
   [M.B.A. Dec. 2010]

■■■

Chapter 3

Capital Budgeting

Contents ...
3.1 Introduction
3.2 Reasons for Capital Investments
3.3 Aspects of Capital Budgeting Process
3.4 Types of Capital Budgeting Decisions
3.5 Steps in Capital Budgeting Process
3.6 Importance of Capital Budgeting
3.7 Evaluation Techniques
3.8 Other Aspects of Capital Budgeting
- Solved Problems
- Points to Remember
- Questions for Discussion
- Case Study
- Suggested Activity
- Questions from Previous Pune University Examinations

Learning Objectives ...
After studying this chapter, you should be able to,
1. Understand the Concept and Importance of Capital Budgeting Decisions
2. Understand the Tools and Techniques of Evaluation of Capital Budgeting Decisions
3. Know the Difference between Non discounted and Discounted Cash Flow Techniques
4. Learn the various Techniques used under Risk and Uncertainty Conditions
5. Grasp the Concept of Capital Rationing

3.1 Introduction

A business organisation has to face the problem of capital investment decisions quite often. Capital investment refers to the investment in projects whose results of which would be available only after a year. The investments in these projects are quite heavy and are to be made immediately but the return will be available only after a period of time. These investment decisions, popularly known as capital budgeting decisions, require comparison of cost against benefits over a long period. Such investments may affect revenues for the time period ranging from 2 to 20 years or more. In other words, the system of capital budgeting is employed to evaluate expenditure decisions, which involve current outlays but are likely to produce benefits over a period of time longer than one year. These benefits may be either in the form of increased revenues or reduction in costs. The following basic features of capital budgeting may be derived from the above discussion.

(i) Capital budgeting involves comparatively a large amount.
(ii) The benefits from these decisions are spread over a large time horizon.
(iii) There is a greater degree of risk involved in these decisions.
(iv) Capital budgeting decisions are either not reversible or reversible at a heavy loss.

3.2 Reasons for Capital Investments

(a) Projects which are means to maintain or improve profitability

(i) Certain projects may result in cost reduction, e.g., Replacement of manual operations by labour saving devices.
(ii) Certain projects may lead to increased output and, therefore, increased earnings.
(iii) It may become necessary to invest in certain projects in order to protect the company's earning potential, in view of growing competition. It may be either a protective investment or even an investment, meant to ward off competition.
(iv) Many Capital Investments become necessary because of technological changes and innovations. If a machine with a better design comes into the market, the existing machines (in the same line) become obsolete. If a new manufacturing process is developed (which results in greater economy and/or more output), the existing process has to be discarded.
(v) If a company wants to acquire or maintain leadership in the industry it spends vast sums of money on Research and Development which may in some cases appear to be output of proportion to its existing level of activities.

The primary motive in making the above types of investment is profitability in contract to the five types of investments classified under (b) below. What we are going to discuss in this chapter is relevant to the investments which are made for reasons of profit.

(b) Projects for which profitability is not the criterion

There are certain projects, in which every company has to invest funds, though such projects do not have any direct impact on increased profitability either in the short–run or in the long–run.

Examples:

(i) Projects, which are statutorily required, e.g., effluent clearing plant in a fertilizer factory, dust collection in a cement factory, special equipment to treat noxious gases by a chemical factory.

(ii) Service Department Projects, e.g., building and furniture for administrative, finance, legal departments etc.

(iii) Welfare Projects such as health clinic, recreation club for employees.

(iv) Educational Projects such as schools for employee's children.

(v) Safety Projects, e.g., fencing equipment, special protective cages, etc.

However, it does not mean that some of these projects do not result in increased productivity and profitability in the long–run, they may. But what is necessary to remember is that in making these investments, profitability is not the chief criterion.

3.3 Aspects of Capital Budgeting Process

The most important part of the capital budgeting process is decision making in some very crucial areas. These areas can be broadly identified as given below:

(i) The total amount that the firm has to invest in capital budgeting proposals.

(ii) The projects in which the amount to be invested have to be identified and accordingly ranking the projects with respect to their relative importance in the overall strategy of the firm.

(iii) The sources from which the required amount is to be raised should also be decided. The cost of funds depends on the sources from which the funds are raised.

(iv) The techniques which are to be used for the evaluation of the capital budgeting proposals should also be decided in advance so that fair evaluation will be possible.

3.4 Types of Capital Budgeting Decisions

Capital budgeting decisions are normally of the following types:

(i) Replacements: Existing fixed assets will need replacements either due to the end of their useful life or due to advancement in technology; otherwise their productivity will come down. For replacing such assets, capital budgeting decisions become essential.

(ii) Expansion: Enhancement of existing capacity becomes necessary due to increased demand for the products. For this enhancement, additional funds will be required.

(iii) Diversification: A firm may be interested in diversification with the objective of reducing the risk. Diversification may be in the form of introducing additional product lines or entering into several markets rather than operating in a single market. In such cases, capital investment decisions become inevitable.

(iv) Other projects: A firm may have to invest money in such projects which are not directly resulting into profits but are mandatory. For example: installation of pollution control equipment, undertaking welfare projects for workers etc.

Capital Expenditure Proposals may also be classified into the following types:

  (a) **Mutually Exclusive Proposals:** These types of proposals are alternatives to each other and the decision making is to be done for selecting any one of these proposals. For example, if a firm wants to replace its Plant and Machinery and two alternatives are available, any one will be selected by applying the decision criteria for the same. Similarly there can be options like buying v/s leasing, which means that either an asset can be purchased or the same can be taken on lease. Comparative costs and benefits of both the options will be worked out and appropriate choice will have to be done.

  (b) **Independent Proposals:** These are independent proposals and do not have any alternatives as such. For example, a company may be considering to expand its production capacity or it may be consider introduction of a new product. These proposals do not have any alternative and the acceptance depends on the comparison of costs and benefits.

  (c) **Dependent Proposals:** Sometimes, it happens that certain proposals are dependent on a particular proposal. For example, if a manufacturing company decides to open an additional production facility in the rural area, along with the plant and machinery, they will have to invest in other infrastructure facilities like housing for workers, roads, hospitals, schools and colleges and so on.

3.5 Steps in Capital Budgeting Process

Capital budgeting decisions have long-term implications and hence careful planning and effective implementation of the same becomes extremely important. The following steps are normally involved in the capital budgeting process.

  (a) **Finding out Investment Avenues:** Before formulating any proposal of capital budgeting, it is essential to find out the profitable investment avenues for capital investment. Identification of proposals is dependent on generation of ideas and the ideas are generated at various levels. It has been observed that several proposals of cost reduction or modernisation or even of product improvement may be generated by workers at the lower or middle level while the expansion or diversification proposals may come from the top management. The various ideas generated at different levels will have to scrutinize carefully before accepting any one of them.

  (b) **Screening and Evaluation of Ideas:** A very careful evaluation of the proposals generated at various levels is of utmost importance in the capital budgeting process. Evaluation of these proposals is done on the basis of the projected cash inflows and the proposed cash outflows. For this development projection of cash inflows is important. In real life situations, this is quite difficult as the future is uncertain and lots of risks are involved in various proposals which may make the prediction rather difficult. Estimation of cash flows requires collection and analysis of all qualitative and quantitative data, both financial and non financial in nature. Large companies would generally have a Management Information System providing such data. While estimating the cash flows, the time horizon over which the estimate is to be made is also to be decided in advance. The time horizon depends on the estimated life of the proposal which may vary from proposal to proposal. However a time horizon of over 10 years is highly risky as lot of uncertainty creeps in. After the estimation of cash flows, appropriate technique is used for evaluation of the proposal for the sake of decision making.

(c) Authorisation of the Proposal: It has been the practice in several organisations that before the commencement of a proposal, there is an authorisation of the proposal in a formal manner. Proposals are presented in a formal manner by submitting a detailed description of the proposal which includes the initial investment required, the description of the proposal, and detailed projections of cash flows with appropriate justification of the same. Additionally the expected annual accounting rate of return along with the pay back period may also be given in the detailed description. Due to the importance of the capital budgeting decisions, it is but natural that the proposal is submitted to the Top Management which may have a committee to look into this matter. However, considering the pressure of time on the Top Management, companies may fix up ceiling limits on the amounts of the proposals and may prescribe that proposals above a particular amount only should be submitted to the Top Management and proposals of lower amounts may be sanctioned at the Department level itself. The authorisation of the proposal signals the start of the proposal.

(d) Implementation: After a careful evaluation of the proposal, if it is found viable, the implementation of the same commences. Care is taken to ensure that there is no time and cost overrun and the project is completed in time. For effective implementation, network analysis proves to be extremely useful. Techniques used in the network analysis, i.e. Project Evaluation and Rating Technique [PERT] and Critical Path Method [CPM] help companies to implement the proposals effectively to ensure that the proposal is completed within given time and there is no cost overrun.

(e) Post Completion Audit of the Cash Flows: It is of paramount importance that there should be constant review of the capital expenditure proposals after their commencement. In this review the actual results are compared with the estimated results that were included in the investment proposal. There should be some method of evaluation similar to the method used for the evaluation of the proposal itself. Post completion audit will compare the actual performance with the standard one, but the difficulty here is that no pre determined standard will exist for any capital expenditure proposal. Comparison of actual and estimated cash flows will be very difficult to evaluate basically because even if there is a deviation between the actual and the projected, ascertaining the reasons for such deviation will be difficult. There may not be any method to find out as to how much of the deviation is due to incorrect forecast and how much is due to other factors. In such situations, what can be done is that the investment proposals should be scrutinized very carefully in the screening stage itself and also incorporate the estimated results of individual projects into departmental operating budgets. Although the results of individual projects cannot be isolated, their combined effect can be examined as part of the conventional periodic performance review.

Another important factor to be considered is that capital investment decisions are long-term decisions. Naturally a forecast of future cash inflows is to be made and if the actual cash inflows do not match with the projections, the project may be a failure. Future is always uncertain and hence even if technique like sensitivity analysis and probability analysis are used, one negative event may severely affect the outcome of the project. Hence, it will not be appropriate to blame any one particular department or person for failure of capital investment proposals. Actually, it is not the intention of the post completion audit also as otherwise it will kill the initiative and promote a policy of over cautious approach. There is a danger that only safe proposals will be undertaken and it may hamper the profitability in the long run.

However, in any case, post completion audit of capital expenditure proposals should be undertaken. A record of the performance and the mistakes committed can be guidance for avoiding such mistakes in the future. Similarly, this audit will also inculcate a tendency among the manager to screen every proposal very carefully and thus have a realistic appraisal of the proposals.

3.6 Importance of Capital Budgeting

Capital budgeting decisions are quite crucial and critical business decisions. The reasons for this can be summarised as given below:

(a) The capital budgeting decisions relate to fixed assets and the fixed assets represent the true earning assets of the firm. They enable the firm to generate finished goods that can be ultimately sold at profit. Thus, it can be said that capital budgeting decisions determine the future destiny of the company. While an opportune investment decisions can yield spectacular returns, a few wrong decisions may force a firm into bankruptcy.

(b) The effect of capital budgeting decisions will be felt by the firm over a long time, and inevitably affect the cost structure of a company. For example, if a particular plant has been purchased by a company to start a new product, the company commits itself to a sizeable amount of fixed costs, in terms of labour, supervisor's salary, insurance etc. If the project is unsuccessful, the entire burden of fixed costs will fall on the firm, thus, affecting its profitability.

(c) In most cases, capital budgeting decisions are irreversible. The reason is that, there may not be any market for second hand plant and equipment and they may have to be sold out only at a loss.

(d) The capital budgeting decisions require an assessment of future events which are uncertain. It is really a difficult task to estimate the probable future events, and the expected benefits and costs in uncertain conditions.

3.7 Evaluation Techniques

Capital budgeting decisions are extremely crucial for any organisation for the following reasons:

(a) The amount involved in these proposals is very huge and after investing such an amount, if the projects prove to be failure, it will result into tremendous amount of losses. Sometimes the entire organisation may be written off due to such failed projects.

(b) Capital budgeting decisions are normally not reversible, and if at all reversed, may lead to loss. For example, if a firm decides to invest in modernisation of machinery and due to some reason, this decision proves to be a failure; reversal of this decision can be done only at a loss.

Therefore, before any capital budgeting decision is taken, careful evaluation of the same should be done and if they are likely to be viable, only then should they be accepted. For evaluation of capital budgeting proposals, the following techniques are used.

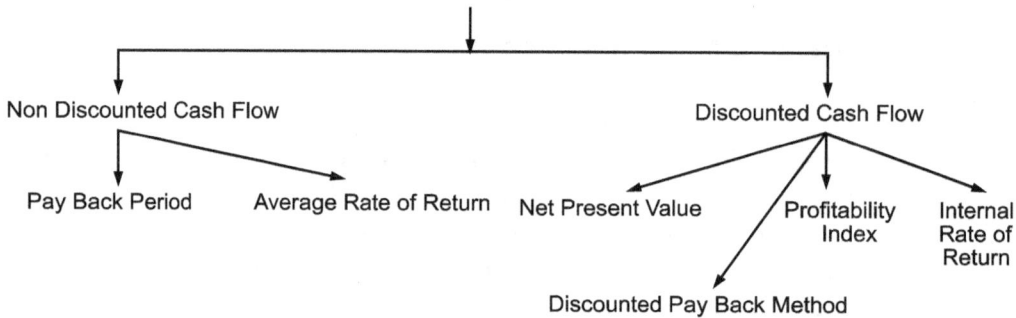

These techniques are discussed in detail in the following paragraphs.

(A) Non Discounted Cash Flow Techniques:

Evaluation of capital budgeting proposals is done on the basis of cash inflows and outflows rather than on the basis of accounting profits.

Non discounted cash flow means, the estimated cash flows during the entire life time of the project, without taking into consideration their time value, i.e. the present value of the future cash inflows.

FINANCIAL MANAGEMENT — CAPITAL BUDGETING

The following techniques are included in this category.

(I) Pay Back Period

The Pay Back Period is the number of years in which the initial investment made in a capital budgeting proposal is recovered. For example, if the initial investment in a proposal is ₹ 20,00,000 and the projected cash inflows per year are ₹ 400000 each, the payback period will be ₹ 20,00,000/₹ 4,00,000 = 5 years. This means that the initial investment made in the proposal will be recovered in a period of 5 years. The pay back period is calculated as given below:

- When the projected cash inflows from a capital budgeting proposal are equal, the pay back period is computed with the help of the following formula.

    Pay Back Period = Initial Investment / Projected Annual Cash Inflows.

- When the projected cash inflows from a capital budgeting are not uniform, the pay back period will be computed as given below:

    Initial Investments: ₹ 50,00,000

Projected Cash Inflows:

Year	Amount [₹]	Cumulative Cash Inflows [₹]
01	12,00,000	12,00,000
02	19,00,000	31,00,000
03	25,00,000	56,00,000
04	27,00,000	83,00,000
05	26,00,000	1,09,00,000
Total	1,09,00,000	

The cumulative cash inflows shown in the third column shows that in the first two years out of the initial investment, ₹ 31,00,000 are recovered while at the end of the third year, total ₹ 56,00,000 are recovered. This indicates that the Pay Back Period is more than two years but less than three years. The following formula will be used to calculate the exact Pay Back Period.

Pay Back Period: 2 + unrecovered balance at the end of the second year/Cash Inflows of the subsequent year.

= 2 + 19,00,000/25,00,000

= 2 + 0.76

= 2.76 years.

The Pay Back Period of 2.76 years shown indicates that the initial investment made in the project, will be recovered in that period. For any proposal, the lesser the pay back, the better it is. Hence, if the Pay Back Period technique is to be used for evaluation of capital budgeting proposals, the decision making will be on the basis of the following points.

(a) In case there are mutually exclusive proposals, i.e. either proposal X or proposal Y is to be accepted the lesser the pay back period, the better it is. In other words, in such cases, the proposal with a lesser pay back period will be selected.

(b) In case, there is only one proposal, which is either to be accepted or rejected, the firm may decide some target pay back period and if the projected pay back period is less than that, then only the proposal will be selected.

For example, if there is a proposal to accept or reject and the target pay back period is 5 years, while the projected pay back period is 4 years, the proposal may be accepted. On the other hand if the projected pay back period is 6 years, it may be rejected.

The Pay Back Period technique has the following merits:

1. It is a rough and ready method of computing the number of years in which the initial investments are recovered.
2. The Pay Back Period is easy to compute and understand, as even a common man can understand the implications of this technique.
3. The number of years in which the initial investment is going to be recovered is known, which facilitates the planning of the investment.

However, the Pay Back Period has the following limitations:

(a) The main limitation of the pay back period is that the present value of money is not taken into consideration. The present value of money goes on declining with the passage of time and therefore projected cash inflows should be adjusted to this factor. However, this is not done in the case of pay back period and hence the utility of this technique is reduced substantially. In order to remove this limitation, discounted pay back period is computed by discounting the cash inflows.

(b) In this technique, the number of years in which the initial investment is recovered is given more importance as the emphasis is on the recovery of the initial investment. However, the post-pay back period profitability is ignored and hence there is a possibility of profitable projects being rejected only because the pay back period of these projects is more. The following illustration will make the point clear.

FINANCIAL MANAGEMENT   CAPITAL BUDGETING

Proposal X

Initial Investments: ₹ 50,00,000.

Projected Cash Inflows:

Year	Amount [₹]	Cumulative Cash Inflows [₹]
01	12,00,000	12,00,000
02	19,00,000	31,00,000
03	25,00,000	56,00,000
04	27,00,000	83,00,000
05	26,00,000	1,09,00,000
Total	1,09,00,000	

As shown in the above illustration, the Pay Back Period in this proposal is 2.76 years.

Now, consider the proposal Y, which also has the initial investment of ₹ 50,00,000 and the estimated life of 5 years. The projected cash inflows are as follows.

Year	Amount [₹]	Cumulative Cash Inflows [₹]
01	10,00,000	10,00,000
02	15,00,000	25,00,000
03	24,00,000	49,00,000
04	35,00,000	84,00,000
05	38,00,000	1,22,00,000
Total	1,22,00,000	

The Pay Back Period in the above case is as follows.

Pay Back Period: = 3 + 1,00,000/3500000

                   = 3.028 years.

Thus, it can be observed that the pay back period for proposal Y is more than that of X and therefore proposal X will be selected on the basis of pay back criteria. However, if the total cash inflows are taken into account, proposal Y is more profitable than X as the total of cash inflows is ₹ 1,22,00,000 while that of X is ₹ 1,09,00,000 but this fact will be ignored as more importance is given to the faster recovery of the initial investment.

(II) Average Rate of Return (ARR) /Accounting Rate of Return

This is an age old technique used for evaluating capital expenditure proposals. It has been defined in many ways, which led to Peter Drucker to say that this is a 'rubber of infinite elasticity'. This rate of return indicates the percentage return projected on the investment made in the proposal. In this method, projected net profit after income tax is computed for the expected life of the proposal and its average is worked out. The percentage of this average net profit to the investments is computed which is the average rate of return or also called as accounting rate of return. The formula for computing this rate is as follows:

Average Rate of Return [Accounting Rate of Return] = Projected Average Incremental Net Profits after income tax/Investments ×100

Average Rate of Return is also computed by taking the average investments made in the proposal which is calculated as given below.

Average Investments = Opening Investments + Closing Investments/2

The illustration of Average Rate of Return is given below.

Illustration:

Initial Investments: ₹ 20,00,000, residual value: nil.

Effective life: 5 years.

Projected Net Profits after depreciation and income tax:

Year	Amount ₹
1	4,50,000
2	6,00,000
3	7,00,000
4	7,50,000
5	7,00,000
Total	32,00,000

Solution:

The average profits will be: ₹ 32,00,000/5 = ₹ 6,40,000

The Average Rate of Return = Average Profits/Average Investments *
= ₹ 6,40,000/₹ 10,00,000 × 100
= 64%

* Average investment is computed by taking the total of the opening balance plus the closing balance and dividing the total by two, i.e. ₹ 20,00,000 + Nil/2 = ₹ 1000000.

Decision Making: In case of a single proposal, the decision-making depends on the cost of funds required for that proposal. If the projected accounting rate of return is more than the cost of funds, the proposal may be accepted, otherwise it may not. In case there are two mutually exclusive proposals, the one with higher rate of return should be accepted.

The main merits of this method are as follows.

(a) This method is easy to understand and simple to compute. Hence it is easily understandable.

(b) Feasibility of a proposal can be understood properly in the form of percentage of rate of return on the investment.

However this method suffers from a major limitation and that is the present value of money is not taken into consideration and hence not much useful for evaluation of proposals, which are of longer duration.

FINANCIAL MANAGEMENT · CAPITAL BUDGETING

(B) Discounted Cash Flow Techniques
[I] Net Present Value (NPV)

The Net Present Value is the difference between the total present value of projected cash inflows arising from a proposal and the initial investment made in the proposal. For computing the Net Present Value, the following steps are taken.

(a) Cash in flows arising out of a capital budgeting proposal are projected for the entire life time of a proposal.

(b) A rate of discount at which the cash inflows are to be discounted should be fixed. The rate of discount depends on the cost of funds required for the proposal and the inflation rate in the economy.

(c) Present value of projected cash inflows is computed by applying the rate of discount selected.

(d) Net present value is computed by deducting the initial investment amount [cash outflow] from the total present value of the cash inflows. If the net present value is positive, the proposal may be accepted and if it is negative, it may be rejected. In case of mutually exclusive proposals, a proposal with higher net present value will be selected.

Illustration:

X Ltd. is considering a proposal of investing ₹ 25,00,000 with an expected life of 5 years and no salvage value at the end of the life. The projected cash inflows are as follows:

1st Year: ₹ 5,00,000, 2nd year: ₹ 7,00,000, 3rd year: ₹ 9,50,000, 4th year: ₹ 10,00,000 and 5th year: ₹ 11,00,000.

The company uses 10% rate of discount. Calculate the Net Present Value of this proposal.

Solution:

Year	Amount ₹	P.V. Factors @ 10%	Present Value of Cash inflows
1st	5,00,000	.909	4,54,500
2nd	7,00,000	.826	5,78,200
3rd	9,50,000	.751	7,13,450
4th	10,00,000	.683	6,83,000
5th	11,00,000	.621	6,83,100
	42,50,000		31,12,250

Net Present Value = Total present value of cash inflows
– Initial investments

₹ 31,12,250 – ₹ 25,00,000 = ₹ 6,12,250

As the net present value is positive, the proposal may be accepted.

[II] Internal Rate of Return (IRR)

This is an alternative technique for use in making capital investment decisions that also takes into consideration the present value of money. The internal rate of return represents the true interest rate earned on an investment over the course of its useful life. This is the rate of discount at which the net present value is neither positive nor negative. In other words, the rate of discount at which the net present value is nil, is the internal rate of return.

The Internal Rate of Return has the following merits:

(a) Time value of money is taken into consideration.
(b) It considers all cash flows occurring over the entire life of the project to calculate the rate of return.
(c) It is consistent with the shareholders' wealth maximisation objectives. Whenever a project's internal rate of return is greater than the opportunity cost of capital, the shareholders' wealth will be maximised.

The computation of internal rate of return involves trial and error process up to a certain stage and then exact internal rate of return is computed by applying a formula. Before applying the formula, the following steps are required to be taken:

(a) Initially, the cash inflows arising out of a particular proposal will be discounted at a particular rate, say 10%.
(b) If the net present value at 10% is positive, a higher rate of discount than 10% will be tried for arriving at negative net present value. In other words, a pair of rate, one with a positive net present value and another with a negative net present value will have to be found out by trial and error process.
(c) After establishing the pair of rate, the next step will be the application of the following formula to find out exact rate of return. The formula for the same is as follows.

Internal Rate of Return = Lower Rate + Net Present Value at lower rate / Difference between the present value ×Difference in rates.

[Illustration is given in the solved examples]

Decision Making: If there is a single proposal, which is either to be accepted or rejected, the internal rate of return is compared with the cost of funds and if it is found that the internal rate of return is more than the cost of funds, the project may be accepted. On the other hand, if the internal rate of return is less than the cost of funds, the project may be rejected.

In case of mutually exclusive proposals, the proposal with a higher internal rate of return may be accepted.

Modified Internal Rate of Return: The assumption in case of internal rate of return is that the cash flows generated during the lifetime of the project are reinvested. The internal rate of return method assumes that the reinvestment of the cash flows at its internal rate of return while the net present value method assumes that the cash flows are reinvested at the opportunity cost of capital. The reinvestment assumption is based on the following computation.

Suppose, Project X and Y are having same internal rate of return and thus they are equally attractive. Further suppose that the terminal value of Y is ₹ 200. It is but natural that the terminal value of X is also ₹ 200 so that both of them have the same internal rate of return. Following the internal rate of return, the terminal value of X would be ₹ 200 only when its cash flows are assumed to be reinvested at its internal rate of return of 20%. For example, ₹ 100 (1 + 20) 2 + ₹ 56 = ₹ 200. Given the initial value of ₹ 115.74 and the terminal value of ₹ 200, the compound average annual return should be equal to internal rate of 20%.

However some experts argue that it is more realistic to use the opportunity cost of capital as the reinvestment rate. If we use 10% as the reinvestment rate, X's terminal value will be ₹ 177 and now project X's compound average annual return would be,

$$\sqrt[3]{\frac{177}{115.74}} - 1 = 0.15 \text{ or } 15\%$$

This 15% is the modified internal rate of return. The Modified Internal Rate of Return [MIRR] is the compound average annual rate that is calculated with a reinvestment rate different than the project's internal rate of return.

[III] Profitability Index (PI)

This is also termed as cost benefit ratio and is computed by dividing the total present value of cash inflows by the initial investment. The profitability index indicates the return available per rupee invested in a proposal and is useful when decision making is to be made from mutually exclusive proposals involving different amount of investments. Profitability Index is defined as the rate of present value of the future cash benefits at the required rate of return to the initial cash outflow of the investment. This is yet another method of evaluating the investment proposals. It is also known as the Benefit Cost Ratio (B/C). The PI approach measures present value of returns per rupee invested. This is similar to NPV approach. Where project with different initial investments are to be evaluated the PI method proves to be the best technique.

[IV] Discounted Pay Back Period

One of the serious limitations of the Pay Back Period discussed above is that the present value of cash inflows is not taken into consideration. In other words, the cash flows are not discounted for the computation of the pay back period. In order to remove this limitation, for the computation of the pay back period, the present value of the cash flows are taken into consideration and then the pay back period is computed. This is called as 'Discounted Pay Back Period'. However, the limitation that post pay back period cash flows are not taken into consideration still continues in spite of the discounting of the cash flows. The computation of discounted pay back period is shown in the illustrations given below.

Comparison of Net Present Value and Internal Rate of Return: The Net Present Value and Internal Rate of Return, both are the techniques of evaluation of capital expenditure proposals by using discounted cash flows. A question arises as to whether these techniques will give same results or whether they will reveal conflicting results in the evaluation of a capital expenditure proposal? For example, suppose a company is evaluating proposal X and proposal Y, which are mutually exclusive and their net present values and internal rate of return reveal the following things.

Proposal	Initial Investments [₹]	Net Present Value [₹]	Internal Rate of Return [%]
X	20,00,000	8,90,000	20%
Y	20,00,000	9,50,000	22%

In the above situation, it is clear that proposal Y is giving higher net present value and its internal rate of return is also greater than that of X, which means that on both the criteria, proposal Y is better. This is confirmed by both the techniques used for the evaluation. Thus it has been observed, that in the case of conventional projects, [in which an initial cash outflow is followed by a series of cash inflows] that are independent of each other [i.e. where the selection of a particular project does not preclude the choice of the other], both Net Present Value and Internal Rate of Return will lead to same accept/reject decisions.

There exist situations where the Internal Rate of Return method may lead to different decisions being made from those that would follow the adoption of the Net Present Value procedure.

The Net Present Value and Internal Rate of Return will give conflicting rankings to the capital expenditure proposals, which are mutually exclusive, under the following conditions.
- The cash flow pattern may differ. That is, the cash flows of one project may increase over time, while those of others may decrease or vice versa.
- The cash outlays, i.e. initial investment may differ for the projects.
- The projects may have different expected lives.

These factors are discussed below.

[I] Timing of Cash Flows

The most commonly found condition for the conflict between the NPV and IRR is the timing of cash flows. The following example will clarify the point.

Suppose, there are two projects, M and N with the following details.

Project	Cash Outlays C0	Cash Inflows C1	Cash Inflows C2	Cash Inflows C3	Net Present Value @ 9%	Internal Rate of Return
M	– 1680	1400	700	140	301	23%
N	– 1680	140	840	1510	321	17%

It can be seen that at 9% rate of discount, the NPV of project M is ₹ 301 which is less than the NPV of project N, but the IRR of project M is higher than that of N. A question arises as to why this happens? In such situation, which project should be accepted?

Let us see how the NPVs of both the projects behave with discount rates. This is shown in the following table.

Discount Rate [%]	Project M	Project N
0	560	810
5	409	520
10	276	276
15	159	70
20	54	– 106
25	– 40	– 257
30	– 125	– 388

It can be seen from the above table that the net present value of project N falls sharply as the rate of discount increases. The reason is that its largest cash inflows are quite late in life, when the compounding effect of time is most significant. This is exactly opposite as compared to project M as this project has larger amounts of cash inflows in the early part of the life when compounding effect is not much. The internal rate of return for both the projects, are 23% and 17% respectively for M and N. The NPV profiles of two projects intersect at 10% rate of discount which is shown below. This is called Fisher's Intersection.

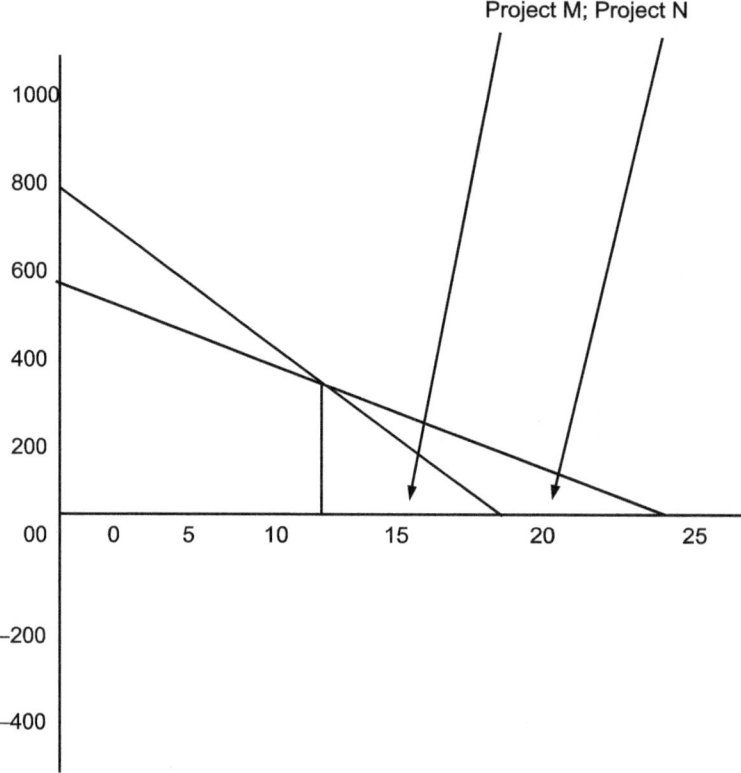

Fisher's intersection occurs at the discount rate where the net present values of both the projects are the same, i.e. ₹ 276. The intersection rate can be determined with the help of the following method.

$$-1680 + 1400/(1 + r^*) + 700/(1 + r^*)^2 + 140(1 + r^*)^3$$
$$= -1680 + 140(1 + r^*) + 840(1 + r^*)^2 + 1510(1 + r^*)^3$$

Solving the above equation we get r* = 10%

It can be noticed from the above graph that at the rate of discount less than the intersection rate [10%], project N has the higher net present value but lower internal rate of return of 17%. On the other hand, at the discount rate higher than the intersection rate of 10%, project M has both, higher net present value as well as higher internal rate of return of 23%. Thus, if the required rate of return is greater than the intersection rate, both, net present value and internal rate of return will yield consistent results. That is, the project with higher internal rate of return will also have higher net present value. However, if the required rate of return is less than the intersection rate, the two methods will give contradictory results. That is, project with higher internal rate of return will have lower net present value and vice versa.

Another question is that in such a conflicting situation, which project should be chosen? Both projects generate positive net present value at 9% but project N is better as it is generating higher net present value. If the internal rate of return criteria is used, project M is generating higher internal rate of return. If project N is chosen, we will be richer by an additional value of ₹ 20. Should we have the satisfaction of earning a higher rate of return or should we like to be richer? The net present value is consistent with the objective of maximising wealth and hence when a choice is to be made between mutually exclusive projects, the project with higher net present value should be selected.

Incremental Approach: It is argued that the internal rate of return method can still be used to choose between mutually exclusive projects, if we adopt it to calculate rate of return on the incremental cash flows. If we prefer project N to project M, there should be incremental benefits in doing so. To see this, let us calculate the incremental flows of project N over project M. The following results are obtained.

Project	Initial Cash Outflows C0	Cash Inflows C1	Cash Inflows C2	Cash Inflows C3	Net Present Value @ 9%	Internal Rate of Return [%]
[N – M]	00	– 1260	140	1370	20	10

The internal rate of return is 10%. It is more than the opportunity cost of 9%. Therefore project N should be accepted. It is better than project M despite its lower internal rate of return because it offers all benefits that project M offers plus the opportunity of an incremental investment at 10%, a rate higher than the required rate of return of 9%. It may be noticed that the net present value of incremental flows is the difference of the net present value of project N over that of project M; this is so because of value adding principle.

The incremental approach is a satisfactory way of salvaging the internal rate of return rule. But the series of the incremental cash flows may result in negative and positive cash flows. [i.e. lending and borrowing type pattern]. This would result in multiple internal rate of return and ultimately the net present value method will have to be used.

Scale of Investment: Another condition, under which the net present value and internal rate of return methods will give contradictory ranking to the projects, is when the cash outlays are of different sizes. Let us consider projects A and B involving following cash flows.

Project	Cash Outflows [Initial] ₹	Cash Inflows 1st year [₹]	Net Present Value at 10%	Internal Rate of Return [%]
A	– 1000	1500	364	50%
B	– 1,00,000	1,20,000	9091	20

The net present value of project A is ₹ 364 at 10% rate of discount and the internal rate of return in 50% while in case of project B, the net present value is ₹ 9091 at 10% rate of discount and the internal rate of return is 20%. Thus these two projects are ranked separately under the two methods.

As discussed earlier, the net present value method gives unambiguous results. Since the net present value of project B is higher, it should be accepted. The same result can be obtained if we calculate the internal rate of return on incremental investment.

Project	Cash Outflows [Initial] ₹	Cash Inflows 1st year [₹]	Net Present Value at 10%	Internal Rate of Return [%]
[A-B]	– 99000	1,18,500	8727	19.7

The incremental investment of ₹ 99000 [₹ 1, 00, 000 – ₹ 1000] will generate cash inflows of ₹ 1, 18, 500 after a year. Thus the return on the incremental investment is 19.7%, which is in excess of 10% required rate of return. Thus project B is preferable to project A

Project Life Span: Difference in the life span of two mutually exclusive projects can also give rise to the conflict between the net present value method and internal rate of return method. The following illustration is given below:

Projects	C0 [Cash Outflows]	Cash Inflows C1	C2	C3	C4	C5	Net Present Value @ 10%	Internal Rate of Return %
X	– 10000	12000					909	20
Y	– 10000	0	0	0	0	20,120	2493	15

Both the projects require initial cash outlays of ₹ 10000 each. Project X generates cash flow of ₹ 12000 at the end of one year, while Project Y generated cash flow of ₹ 20 at the end of the fifth year. At 10% required rate of return, the net present value of the project X is ₹ 909 while that of Y is ₹ 2493. Internal rate of return in case of project X is 20% while that of Y is 15%. Thus the two methods rank the projects differently. The net present value can be used to choose between the projects since it is always consistent with the wealth maximising principle. Thus project Y should be preferred since it has higher net present value.

3.8 Other Aspects of Capital Budgeting
Capital Rationing
1. **Meaning:** A firm may have several projects which may yield positive net present value. However there is a situation where some ceiling limit is to be put on the total capital expenditure that a firm wishes to incur. Financial constraints may force a firm to put restrictions on the total volume of capital expenditure that may be incurred in a particular period. Thus capital rationing is a situation where a firm cannot undertake all positive net present value projects it has identified because of shortage of capital.

It is quite natural that in such a situation, even some viable proposals have to be rejected due to shortage of funds. A firm has to answer a question in this situation that how to allocate available funds to the acceptable proposals which require more funds than they are available? Various aspects of capital rationing are discussed in detail in the following paragraphs.

2. **Factors Responsible for Capital Rationing:** Capital rationing situation may arise in the following situations:

    (a) **External Factors:** Capital rationing may arise due to external factors like imperfections of capital market or deficiencies in the market information which may affect the availability of capital. Sometimes the market is not able to mop up the necessary financial resources required by a firm. It may also happen that the Government may put some restrictions on the market which will limit the capital availability in the market.

    For example, to control inflation, the Government may increase the rate of interest which will affect the capital flow adversely in the market. Due to these restrictions, a firm may not be able to mop the amount of capital required by them for various projects.

    (b) **Internal Factors:** Internal factors responsible for capital rationing are as follows.

    (i) Apprehension of the Management regarding the issue of fresh equity share capital for the fear of loosing the control over the company.

    (ii) Conservative policy of the Management regarding raising funds through debt may affect the financing of a particular proposal.

    (iii) Reluctance to accept some viable proposals because of its inability to manage the firm in the scale of operation resulting from inclusion of all the viable projects.

3. **Decision Making in Capital Rationing Situations:** Under capital rationing situations, the crucial decision is that how to distribute the scarce capital amongst the most profitable proposals. The Management has to decide not only the profitable investment opportunities but also decide that combination of the profitable projects which will give the highest net present value within the available funds amount.

   As per the theoretical principles, proposals should be undertaken to the point where the return is just equal to the cost of financing these proposals. However, in capital rationing situations, it may so happen that a firm may have to sacrifice some of the profitable proposals due to paucity of funds. Hence, as mentioned above, funds should be allocated amongst different proposals in such a manner that the net present value from all these proposals will be the highest.

The following illustrations will make the concept further clear.

FINANCIAL MANAGEMENT   CAPITAL BUDGETING

Illustration 1: The following proposals are available for a firm. Their net present values and initial investments are given below.

Proposal	Required Initial Investments [₹]	Net Present Value at appropriate cost of capital [₹]
A	1,00,000	20,000
B	3,00,000	35,000
C	50,000	16,000
D	2,00,000	25,000
E	1,00,000	30,000

Total funds available are ₹ 300000. Determine the optimal combination of proposals assuming that the projects are divisible.

Solution: The various proposals will have to be ranked as shown below for arriving at the optimum combination.

Proposal	Required Initial Investments [₹]	Net Present Value at the Appropriate Cost of Capital [₹]	Profitability Index (3/2)	Rank
(1)	(2)	(3)	(4)	(5)
A	1,00,000	20,000	0.2	3
B	3,00,000	35,000	0.117	5
C	50,000	16,000	0.32	1
D	2,00,000	25,000	0.125	4
E	1,00,000	30,000	0.3	2

From the above table, it is clear that the proposal C has the highest rank and then there are other proposals according to their profitability index. The profitability index is used for ranking the proposals.

The following table shows the allocation of the funds amongst different projects to maximise the return.

Rank of Investment	Project	Required Initial Investment [₹]
1	C	50,000
2	E	1,00,000
3	A	1,00,000
4	1/4th of D [1/4th of ₹200000]	50,000
Total		3,00,000

Thus it can be seen that the optimum combination of proposals in capital rationing situation is C, E, A and 1.4th of D. This combination will optimise the return.

FINANCIAL MANAGEMENT   CAPITAL BUDGETING

Illustration 2: X Ltd, has six proposals in hand. Their cash flows are given below.

[₹ 000s]

Year	A	B	C	D	E	F
0	(100)	(50)	----	(10)	(100)	-------
1	(50)	(70)	(100)	(20)	(100)	--------
2	(25)	100	(30)	50	200	(200)
3	100	100	150	(100)	100	300
4	100	-----	200	100	50	100
5	100	-------	-------	100	--------	100

The required rate of return for the proposals is 10%. This rate is expected to remain constant over the next five years. Based on the 10% rate of discount, the net present values of the proposals are as follows.

Project	Net Present Value [₹ 000s]
A	39.4
B	44.1
C	133.6
D	68.4
E	83.6
F	190.5

In order to implement the above proposals, the following investments are required.

Year	₹
0	2,60,000
1	3,40,000
2	2,55,000
3	1,00,000
4	------------
5	------------

Impact of Taxation on Investment Decisions

Taxation laws differ from country to country and also there are various types of allowances given to firms as an incentive for capital investments. The taxation has an impact on the evaluation of a particular proposal as it affects the cash outflows as the tax payments are to be made in cash only. Therefore in several situations the taxation aspects have a dominant influence on the proposal evaluation.

As discussed earlier, the appraisal of a capital expenditure proposal is done on the basis of the incremental cash inflows arising from that proposal. In most of the situations, the taxes will have an adverse impact on the cash inflows as the taxes will result in cash outflows. However in some few situations, the impact of taxation is favourable on the cash inflows, i.e. it will result in some savings. The effects of taxation on the capital expenditure proposals can be of the following types.

(a) Corporate taxes on the projected profit or losses.

(b) Investment incentives [cash grants/subsidies/investment allowances].

(c) The reduction of the weighted average cost of capital due to the fact that the interest on debt is allowable for computing taxation.

(d) Where the proposal results into loss, and where the firm has sufficient profits from other operations, the loss on the proposal will reduce the overall taxation liability of the firm. This reduction of tax is equivalent to cash inflow to the proposal and is computed by multiplying loss by the relevant corporate tax.

(e) Where the proposal incurs a loss and the firm also has incurred an overall loss, the resulting cash inflows from the loss can be carried forward to a future profit making year. Similarly the equivalent cash inflows will be shown against the project in the future year when sufficient profits become available.

[Impact of taxation on capital expenditure proposals is illustrated in the solved problems given in the chapter]

Impact of Inflation on Investment Decisions

Inflation can be simply defined as an increase in the average price of goods or services. The accepted measure of general inflation is the Retail Price Index which is based on the assumed expenditure patterns of an average family. General inflation is a factor in investment appraisal but of more concern is that may be termed specific inflation, i.e. the changes in price of the various factors which may increase the cash outflows, for example, wage rates, material costs, energy costs, transportation charges etc. In view of this every effort should be made to estimate the rate of inflation and its likely impact on the inflows and outflows. Every attempt should be made to estimate specific inflation for each element of the project in a detailed manner. The following factors are quite important in this respect.

(a) **Synchronised and differential Inflation:** Inflation is differential when costs and revenues change at differing rates of inflation or where the various items of cost and revenues move at different rates. This is the normal situation but the concept of synchronised inflation, where costs and revenues are changing at the same rate may occur very rarely.

(b) Money Cash Flows and Real Cash Flows: Money cash flows are the actual amounts of money changing hands whereas real cash flows are the purchasing power equivalents of the actual cash flows. In a world of zero inflation there would be no need to distinguish between money and real cash flows as they would be identical. However, this situation will take place very rarely and in the real life situations, a firm will have to encounter some degree of inflation. Where inflation does exist, then a difference arises between money cash flows and their real value and this difference is the basis of the treatment of inflation in project appraisal. The real discount factor can be calculated with the help of the following formula.

$$\text{Real discount factor} = \frac{1 + \text{Money discount factor}}{1 + \text{Inflation rate}} - 1$$

Illustration: A machine costs ₹ 10000 and is expected to yield the following net cash flows. [Estimated at current prices]

Year	1	2	3
₹	5000	8000	6000

Expected rate of inflation is 5% p.a. and the cost of capital is 15.5%.

The impact of inflation on the cash flows is computed as given below.

₹

Year	Current Prices	Actual Cash Flows
0	(10000)	(10000)
1	5000×1.05	5250
2	$8000 \times (1.05)^2$	8820
3	$6000 \times (1.05)^3$	6946

For each flow, we have added inflation @ 5% by multiplying by $(1.05)^n$ where n is the number of years inflation. Having calculated the actual cash flows, we will not compute the net present value by discounting in the usual manner. This is shown below.

₹

Year	Cash flows	Discount Factor @ 15.5%	Present Value
0	(10000)	1	(10000)
1	5250	1/1.155	4545
2	8820	$[1/1.155]^2$	6612
3	6946	$[1/1.155]^3$	4508
Total			NPV = 5665

Since the net present value is positive, the proposal may be accepted.

FINANCIAL MANAGEMENT   CAPITAL BUDGETING

Solved Problems

Problem 1

ABC Ltd. is considering investing in a project that is expected to cost ₹ 12,00,000 and has an effective life of 5 years. The projected cash inflows for this period are as follows.

Year	Amount [₹]
1	3,00,000
2	3,00,000
3	4,50,000
4	4,50,000
5	7,50,000
Total	22,50,000

Calculate: [A] Pay Back Period [B] Net Present Value @ 10% rate of discounts [C] Profitability Index. [D] Discounted Pay Back Period at 10% rate of discount.

Solution:

[A] Pay Back Period

Year	Amount [₹]	Cumulative Cash Inflows [₹]
1	3,00,000	3,00,000
2	3,00,000	6,00,000
3	4,50,000	10,50,000
4	4,50,000	15,00,000
5	7,50,000	22,50,000
Total	22,50,000	22,50,000

Thus from the above table, it is clear that out of the initial investment of ₹ 12,00,000, at the end of the third year ₹ 10,50,000 are recovered and at the end of the fourth year ₹ 15,00,000 are recovered. This means that the Pay Back Period is more than 3 years and less than 4 years. For calculating the exact pay back period, the following formula will be utilised.

Pay Back Period = 3 + 1,50,000/4,50,000 = 3.

Note: ₹ 1,50,000 is the unrecovered balance of the initial investment at the end of the third year, while ₹ 4,50,000 is the cash inflow of the subsequent year, i.e. cash inflow of the fourth year.

[B] Net Present Value @ 10%

Year	Amount [₹]	Present Value Factors @ 10%	Present Value of Cash Inflows
1	3,00,000	.909	2,72,700
2	3,00,000	.826	2,47,800
3	4,50,000	.751	3,37,950
4	4,50,000	.683	3,07,350
5	7,50,000	.621	4,65,750
Total	22,50,000		16,31,550

Net Present Value = Total Present Value of Cash Inflows – Initial Investments
= ₹ 1631550 – ₹ 1200000 = ₹ 431550

[C] Profitability Index

The formula for the Profitability Index is as follows.

Total Present Value of Cash Inflows/Initial Investments
= ₹ 16,31,550/₹ 12,00,000 = 1.359

[D] Discounted Pay Back Period

The following table, similar to the table prepared for computing the Net Present Value is prepared to compute the cumulative discounted cash inflows and then the Discounted Pay Back Period.

Year	Amount [₹]	Present Value Factors @ 10%	Present Value of Cash Inflows	Cumulative Cash Inflows [₹]
1	3,00,000	.909	2,72,700	2,72,700
2	3,00,000	.826	2,47,800	5,20,500
3	4,50,000	.751	3,37,950	8,58,450
4	4,50,000	.683	3,07,350	11,65,800
5	7,50,000	.621	4,65,750	16,31,550
Total	22,50,000		16,31,550	

Thus it is clear from the above computation, that the Discounted Pay Back Period is more than 4 years but less than 5 years. The following formula will have to be used for computing the exact Discounted Pay Back Period

Discounted Pay Back Period = 4 + 34,200 * / 7,50,000** = 4.045 years

* Unrecovered balance at the end of the 4th year
** Cash inflows of the subsequent year, i.e. 5th year.

FINANCIAL MANAGEMENT — CAPITAL BUDGETING

Problem 2

A firm whose cost of capital is 10% is considering two mutually exclusive proposals, X and Y, the details of which are as follows.

Particulars	Proposal X [₹]	Proposal Y [₹]
Initial Investments	15,00,000	15,00,000
Projected Cash Inflows		
1st year	1,00,000	6,50,000
2nd year	2,50,000	6,00,000
3rd year	3,50,000	6,00,000
4th year	5,50,000	5,75,000
5th year	7,50,000	5,25,000
Total	20,00,000	29,50,000

Calculate:

[A] Pay Back Period
[B] Net Present Value @ 10% rate of discount
[C] Profitability Index
[D] Internal Rate of Return.

Solution:

[A] Pay Back Period

Particulars	Proposal X [₹]	Proposal Y [₹]	Cumulative Cash Inflows Proposal X	Cumulative Cash Inflows Proposal Y
Projected Cash Inflows				
1st year	1,00,000	6,50,000	1,00,000	6,50,000
2nd year	2,50,000	6,00,000	3,50,000	12,50,000
3rd year	3,50,000	6,00,000	7,00,000	18,50,000
4th year	5,50,000	5,75,000	12,50,000	24,25,000
5th year	7,50,000	5,25,000	20,00,000	29,50,000
Total	20,00,000	29,50,000		

Proposal X: From the cumulative cash inflows, it is clear that the pay back period is more than 4 years but less than 5 years. The exact period is calculated with the help of the following formula.

Pay Back Period [Proposal X] = 4 + 2,50,000*/7,50,000** = 4.33 years.

Pay Back Period [Proposal Y] = 2 + 2,50,000*/6,00,000** = 2.41 years.

* Unrecovered balance at the end of the particular year, i.e. 4th year in case of Proposal X and 2nd year in case of Proposal Y.

** Cash inflows of the subsequent year.

[B] Net Present Value

(a) Proposal X

Particulars	Projected Cash Inflows [₹]	Present Value Factors @ 10%	Present Value of Cash Inflows [₹]
Projected Cash Inflows			
1st year	1,00,000	.909	90,900
2nd year	2,50,000	.826	2,06,500
3rd year	3,50,000	.751	2,62,850
4th year	5,50,000	.683	3,75,650
5th year	7,50,000	.621	4,65,750
Total	20,00,000		14,01,650

Net Present Value = Total Present Value of cash inflows – Initial Investment
= ₹ 1401650 – ₹ 1500000
= (–) ₹98,350

(b) Proposal Y

Particulars	Proposal Y [₹]	Present Value Factors @ 10%	Present Value of Cash Inflows [₹]
Projected Cash Inflows			
1st year	6,50,000	.909	5,90,850
2nd year	6,00,000	.826	4,95,600
3rd year	6,00,000	.751	4,50,600
4th year	5,75,000	.683	3,92,725
5th year	5,25,000	.621	3,26,025
Total	29,50,000		22,55,800

Net Present Value = Total Present Value of cash inflows – Initial Investment
= ₹ 22,55,800 – ₹ 15,00,000 = ₹ 7,55,800

[C] Profitability Index

Proposal X = Total present value of cash inflows / Initial investments
= ₹ 14,01,650 / ₹ 15,00,000 = .934

Proposal Y = ₹ 22,55,800 / ₹ 15,00,000 = 1.503

[D] Internal Rate of Return: Internal rate of return is trial and error process up to a certain stage, before the application of the formula. In case of Proposal X, the net present value at 10% rate of discount is coming negative and hence we will have to find out another rate at which the net present value will come positive. The calculation is done as shown below. For having positive net present value, a lower rate than 10% will have to be tried and hence the net present value is computed at 5% rate of discount.

FINANCIAL MANAGEMENT — CAPITAL BUDGETING

Proposal X

Particulars	Projected Cash Inflows [₹]	Present Value Factors @ 5%	Present Value of Cash Inflows [₹]
Projected Cash Inflows			
1st year	1,00,000	.952	95,200
2nd year	2,50,000	.907	2,26,750
3rd year	3,50,000	.864	3,02,400
4th year	5,50,000	.823	4,52,650
5th year	7,50,000	.784	5,88,000
Total	20,00,000		16,65,000

If the net present value at 5% rate of discount is worked out it will be ₹ 1665000 − ₹ 1500000 = ₹ 165000. Now we have two rates, one is 5% at which the net present value is positive and the other one is 10% at which the net present value is negative. This means that the Internal Rate of Return is between 5% and 10%. For computing exact Internal Rate of Return, the following formula will have to be used.

Internal Rate of Return = Lower Rate + Net Present Value at lower rate/ Difference between the present values × Difference in rates.

= 5% + ₹ 1,65,000*/₹ 16,65,000** − ₹ 14,01,650 × 5%

= 5% + 1,65,000/2,63,350 × 5%

= 8.13%

*Net present value at 5%, ** Difference in the present values

Proposal Y: For proposal Y, the net present value at 10% rate of discount is coming positive and hence we will have to try a rate which is higher than 10% to get a negative net present value. The calculations are shown below.

Proposal Y

Particulars	Proposal Y [₹]	Present Value Factors @ 35%	Present Value of Cash Inflows [₹]
Projected Cash Inflows			
1st year	6,50,000	.740	4,81,000
2nd year	6,00,000	.548	3,28,800
3rd year	6,00,000	.406	2,43,600
4th year	5,75,000	.301	1,73,075
5th year	5,25,000	.223	1,17,075
Total	29,50,000		13,43,550

FINANCIAL MANAGEMENT   CAPITAL BUDGETING

The total present value of cash inflows is ₹ 13,43,550, which is less than the initial investment of ₹ 1500000 and hence the net present value at 35% is negative. Now, we have two rates, one is 10% at which the net present value is positive and the second is 35% at which the net present value is negative. This means that the internal rate of return is between 10% and 35%. For computing the exact internal rate of return, the following formula will have to be used.

Internal Rate of Return

Lower Rate + Net Present Value at lower rate/Difference between the present values × Difference in rates

= 10% + ₹ 7,55,800/₹ 22,55,800 – ₹ 13,43,550 × 25%

= 30%

Problem 3

Z Ltd. is examining two mutually exclusive proposals for new capital investment. The data on the proposals are as follows:

Particulars	Proposal A [₹]	Proposal B [₹]
Initial cash outflow	27,00,000	30,00,000
Salvage value	Nil	Nil
Expected life	6 years	6 years
Depreciation	Straight line method	Straight line method

Earnings before depreciation and income-tax year	[₹]	[₹]
1	6,50,000	9,75,000
2	7,25,000	10,00,000
3	8,75,000	11,00,000
4	9,50,000	10,25,000
5	9,00,000	9,50,000
6	8,00,000	8,50,000
Total	**49,00,000**	**59,00,000**

The corporate income-tax rate is 30%. Calculate the following:

(i) Pay-back period

(ii) Net present value at 15%

(iii) Average rate of return.

Rank the proposals under each of the technique.

FINANCIAL MANAGEMENT CAPITAL BUDGETING

Solution:

For calculation of the (i) and (ii) above, it will be necessary to calculate cash inflows from the given figures of earnings before depreciation and tax. Depreciation in case of both the proposals is computed as: Cost – Scrap /Effective life in years.

Proposal A

Year	I EBDT	II Depreciation	III EBT	IV Income tax at 30%	V EAT	VI Depreciation	VII Cash inflows
	[₹]	[₹]	[₹]	[₹]	[₹]	[₹]	[₹]
1	6,50,000	4,50,000	2,00,000	60,000	1,40,000	4,50,000	5,90,000
2	7,25,000	4,50,000	2,75,000	82,500	1,92,500	4,50,000	6,42,500
3	8,75,000	4,50,000	4,25,000	1,27,500	2,97,500	4,50,000	7,47,500
4	9,50,000	4,50,000	5,00,000	1,50,000	3,50,000	4,50,000	8,00,000
5	9,00,000	4,50,000	4,50,000	1,35,000	3,15,000	4,50,000	7,65,000
6	8,00,000	4,50,000	3,50,000	1,05,000	2,45,000	4,50,000	6,95,000
Total	49,00,000				15,40,000		42,40,000

Calculation of (i) Pay-back, (ii) NPV and (iii) ARR:

Year	Cash inflows [₹]	P.V. Factors @ 15%	P.V. of cash inflows
1	5,90,000	.869	5,12,710
2	6,42,500	.756	4,85,730
3	7,47,500	.657	4,91,108
4	8,00,000	.571	4,56,800
5	7,65,000	.497	3,80,205
6	6,95,000	.432	3,00,240
Total	42,40,000	Total	26,26,793

(i) **Pay-back period** = 3 + 7,20,000/8,00,000 = 3.9 years

(ii) **NPV** = Present values of cash inflows – Initial cash outflows
= 26,26,793 – 27,00,000
= (–) 73,207

(iii) **Average rate of return:** This is calculated as follows:

$$\text{ARR} = \frac{\text{Average income}}{\text{Average investment}} \times 100$$

= ₹ 2,56,667/13,50,000 × 100
= 19.01%

FINANCIAL MANAGEMENT   CAPITAL BUDGETING

Note: Average income is total of Earnings After Tax, [Column 'V' in the table I] divided by number of years i.e. 6 years [₹ 15,40,000 ÷ 6 = ₹ 2,56,667].

Average investment is Initial Investment + Salvage value divided by 2

i.e. ₹ $\frac{27,00,000 + Nil}{2}$ = ₹ 13,50,000.

Proposal B

Year	I EBDT	II Depreciation	III EBT	IV Income tax at 30%	V EAT	VI Depreciation	VII Cash inflows
	[₹]	[₹]	[₹]	[₹]	[₹]	[₹]	[₹]
1	9,75,000	5,00,000	4,75,000	1,42,500	3,32,500	5,00,000	8,32,500
2	10,00,000	5,00,000	5,00,000	1,50,000	3,50,000	5,00,000	8,50,000
3	11,00,000	5,00,000	6,00,000	1,80,000	4,20,000	5,00,000	9,20,000
4	10,25,000	5,00,000	5,25,000	1,57,500	3,67,500	5,00,000	8,67,500
5	9,50,000	5,00,000	4,50,000	1,35,000	3,15,000	5,00,000	8,15,000
6	8,50,000	5,00,000	3,50,000	1,05,000	2,45,000	5,00,000	7,45,000
	59,00,000				20,30,000		50,30,000

Calculation of (i) Pay-back, (ii) NPV, (iii) ARR.

Year	Cash inflows [₹]	P.V. Factors @ 15%	P.V. of cash inflows
1	8,32,500	.869	7,23,443
2	8,50,000	.756	6,42,600
3	9,20,000	.657	6,04,440
4	8,67,500	.571	4,95,343
5	8,15,000	.497	4,05,055
6	7,45,000	.432	3,21,840
Total	50,30,000		31,92,721

(i)   **Pay-period** = 3 + 3,97,500/8,67,500 = 3.45 years

* = Unrecovered balance at the end of the 3rd year

+ = Cash inflow of the subsequent year, i.e. of the 4th year.

(ii)   **NPV** = ₹ 31,92,721 − ₹ 30,00,000 = ₹ 1,92,721

(iii)   **ARR** = 3,38,333/15,00,000 × 100 = 22.55%

Summary

Particulars	Proposal A [₹]	Proposal B [₹]
(i) Pay-back period	3.9 years	3.45 years
(ii) NPV	(−) ₹ 73,207	₹ 1,92,731
(iii) ARR	19.01%	22.55%

From the above mentioned summary, Proposal B is better than Proposal A in all respects, its pay-back period is lesser than A while ARR is more than A. In case of NPV, proposal A is showing negative net present value while proposal B is showing positive net present value.

Problem 4

Y Ltd. is considering to purchase a machine in order to produce a new product. It is expected that the new product will generate an annual profit of ₹ 1500000 per year for first 5 years. The material cost required for this production is expected to be ₹ 450000 p.a., labour of ₹ 550000 and other expenditure ₹ 150000 p.a. The cost of the machine is ₹ 500000 with expected scrap value nil, with a life of 5 years. The company uses a straight line method of depreciation. The income–tax rate is 30% and the cost of capital 12%. The machine will also require an investment of working capital of ₹ 75,000 which will be recovered at the end of the 5th year.

Advise the company about purchase of the machine by using net present value method.

Solution:

The total cash outflow from the machine is as follows:

Cost	₹ 5,00,000
Working capital	₹ 75,000
Total	**₹ 5,75,000**

The cash inflows are calculated as follows:

Statement showing cash inflows

Particulars	[₹]	Amount [₹]
Sales:		15,00,000
Less: Expenses		
(i) Material	4,50,000	
(ii) Labour	5,50,000	
(iii) Other expenses	1,50,000	11,50,000
Profit before depreciation:		3,50,000
Less: Depreciation		
[₹ 5,00,000 ÷ 5]		1,00,000
Profit before tax		2,50,000
Less: Income–tax @ 30%		75,000
Profit after tax		1,75,000
Add: Depreciation		1,00,000
Cash inflows		2,75,000

3.33

FINANCIAL MANAGEMENT   CAPITAL BUDGETING

Present value of cash flows

1 – 5 year @ 12% p.v. factors ₹ 2,75,000 × 3.605 [Cumulative p.v. factors]		= 9,91,375
Add: Working capital recovery ₹ 75,000 × .567		42,525
		10,33,900
Less: Cash outflow		5,75,000
Net present value		4,58,900

Conclusion: Since the NPV is positive, the machine should be purchased.

Problem 5

An existing machine has been in operation for the last 2 years with remaining useful life of 10 years. The management of the company is considering to replace it with an improved model which will result in greater productivity. The existing machine can be sold at a price of ₹ 100000. The relevant particulars are as follows:

Particulars	Existing machine	New machine
Purchase price	₹ 2,40,000	₹ 4,00,000
Estimated life	12 years	10 years
Salvage value	Nil	Nil
Annual operating hours	2,000	2,000
Selling price per unit	₹ 10	₹ 10
Output per hour	15 units	30 units
Material cost per unit	₹ 2	₹ 2
Labour cost per hour	20	40
Consumable stores p.a.	2,000	5,000
Repairs & maintenance p.a.	9,000	6,000
Working capital	25,000	40,000

The company follows the straight line method of depreciation and is subject to 50% tax. Whether the present machine should be replaced? The cost of capital is 15%.

Solution:

I. Cash outflows:

		₹
Purchase price		400000
Add: Additional working capital		15,000
		4,15,000
Less: Sale price of old machine:	1,00,000	
Tax savings due to loss on sale [Book value ₹ 2 – ₹ 1 sale price = ₹ 1 loss]	50,000	1,50,000
Net cash outflows		2,65,000

FINANCIAL MANAGEMENT — CAPITAL BUDGETING

II. Cash inflows:

Particulars	Existing machine	New machine	Difference
1	2	3	4
A. Sales–units	30,000	60,000	30,000
B. Sales value	₹ 3,00,000	₹ 6,00,000	₹ 3,00,000
C. Expenses:			
(i) Material	60,000	1,20,000	60,000
(ii) Labour	40,000	80,000	40,000
(iii) Consumable stores	2,000	5,000	3,000
(iv) Repairs & Main.	9,000	6,000	(3,000)
(v) Depreciation	20,000	40,000	20,000
Total – [C]	1,31,000	2,51,000	1,20,000
D. Earnings before tax [B – C]	1,69,000	3,49,000	1,80,000
E. Earnings after tax [Tax 50%]	84,500	1,74,500	90,000
F. Cash inflow [E + Depreciation]	1,04,500	2,14,500	1,10,000

Net Present Value

Year	Cash inflows [₹]	P.V. Factors at 15%	P.V. of cash inflows
1 – 10	1,10,000	5.019*	5,52,090
	15,000*	.247	3,705
	*Working capital Recovery		
		Cash inflow	5,55,795
		(–) Cash outflow	2,65,000
		Net present value	**2,90,795**

*Cumulative present value factors @ 15% for 10 years

The NPV is positive and, therefore, the machine can be replaced.

FINANCIAL MANAGEMENT — CAPITAL BUDGETING

Problem 6

A manufacturing company is considering to purchase a machine for improving its productivity. Two choices in the form of Machine C and Machine D are available. The details of the two machines are as follows:

Particulars	Machine C	Machine D
Purchase price (₹)	6,00,000	6,00,000
Expected life	10 yrs.	10 yrs.
Additional fixed costs [Excluding depreciation]	30,000	32,000
Additional capacity	2 Hrs.	2 Hrs.
Salvage value	Nil	Nil
Installation cost	1,00,000	1,25,000

The company at present is producing three products viz. X, Y and Z. The additional demand of the product that can be met with the new machine and the contribution per unit is as follows:

Particulars	X	Y	Z
	[₹]	[₹]	[₹]
Contribution per unit	40	52	46
Additional demand [units]	2,000	2,500	4,000
No. of machine hrs. per unit	25	30	23

The income–tax rate is 30%. The required rate of return is 10%. Advise the company about proper choice.

Solution:

In order to take the decision about X or Y, net present value of both the machines have to be calculated. For calculation of cash inflows, sales mix will have to be calculated. Since three products are being produced and number of available machine hours is limited for both the machines, priority will have to be decided among the three products on the basis of contribution per machine hour. This is done in the following manner.

Machine C

I. Statement showing priority of the products

Particulars	X	Y	Z
Contribution per unit [₹]	40	52	46
Machine hrs. per unit	25	30	23
Contribution per machine hour	1.6	1.73	2
Priority	III	II	I

3.36

FINANCIAL MANAGEMENT — CAPITAL BUDGETING

II. Statement showing no. of units of each product

	Units	Hrs. per unit	Total Hrs.
Product Z [Highest possible units to be produced]	4,000	23	92,000
Product Y	2,500	30	75,000
Product X	1,320	25	Balance Hrs. 33,000

III. Statement showing cash inflows

Particulars		[₹]
Contribution:		
Z 4000 units × ₹ 46 =		1,84,000
Y 2500 units × ₹ 52 =		1,30,000
X 1320 units × ₹ 40 =		52,800
		3,66,800
Less: (i) Fixed costs	30,000	
(ii) Depreciation [7,00,000 ÷ 10]	70,000	1,00,000
Profit before tax		2,66,800
Less: Income–tax 30%		80,040
Profit after tax		**1,86,760**
Add: Depreciation		70,000
Cash inflows		**2,56,760**
Present value of cash inflows at 10%		
From year 1 to year 10		
₹ 2,56,760 × 6.145 =		15,77,790
Less: Initial cash outflow		7,00,000
Net Present value		**8,77,790**

Machine D

Like Machine C, firstly the product mix will have to be decided on the basis of priority decided earlier.

I. Statement showing no. of units of each product

	Units	Hrs. per unit	Total hours
Z	4000	23	92,000
Y	2,500	30	75,000
X	1,720	25	Bal. 43,000
			2,10,000

FINANCIAL MANAGEMENT CAPITAL BUDGETING

II. Statement showing cash inflows

Particulars		[₹]
Contribution:		
Z 4000 units × ₹ 46 =		1,84,000
Y 2500 units × ₹ 52 =		1,30,000
X 1,720 units × ₹ 40 =		68,800
Total contribution		**3,82,800**
Less: (i) Fixed costs	32,000	
(ii) Depreciation	72,500	1,04,500
Profit before tax		2,78,300
Less: Income–tax 30%		83,490
Profit after tax		**1,94,810**
Add: Depreciation		72,500
Cash inflows		**2,67,310**
Present value of cash inflows		
1 year – 10 years – 2,67,310 × 6.145		16,42,620
Less: Initial cash outflows		7,25,000
Net present value		**9,17,620**

Conclusion: NPV of machine D is greater than NPV of Machine C and, therefore, Machine D can be selected.

Unsolved Problem [For self study]

A machine can be purchased outright for ₹ 5. The life of the machine is expected to be five years and expected scrap value at the end of fifth year is ₹ 50,000.

Alternatively, it can be acquired on lease on a lease rent of ₹ 1 p.a. payable at the beginning of each year.

If purchased outright, a bank loan @ 18% p.a. is available where interest is to be paid annually and principal to be repayable in full after five years.

Taxation rate is 30% and straight line method of depreciation is used. Advise the company.

Points to Remember

- **Capital investment** refers to the investment in projects results the results of which would be available only after a year.
- Capital budgeting decisions require comparison of cost against benefits over a long period.
- Before any capital budgeting decision is taken, a careful evaluation of the same should be done.
- For evaluation of capital budgeting proposals, many different techniques such as NPV, IRR, PI and ARR are used.
- In Non-Discounted Cash Flow Techniques, evaluation of capital budgeting proposals is done on the basis of cash inflows and outflows rather than on the basis of accounting profits.

- **The Pay Back Period** is the number of years in which the initial investment made in a capital budgeting proposal is recovered.
- For Average Rate of Return/Accounting Rate of Return, projected net profit after income tax is computed for the expected life of the proposal and its average is worked out.
- Net present value is computed by deducting the initial investment amount [cash outflow] from the total present value of the cash inflows.
- Internal Rate of Return is an alternative technique for use in making capital investment decisions that also takes into consideration the present value of money.
- The internal rate of return represents the true interest rate earned on an investment over the course of its useful life.
- The computation of internal rate of return involves trial and error process up to a certain stage and then exact internal rate of return is computed by applying a formula.
- **Profitability** Index is also termed as cost benefit ratio and is computed by dividing the total present value of cash inflows by the initial investment.
- In order to remove this limitation of the Pay Back Period, the present value of the cash flows is taken into consideration and then the payback period is computed.
- The Net Present Value and Internal Rate of Return, both are the techniques of evaluation of capital expenditure proposals by using discounted cash flows.
- The most commonly found condition for the conflict between the NPV and IRR is the timing of cash flows.
- Fisher's intersection occurs at the discount rate where the net present values of both the projects are the same.
- Difference in the life span of two mutually exclusive projects can give rise to the conflict between the net present value method and internal rate of return method.
- Capital rationing is a situation where a firm cannot undertake all positive net present value projects it has identified because of shortage of capital.

Questions for Discussion

1. What do you understand by 'Capital Budgeting'? Explain with illustrations
2. Discuss the importance of capital budgeting in details.
3. As a Finance Management, which steps you will take before sanctioning the capital budgeting proposal?
4. How will you evaluate capital expenditure proposals?
5. Write a detailed note on capital rationing.
6. Write short notes:
   (a) Types of capital budgeting
   (b) Pay-back period
   (c) Net Present Value

FINANCIAL MANAGEMENT — CAPITAL BUDGETING

Case Study

The initial investment for an investment proposal is ₹ 100 lakhs and Machinery and ₹ 40 lakhs for working capital. Other details are as follows:

Sales – units: 1 lakh units of output per year for years 1 to 5
Sales price: ₹ 120 per unit
Variable cost: ₹ 60 per unit of output
Fixed overheads: [excluding depreciation] ₹ 15 lakhs per year for the first 5 years
Depreciation: 25% on written down value method
Salvage value of machine: Equal to the written down value at the end of the 5th year
Income tax rate: 35%
Cost of capital: 10%

Required:
[A] Indicate the financial viability of the project by computing the Net Present Value
[B] Determine the sensitivity of the project's net present value under each of the following conditions
   [i] Decrease in selling price by 5%
   [ii] Increase in variable cost by 10%
   [iii] Increase in cost of plant and machinery by 10%

Suggested Activity

Collect examples of capital expenditure proposals undertaken by various companies in the previous year.

Questions from Previous Pune University Examinations

1. Explain the various Techniques used for Evaluating Capital Expenditure Proposals. **[P.G.D.B.M. April 2006]**
2. Write Short Notes on:
   (a) Return on Investment. **[P.G.D.B.M. Dec. 2006]**
   (b) Average Rate of Return. **[P.G.D.B.M. April 2006]**
   (c) Pay-back Period. **[P.G.D.B.M. Dec. 2006]**
   (d) Time Value of Money. **[P.G.D.B.M. Dec. 2006, April 2007]**
   (e) Internal Rate of Return. **[P.G.D.B.M. April 2006]**
3. Explain the Different Methods of Evaluating Capital Expenditure Decisions. **[M.B.A. April 2007]**
4. Explain Different Methods of Evaluating Capital Expenditure Methods. **[P.G.D.B.M. April 2009]**
5. What exactly I.R.R. Signifies? **[M.B.A. April 2010]**
6. Write Short Notes:
   (a) Internal Rate of Return. **[M.B.A. Dec. 2010]**
   (b) Time Value of Money. **[P.G.D.B.M. April 2009]**
7. Explain any three methods of evaluating capital expenditure proposals. **[M.B.A. Dec. 2011]**

■■■

Chapter 4

Working Capital Management

Contents ...

4.1 Introduction
4.2 Concept of Working Capital
4.3 Nature of Working Capital Management
4.4 Scope for Working Capital Management
4.5 Operating Cycle
4.6 Types of Working Capital
4.7 Factors Affecting Working Capital
4.8 Working Capital Policy
4.9 Financing of Working Capital
4.10 Assessment of Working Capital Requirements
4.11 Factoring
4.12 Receivables Management / Management of Accounts Receivables
4.13 Management of Cash
4.14 Inventory Management
- Solved Problems
- Points to Remember
- Questions for Discussion
- Case Study
- Suggested Activity
- Questions from Previous Pune University Examinations

Learning Objectives ...

After studying this topic, you should be able to,
1. Understand the concept and types of working capital
2. Understand the determinants of working capital
3. Study the operating cycle
4. List methods of financing
5. Assess working capital required by an organisation
6. Understand the method of preparation of working capital budget

4.1 Introduction

The discussion in the chapter of Capital Budgeting was mainly in relation to the investments in the fixed assets. In this chapter, the concept of working capital and its management is discussed in detail.

The management of fixed assets and current assets differs from each other in three different ways. The difference can be summarised as given below:
   (a) Time factor plays a minor role in managing current assets while it is a major factor in managing fixed assets. Therefore, in fixed assets management present values of expected future cash inflows and outflows are taken into account.
   (b) If a firm maintains a large holding of current assets, especially cash, the risk is reduced but it also reduces the overall profitability.
   (c) Though the fixed and current assets levels depend upon sales, only current assets can be adjusted with sales fluctuations.

The amount invested by an organisation in fixed assets is called 'fixed capital' and a business organisation invests some portion of its total capital in the fixed assets. Some portion of the total capital is kept for the working capital requirements of the business.

Management of the working capital of an organisation is extremely important as it decides the amount of current assets that are to be maintained in the business as well as that of the current liabilities.

Working capital is required to run the day to day activities of the business and hence it not only involves managing of current assets but also involves raising the amount of working capital required, through various sources including short-term and long-term sources.

4.2 Concept of Working Capital

The concepts of working capital can be broadly divided into two categories: (i) Gross working capital (ii) Net working capital

   (i) Gross working capital: This concept implies the total of all current assets of a business firm. A current asset is that asset which can be converted into cash or into other current assets within an accounting year or an operating cycle.

Current assets include cash and bank balances, debtors, bills receivables, inventories, prepaid expenses and short-term investments.

   (ii) Net working capital: This concept of working capital is the difference between current assets and current liabilities. While current assets have been defined above, current liabilities can be explained as those liabilities which are expected to mature for payment within an accounting year and will be paid either out of existing current assets or by creating other current liabilities.

Current Liabilities include creditors, bills payable, outstanding expenses, bank overdraft and other short-term loans.

Net working capital can be positive or negative. If current assets exceed current liabilities, the difference is positive net working capital and when current liabilities exceed current assets, the difference is negative working capital.

Working capital can also be divided into categories:
(i) fixed working capital
(ii) fluctuating working capital.

Every business requires some minimum amount of working capital inspite of the level of operations, throughout the year. This amount represents the fixed amount of working capital.

In many business firms, the levels of operations fluctuate from time to time depending upon the demand pattern. In case, the demand picks up in a particular season, the need for working capital also increases and during low demand periods, the need for working capital also comes down. This aspect of working capital can be shown in a better way with the help of the following diagram.

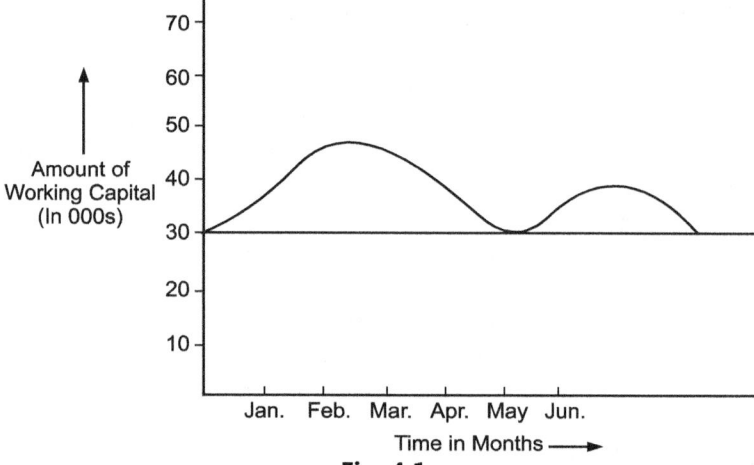

Fig. 4.1

The fixed amount of working capital also go on increasing as the time passes because of the growth of the firm. This can be shown in the following diagram.

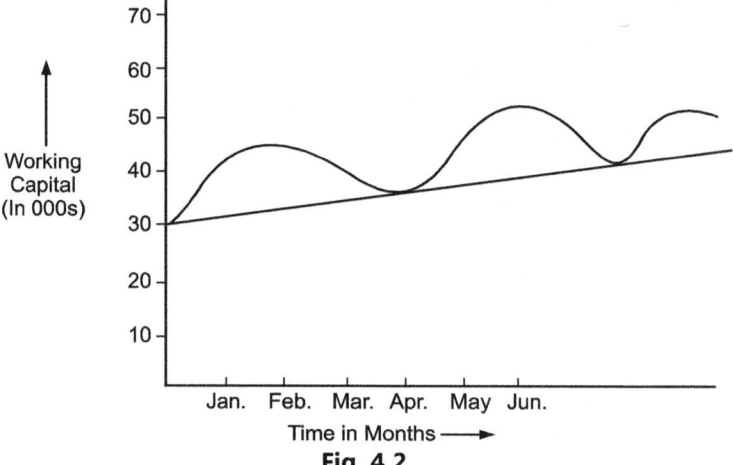

Fig. 4.2

4.3 Nature of Working Capital Management

Working Capital means current assets such as cash, accounts receivable and inventory and so on, minus the current liabilities. The management of current assets is as important as or rather more important than the management of fixed assets. This is because the fate of most of the business very largely depends upon the manner in which their working capital is managed.

The study of working capital management is incomplete unless we have an overall look on the management of current liabilities. Determining the appropriate level of current asset, current liabilities and of working capital involves fundamental decisions regarding firm's liquidity and the composition of firm's debts.

There are two fold objectives of the Management of Working Capital:
   (i)   Maintenance of working capital at appropriate level and
   (ii) Availability of ample funds as and when they are needed.

In the accomplishment of these two objectives the management has to consider the composition of current assets pool. The working capital position sets the various policies in the business with respect to general operation, purchasing, financing, expansion and dividend etc.

4.4 Scope for Working Capital Management

1. There is a positive correlation between the sale of the product of the firm and the current assets. An increase in the sale of the product requires a corresponding increase in current assets. It is therefore indispensable to manage the current assets properly and efficiently.

2. More than half of the total capital of the firm is generally invested in current assets. It means less than half of the capital is blocked in fixed assets. We pay due attention to the management fixed assets through the capital budgeting process. Management of working capital too, therefore, attracts the attention of the management.

3. In emergency (non-availability of funds etc.) fixed assets can be acquired on lease but there is no alternative for current assets. Investment in current assets, i.e., inventory or receivables can in no way be avoided without sustaining loss.

4. Working capital needs are more often financed through outside sources so it is necessary to utilise them in the best possible way.

5. The management of working capital is more important for small units because they scarcely rely on long term capital market and have an easy access to short term financial sources i.e. trade credit, short term bank loan etc.

6. In the modern system approach to management, the operations of the firm are viewed as a total that is an integrated system. In this sense it is not possible to study one segment of the firm individually or leave it out completely. Hence an overall look on the management of working capital is necessary.

4.5 Operating Cycle

As explained above, the net working capital is the difference between current assets and current liabilities. A firm acquires current assets to convert them into cash so that the current liabilities can be satisfied. On the other hand, fixed assets such as land and building, plant and machinery etc. are acquired with a long-term objective. The amount of capital invested in fixed assets is recovered after a long period of time. On the other hand, amount blocked in current assets is expected to recover as early as possible. The concept of operating cycle is based on this aspect.

Operating cycle: The concept of operating cycle implies the time period that is required from the time cash is put in the business along with other inputs to the time it is recovered from the amount of sales made by the firm.

A firm puts cash as an input and the inputs like raw materials are purchased with the help of cash. The raw material is converted into finished product and for this additional cash may be required. The finished product is converted into sale and if the sale is made for cash, the operating cycle is complete as cash is recovered back. On the other hand, if sales are on credit, sales are converted into debtors and debtors are converted into cash.

The length of the operating cycle depends upon several factors. These factors are as follows:

(i) Length of the manufacturing process: If the manufacturing process is quite lengthy, the operating cycle will be prolonged. On the other hand, if the manufacturing process is of shorter duration, the length of the operating cycle will also be of a shorter duration.

For example, in case of hotels and restaurants, the manufacturing process is relatively short which reduces the duration of operating cycle. In case of heavy engineering industries, since the manufacturing process itself is very lengthy, the operating cycle also becomes very long.

(ii) Holding period of inventories: On an average for how long the firm holds inventory is also one of the factors affecting operating cycle. If the firm holds inventory of raw material for a longer duration due to safety precautions, operating cycle is prolonged. Firms following hand to mouth policies regarding inventories of raw materials will have a shorter operating cycle.

Similarly, in case of work-in-process, if the time duration is long before being converted into finished product, operating cycle will be of a longer period. In case of finished goods inventory also, the same principle exists. If finished goods are quickly converted into sales, operating cycle will be shorter. But if finished goods inventory is not converted into sale quickly and liberal credit is extended to the customers, operating cycle becomes lengthy.

4.6 Types of Working Capital

Various types of working capital are as discussed below:

(a) **Gross Working Capital:** Gross working capital is equal to total current assets only. It indicates the quantum of working capital available to meet current liabilities.

(b) **New Working Capital:** Net working capital is the excess of current assets over current liabilities. It is a qualitative concept.

(c) **Permanent Working Capital:** It is the minimum aggregate of cash, inventory and debtors maintained to carry on business operations smoothly at any time during an accounting period.

(d) **Temporary Working Capital:** It is also called as 'circulating working capital'. It is influenced by seasonal fluctuations of businesses concerned.

(e) **Special Working Capital:** This is the amount of working capital to meet unforeseen eventualities that may arise during the course of operations.

(f) **Regular Working Capital:** This is the amount of working capital required for the continuous operations of an enterprise.

4.7 Factors Affecting Working Capital

The working capital needs of a firm are affected by numerous factors. The important factors are as follows:

(a) **Nature of business:** In some business organisations, the sales are mostly on cash basis and the operating cycle is also very short. In these concerns, the working capital requirement is comparatively less. Mostly service giving companies come in this category. In some of the manufacturing concerns, usually the operating cycle is very long and a firm has to give credit to customers for improving sales. In such cases, the working capital requirement is more.

(b) **Production policy:** Working capital requirements also fluctuate according to the production policy. Some products have a seasonal demand but in order to eliminate the fluctuations in working capital, the manufacturer plans the production in a steady flow throughout the year. This policy will even out the fluctuations in working capital.

(c) **Market conditions:** Due to competition in the market, the demands for working capital fluctuate. In a competitive environment, a business firm has to give liberal credit to customers. Similarly, it will have to maintain a large inventory of finished goods to service the customers promptly. In this situation, larger amount of working capital will be required.

On the other hand, when a firm is in seller's market, it can manage with a smaller amount of working capital because sales can be made on cash basis and there will be no need to maintain large inventory of finished goods because customers can be serviced with delay.

(d) Seasonal fluctuations: A firm which is producing products with seasonal demands requires more working capital during peak seasons while the demand for working capital will go down during slack seasons. During the season, all activities such as production, purchase and sales are at their peak and hence the working capital need increases.

For example, a sugar factory has the crushing season from October to April and during this period all activities are in full swing. The need for working capital is high during this period. On the other hand, after the crushing season ends, level of different activities is reduced and hence the working capital requirements also come down.

(e) Growth and expansion activities: The working capital needs of the firm increase as it grows in terms of sales or fixed assets. A growing firm may need to invest funds in fixed assets in order to sustain its growth of production and sales. This will in turn increase investments in current assets which will result in increase in working capital needs.

(f) Operating efficiency: For any business organisation, resources available are always scarce and it is of paramount importance that they should be used with utmost care. Thus a firm's operations can be called as efficient if the scarce resources are used extremely effectively so that the productivity is highest and the cost is minimum. Due to the operational efficiency, the working capital is used efficiently and the need for it is reduced. On the other hand, the need for working capital will go on increasing if the operating efficiency cannot be achieved.

(g) Credit policy: The working capital requirements of a firm depend to a great extent on the credit policy followed by a firm for its debtors. A liberal credit policy followed by a firm will result in huge funds blocked in debtors which will enhance the need for working capital. The situation will be further deteriorated if the collection procedure is also slack. If a liberal credit policy is followed without inquiring into the credit worthiness of customers, there can be a problem of recovery in future which will further push up the working capital requirements.

The need for working capital is also affected by the credit policy followed by the firm's creditors. If the creditors are ready to supply materials and goods on liberal credit, working capital requirements are substantially reduced. On the other hand, if purchases are mainly for cash, working capital needs go up. While planning the working capital, due attention should be given towards the credit policies followed by the firm and its creditors.

(h) Sales growth: As the sales grow, the working capital needs also go up. Actually it is very difficult to establish an exact proportion of increase in current assets, as a result of increase in sales. Advance planning of working capital becomes essential because current assets will have to be employed even before growth in sales takes place.

Once sales start increasing, they must be sustained. For this a firm will have to expand its production facilities which will require more investments in fixed assets. This will in turn result in more requirements of current assets which will increase working capital needs.

(i) Dividend policy: A firm pays dividend out of profits earned by it. As per the provisions of the Companies Act 1956, if dividend is to be paid, it must be paid in cash and not in kind. This means that if a firm follows a liberal dividend policy, it will have to make provision for sufficient liquidity and it will result in increasing the need of the working capital. On the other hand, if the dividend policy is kept on conservative basis, the requirements of working capital will be lower.

4.8 Working Capital Policy

The basic objective of working capital management is that there should be an optimum investment in working capital. There should not be either excessive working capital or shortage of working capital. In order to decide the optimum investment in working capital, there is a need to consider different policies of working capital. The different policies are discussed below:

(a) Ratio of current assets to sales: The current assets change as a result of changes in the sales. A firm has to decide about the proportion of current assets to be maintained in relation to sales. There can be aggressive, moderate or conservative current assets policies.

If an aggressive current assets policy is followed, a firm will maintain a very low level of current assets in relation to sales. On the other hand, a conservative policy implies carrying of a very high level of current assets in relation to sales. A moderate policy is a via media between the two extreme policies mentioned above and results into a moderate proportion of current assets to sales. The result of a conservative current asset policy is that the risk is reduced. The surplus current assets will ensure that the firm is able to cope up with fluctuation in sales as well as production. Besides this, the higher liquidity in this method will help in eliminating the risk of technical insolvency. However, profitability will have to be sacrificed in this method.

An aggressive current policy implies that there is a minimum investment in current assets in relation to sales. This means that the firm is taking greater risk. This method definitely ensures higher profitability but at the same time, it exposes the firm to greater risk of technical insolvency as well as lack of capacity to cope up unanticipated changes in market changes in the market place and operating conditions. A moderate current asset policy tries to balance risk and profitability by keeping moderate level of current assets in relation to sales.

The various policies discussed above are shown in the following figure.

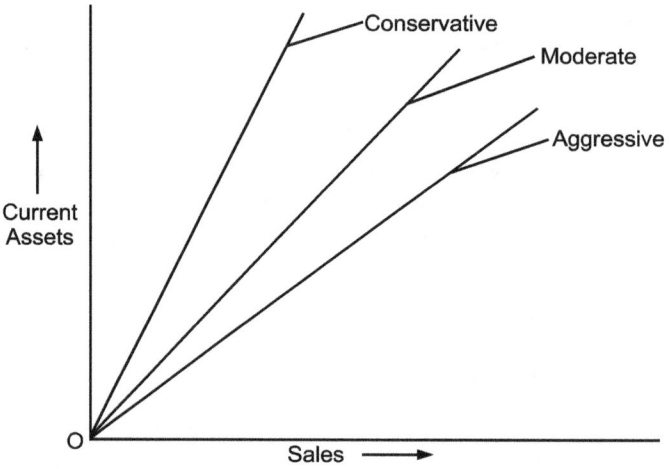

Fig. 4.3

(b) Financing of current assets: Short term vs Long-term financing. Another important question which a finance manager has to answer is that how to finance the current assets? What should be the mix of short term and long-term financing? There are two broad policy options i.e. (i) Conservative current asset financing policy and (ii) An aggressive current asset financing policy.

In conservative current asset financing policy, a firm relies more on long-term financing such as shares, debentures, preference shares, long-term debt and retained earnings. In this method, as the emphasis is on long-term financing, the firm has less risk of facing problems of shortage of funds.

An aggressive policy is said to be followed by a firm, when it relies heavily on short-term bank financing and other short term sources. Even some part of fixed assets is financed by short-term funds. The policy exposes the firm to a higher degree of risk but reduces the average cost of financing. Conservative current assets financing policy reduces the risk but has a higher cost of financing.

In addition to the above mentioned ways of financing, there is one more way which is called as hedging approach. In this approach long-term sources are used for financing fixed assets and permanent current assets while short-term funds are used for financing temporary or variable current assets. However, exact matching is not possible because of the uncertainty about the expected lives of the assets. The different approaches explained above are shown in the following figures.

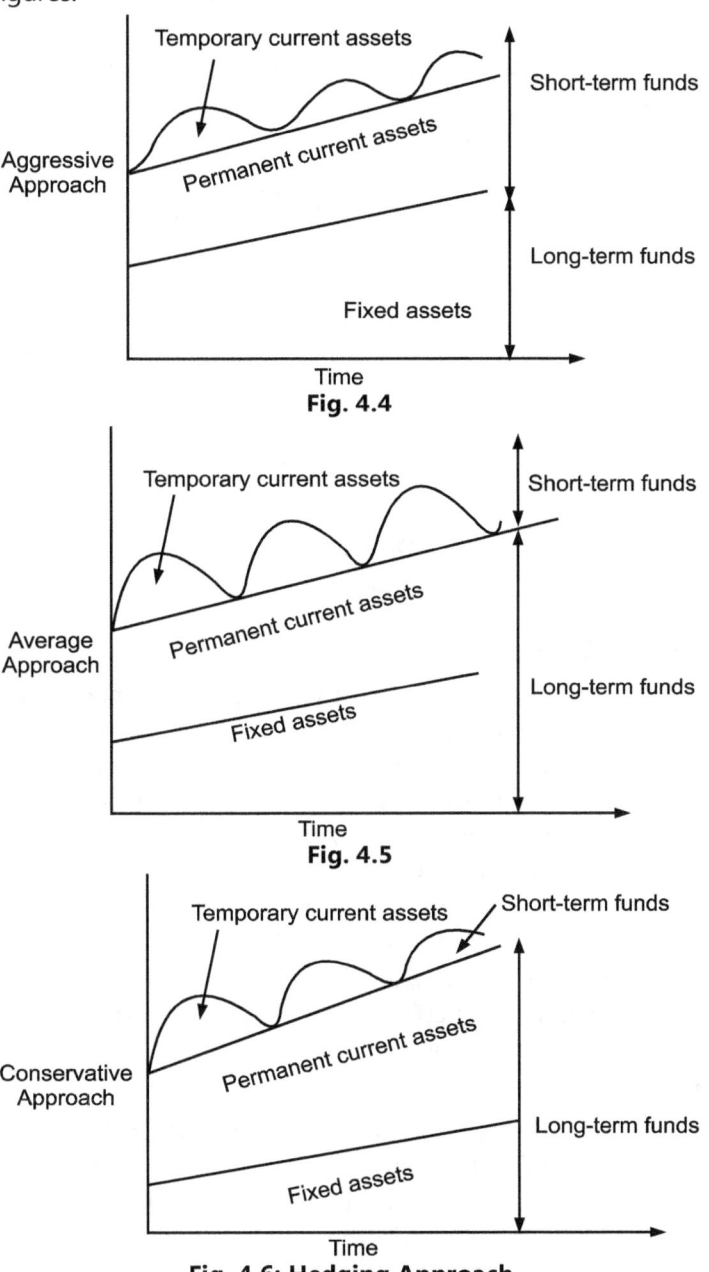

Fig. 4.4

Fig. 4.5

Fig. 4.6: Hedging Approach

(c) Ratio of current assets to fixed assets: A firm needs fixed assets and current assets to support a particular level of output. When level of output is increased, the level of current assets is increased but not in the proportion of the increase in output. A ratio of current assets to fixed assets indicates the level of current assets. This ratio is calculated by dividing current assets by fixed assets. Assuming a constant level of fixed assets, higher current assets to fixed assets ratio indicates a conservative current assets policy while a lower ratio indicates an aggressive current assets policy. This is illustrated with the help of the following figure.

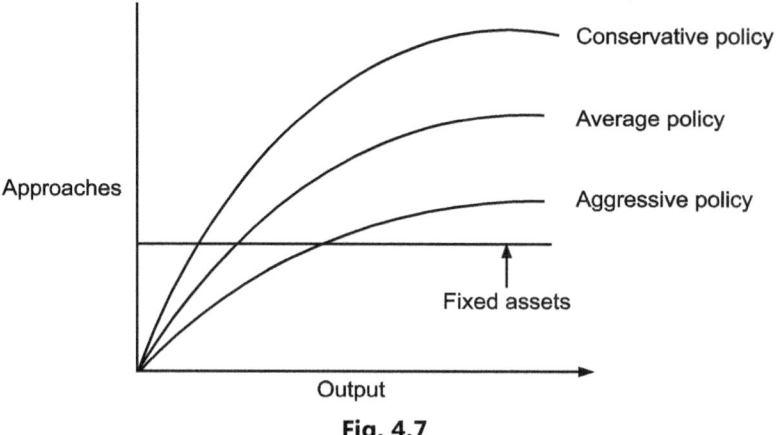

Fig. 4.7

4.9 Financing of Working Capital

In the previous sections various aspects of working capital management are discussed. The important aspect of working capital management is to finance the working capital needs. There are different approaches for financing working capital needs of a business firm. Exclusive long-term sources of funds can be used for financing working capital or exclusively short-term sources can also be used for financing the working capital. A compromise approach in the sense that short-term sources of funds to be used for financing fluctuating amount of working capital and long-term sources of funds should be utilised for financing permanent or core amount of working capital can also be used. Normally funds available for a period of less than one year or for one year are called as short-term sources. In India, borrowings from bank and trade credit are the two short-term sources which are very popular in financing the working capital.

(A) Trade Credit

The trade credit implies the credit allowed by the supplier to the purchasing firm. Trade credits do not actually mean raising of money from outside but is only the postponement of the payment to the creditors. Trade credit is quite a useful mode of financing working capital needs and many firms rely on such credit. However, any supplier would investigate the credit worthiness of its customers before granting such credit.

Credit granted by the supplier can be on open account which implies that goods are sold on credit without any formal instrument and the customer is expected to make the payment according to the credit period. In some cases, the creditor [supplier] prepares an instrument known as bill of exchange which is accepted by the purchaser [firm]. From the purchaser's angle it is a bills payable. The amount of the bills payable is to be paid after the expiry of the period of credit.

The biggest advantage of trade credit to the purchaser is that it is available easily or almost instantly. Of course, the credit worthiness of the purchaser is verified. Similarly, if the relations between the supplier and the purchaser are informal, the trade credit can be highly flexible. It can be adjusted to suit the individual needs.

(B) Bank Financing

Another commonly used source for financing working capital needs is the bank finance. Normally a bank assesses the requirements of customers for working capital needs. This assessment is done on the basis of the sales level as well as production plans of the firm. How much amount of current assets should be maintained is also assessed by the bank.

After deducting the margin money from the total requirements, the balance amount is financed by the bank. There may be separate financing limits for peak periods and non-peak periods. The bank borrowing may be in the following forms:

(i) Bank Overdraft: This is most common method of bank financing. A customer is allowed to withdraw more amount than the balance at his credit in the account.

For example, if bank balance to the credit of a customer is ₹ 20,000 he may be allowed to withdraw ₹ 30,000 thus indicating that there is a bank overdraft of ₹ 10,000. How much amount is allowed to be withdrawn as overdraft depends upon the limit sanctioned by the bank. The limits are decided after a careful scrutiny of the bank account transactions of the customer. Interest is charged only on the amount which is withdrawn as overdraft.

Like trade credit, bank overdraft arrangements can also offer wide flexibility once relations between the bank and the customer are developed.

(ii) Cash Credit: Like overdraft, in this method also, a bank sanctions a particular limit up to which a borrower can borrow. It is not necessary for a borrower to withdraw the entire amount of borrowing immediately. He can withdraw the amount as per his requirements. Interest is charged only on the amount withdrawn and not on the entire amount sanctioned. A bank may demand security in the form of a current asset.

Similar to overdraft, cash credit also offers wide flexibility and, therefore, is very popular method of financing.

(iii) Bills Discounting: A bill of exchange which is drawn by a creditor on his debtor is a negotiable instrument. It contains an unconditional order to pay a certain sum of money after a certain period of time to the creditor. But the creditor has to wait till the maturity date before he receives the payment. His money remains blocked till the period is over. In order to remove this difficulty, the creditor can discount the bill with his bank. The bank deducts certain amount as discount from the amount of the bill and the remaining amount is paid to the creditor. However, before giving this facility to the drawer or the creditor, the credit rating of the drawer is checked by the bank.

(iv) Letter of Credit: In international trade as a security, the sellers insist on the buyers to get letter of credit. When the letter of credit is issued by the buyer's bank, the bank undertakes to pay in case the buyer fails to pay the price of the purchases made. A bank opens a letter of credit in the name of the buyer and payment is made by the bank in case the buyer fails to make the payment. Thus the risk is passed on to the bank from the buyer.

Cash credits or overdrafts are direct ways of financing the working capital requirements while letter of credit is an indirect way of financing and bank's liability arises only if the purchaser fails to make the payment.

(v) Working Capital Loans: In addition to the above mentioned methods, sometimes temporary working capital loans may also be sanctioned by the bank.

For all the financing modes discussed above, a bank will usually demand some kind of security. The security may be in the form of hypothecation, pledge, mortgage or lien.

In addition to the sources of raising finance for working capital needs, one more source in the form of accrued expenses or outstanding expenses is available. Like trade credit, this source also does not actually generate funds but it only postpones the payment of certain expenses. The greater the postponement, the greater is the amount available for financing. Legal aspects should be taken into consideration before using this source.

(C) Regulations of Bank Finance

As described above, bank credit is a very popular source of financing working capital needs. This is due to various reasons like easy availability, higher degree of flexibility etc. But it has been observed that in the past there has been a misuse of bank finance by the borrowers. Loans taken for working capital purposes were diverted to finance long term requirements. Similarly, the management of funds by many companies was unprofessional and unscientific. As a result, many companies became sick and a large amount of bank money was blocked in the sick units. All these reasons made it necessary to have some regulations on the bank financing and accordingly, various study groups were appointed by the Reserve Bank of India to have guidelines for providing bank finance.

The norms of working capital finance followed by banks were based on Tandon Committee Report (Mid 70's). The Chore Committee further made recommendations to follow certain norms and procedure for providing working capital finance. The important norms and guidelines suggested by these committees are summarised in the following paragraphs.

(I) Tandon Committee: The Reserve Bank of India appointed a study group headed by Mr. P. L. Tandon who was the then Chairman of Punjab National Bank. The group suggested some guidelines regarding the bank borrowing for working capital purpose. The Tandon Committee suggested that the borrower should be allowed to hold a reasonable level of current assets. Particularly in the case of inventories, the Tandon committee suggested that the level of inventory should be as per the requirement only and in any case excessive investments in the inventories should be avoided. The banker should finance only those receivables which are in tune with the practices of the borrower's company and industry. In order to avoid excessive investments in inventories, there is a need for having some uniform norms. The Tandon Committee in its final report has suggested norms for 15 industries. Industries like heavy engineering and sugar were omitted.

The Tandon Committee has also suggested norms for determining borrowing limits. As per the norms, the banker is required to finance only a part of working capital gap and the remaining amount should be financed through long-term sources. The following three methods are suggested by the committee:

(i) In the first method, 25% of the working capital gap will be contributed by the borrower and 75% will be financed by bank borrowings. This method will give a minimum of current ratio of 1:1.

(ii) In the second method, 25% of the total current assets will be contributed by the borrower and the remaining will be financed by bank. This method will give a current ratio of 1.3: 1.

(iii) In the third method, borrower will contribute 100% of core assets and 25% of the balance of current assets. The remaining of the working capital gap can be financed by the borrowings.

The committee recommended that the first method should be used mainly as stop gap and the borrowers ultimately should move to the third method. The borrowers who are already in the second stage should not be allowed to enter into first stage. They should be encouraged to enter into the third stage. The committee has also suggested a change in the style of bank lending. The total credit limit should be divided into fixed part and fluctuating part. The fixed part shall be treated as a demand loan and will be minimum borrowing level. The fluctuating part will be taken care of by a demand cash credit. The interest rate on the loan component should be lower than cash credit system.

The committee also recommended that there should be regular supply of information from the borrower to the lender. Projected financial statements, funds flow statements and budgets should be supplied on regular basis. Actual figures supplied quarter wise give idea about the performance of the borrower's business. There is a responsibility on the part of the bank that the stipulated credit limit is not exceeded and also to see that the bank borrowings are used for the purpose of which it is taken.

(II) Chore Committee Recommendations: A working group under the chairmanship of Mr. K. B. Chore was formed in April 1979 by the Reserve Bank of India. The main terms of reference for this group were to review the cash-credit system and suggest modifications and if required, suggest alternate credit system. The important recommendations made by this committee are as follows:

(i) As far as possible, the borrower, should try to reduce the dependence on bank credit. Therefore, the second method suggested by Tandon committee is recommended. If necessary, the borrower should be granted a working capital term loan which should be repaid in semi-annual installments of 5 years with a higher rate of interest than the cash credit.

(ii) For every borrower, limits should be fixed according to 'peak level' and 'normal non-peak level'. This limit is to be fixed for all the borrowers borrowing in excess of ₹ 10 lakhs and will be according to peak and non-peak periods. It will be the duty of the borrower to indicate his needs well in advance. If actual borrowing exceeds this limit by more than 10%, appropriate action will be taken against the borrower. Ad-hoc or temporary credit limits should be discouraged by the banks.

(iii) All borrowers [except sick units] with working capital requirements of ₹ 10 lakhs and above to be placed under second method of lending recommended by Tandon Committee.

(iv) The banks should continue the existing system of three types of lending viz., cash credits, loans and bills. However, cash credit system should be gradually replaced by loans and bills. The division of cash credit account into fixed and fluctuating components as per suggestions of Tandon committee should be discontinued. Advances against book-debts should be converted to bills wherever possible and at least 50% of the cash credit limit utilised for financing of raw material inventory should be changed to bills system.

(v) The requirement of submitting information on quarterly basis should be continued and should be made more strict. However the format should be simpler.

(III) Nayak Committee Recommendations: The Nayak Committee's recommendations were accepted by the Reserve Bank of India, keeping in view the contribution of small scale industry in providing employment, promoting exports and in its support in the overall industrial production. This committee headed by Mr. P. R. Nayak made the following important recommendations.

- There should be priority given to village industries, tiny sector and small scale sector in the same order while giving credit to the small scale sector.
- For the requirements of credit of village industries, tiny sector units and other small scale units upto aggregate fund based working capital limits up to ₹ 50 lakhs from

the banking sector, the norms for inventory and receivables as also the methods of lending as per Tandon Committee will not apply. On the contrary, for such units, the working capital limit will be computed at 20% of their projected annual turnover for new as well as existing units. Margin money requirements for these units which will have to be brought by these units will be 5% of their annual turnover. This means that 25% of their output value should be computed as working capital requirements out of which 20% should be provided by banking sector and remaining 5% will be the margin money which is the contribution of the borrower.

- The SSI unit, who has availed of the bank credit should prepare budget every year in case of the working capital requirement on the basis of 'bottom ups'.
- The banks should follow a 'single window system' for working capital loans as well as term loans. This system will help bank to provide term loans and working capital loans to small scale sector whose project investments are upto ₹ 20 lakhs and working capital requirements are up to ₹ 10 lakhs.
- A grievance cell should be established by banks so that in case of difficulties the small scale units can approach it.
- In order to have speedy disposal of the loan applications from the small scale sector, the banks should process and dispose of the applications from the small scale sector at the earliest and hence, the time limit laid down is that the applications up to ₹ 25000 should be disposed off within 15 days while in other cases it should be disposed off within a period of 8 to 9 weeks. Similarly in order to expedite the processing of the loan applications, the banks are advised to adopt a committee approach, in which decisions are taken by the competent authority after discussion with the concerned Branch Manager.
- There should be a system of appealing in the sense that in case of rejection by an authority, there should be a higher authority to whom the applicant can approach.
- There should not be a pre-condition of deposit mobilisation.
- The bank officers should have right approach, attitude and skills to handle the small scale sector.

(IV) Vaz Committee Recommendations: The Vaz Committee recommended that the recommendations of Nayak Committee should be extended to all the business organisations and these recommendations are accepted. The borrower will have to provide margin money of 5% of the projected turnover, from the long term sources and 20% will be provided by the bank. In arriving this 25%, four working capital cycles have been assumed by the Committee.

4.10 Assessment of Working Capital Requirements

As explained in the earlier sections, excessive current assets result into higher amount of working capital which ensures safety but at the cost of profitability. On the other hand, if investment in current assets is reduced, it will lower the amount of working capital but there will be a greater risk accompanied by higher profitability.

A firm has to ensure a balance between the two and for doing this it is of paramount importance to prepare an estimate of working capital. A statement showing estimate of working capital is also known as *working capital budget*. The greatest advantage of preparation of working capital budget is that it facilitates planning of the level of holding current assets. Similarly, it also helps to compare the projected working capital and actual working capital.

The following steps are taken in predicting the working capital needs:

(i) **Estimating current assets:** In the prediction of working capital, it is essential to predict the current assets. Current assets include the following assets.
   (i) Stock of raw materials, work-in-process and finished goods.
   (ii) Sundry debtors.
   (iii) Any advance payment of expenses.
   (iv) Cash and bank balances.

For predicting the level of inventories, it is necessary to calculate the expected holding period of each type of inventory or stock. In case of debtors, on an average how much credit will be allowed to the debtors should be estimated. For advance payments it is necessary to estimate the amount that will have to be paid as advance. As far as cash and bank balance is concerned, how much amount the firm wants to hold as cash and bank balance should be estimated.

(ii) **Estimating current liabilities:** The second step in estimating working capital requirement is to estimate the current liabilities. The current liabilities include trade creditors, bills payable, bank overdraft, expenses due but not paid and other short-term liabilities. In estimating creditors and bills payable, how much credit will be allowed by the creditors, should be estimated carefully. In case of other current liabilities, what will be expected, delay in the payment of such liabilities should be estimated.

(iii) **Contingency margins:** The difference between estimated current assets and estimated current liabilities will be net working capital requirements. To be on the safer side of contingency margin of 10% to 15% may be added in the net figure calculated as per the above explanation.

In addition to the above mentioned points, any proposed additions in fixed assets should also be taken into consideration if it is going to affect the working capital position. Similarly, how far changes in sales are going to affect the level of current assets should also be taken into consideration.

The format of working capital budget is given below.

Working Capital Budget

Particulars	Amount [₹]	Amount [₹]
[A] Current Assets:		
(i) Stock-in-trade		
(a) Raw materials		
(b) Work-in-process		
(c) Finished goods		
(ii) Debtors		
(iii) Prepaid expenses		
(iv) Cash and bank balance		
Total [A]		
[B] Current Liabilities:		
(i) Creditors		
(ii) Delay in payment of expenses		
Total [B]		
[C] Net Working Capital:		
[A – B]		
[D] Add: Contingency margin if any		
[E] Total working capital requirement		

4.11 Factoring

A firm has to strike a balance between too liberal credit and too strict credit policy. In case of a very liberal credit policy, the amount of sales will increase considerably but at the same time the cost of holding the investments and the amount of bad debts will increase substantially. If the credit policy is too strict and the firm is very much selective in granting credit, some amount of sales is bound to be lost. The ideal credit policy should be such that the difference between the benefits and costs is maximum. One thing which can be understood from the discussion is that granting of credit to the customers cannot be avoided. For surviving in the competitive environment, some credit facility to the customers is a must and it means that certain amount is locked in debtors or accounts receivable. A firm has to wait for some time before the amount is recovered. If there is some agency which can be given some relief to the firm by providing money immediately by purchasing the book debts, it will be most welcome for the firm. The factoring services concept was born out of this need only.

(A) Nature of Factoring

As described above, granting credit to customers results into blocking of funds in accounts receivable. A factor purchases a book debt from the firm and makes instant payment to the firm. Later on the amount is recovered from the debtors by the factor. In the modern days, the factors also provide administrative support in credit collection and also other financial services. The procedure to be followed between the factoring company and the client depends upon the agreement between the two. Before purchasing the book debts, the factor may like to evaluate the credit worthiness of the customer and if he is satisfied, the book-debts will be purchased and cash payment will be made instantly. Information will have to be given to the customer that the payment is to be made directly to the factor. Purchasing the book debts of the client are the basic services provided by the factoring company. However, in addition to these services, a factoring company may provide services regarding credit administration to the clients. Under this a factor may offer full consultancy services to the clients regarding granting credit to the customers. Full details of the customer's accounts are maintained with factoring company and it facilitates the collection from customer. As stated earlier, advance even upto 80%, 90% against the book debts may be paid to the client and the risk of bad debts may also be assumed by the factoring company depending upon the agreement.

(B) Types of Factoring

The following are the types of factoring services available to the clients:

1. **Full service non-recourse:** In this type of factoring, the factor assumes 100% of the risk involved in the collection of debtors. In other words, if some amount becomes bad, the factor bears this loss and the client gets the entire amount of book debts. Usually, 80 – 90% amount of the debtors is paid in advance to the clients and the balance on recovery. Since the customer gets full amount from the factor, this method is widely welcomed by the clients.

2. **Full service recourse factoring:** Under this method, the risk of bad debts is not assumed by the factor. The client has to bear the loss on account of bad debts if any. Naturally, if 100% amount is advanced to the client and subsequently if there are bad debts, some amount will have to be refunded. This type of factoring is comparatively less risky from factoring company's point of view.

3. **Bulk/Agency factoring:** This type of factoring is used as a method of financing book-debts. Under this method, the credit administration is maintained by the client himself and only advance is given either with or without recourse. Clients having efficient credit administration prefer this type of factoring.

4. **Non-notification factoring:** Under this system the factoring company does not maintain the accounts of the customers. Similarly, the customers are not informed about assignment of their accounts to the factor. The factor collects the money through the client company with or without recourse. In other words, the factor performs all his functions without informing the client that he owns the book-debts.

Solved Problems

Working Capital Management

Problem 1

The Board of directors of XYZ Engineering Co. Pvt. Ltd. requests you to prepare a statement showing the working capital requirements for a level of activity of 1,56,000 units of production. The following information is available for your consideration.

Per unit	(₹)
[A] Raw materials	90
Direct labour	40
Overheads	75
Total cost	**205**
Profit	60
Selling price per unit	**265**

[B] (i) Raw materials are in stock on an average one month.

(ii) Materials are in process 50% complete on an average two weeks.

(iii) Finished goods are in stock on an average one month.

(iv) Credit allowed by suppliers one month.

(v) Time lag in payment from debtors two months.

(vi) Lag in payment of wages 1½ weeks.

(vii) Lag in payment of overheads one month. 20% of the output is sold against cash. Cash in hand and bank expected ₹ 60,000.

Assume that production is carried on evenly throughout the year, wages and overheads accrue similarly and a time period of 4 weeks is equivalent to a month.

FINANCIAL MANAGEMENT   WORKING CAPITAL MANAGEMENT

Solution:

XYZ Engineering Co. Pvt. Ltd.
Statement Showing Working Capital Requirements

Particulars

[A] Current Assets   **Amount (₹)**

(i) Stock of raw materials for one month

$$\left[\frac{1,56,000 \times ₹\,90 \times 1}{12}\right]$$ 11,70,000

(ii) Work in process for 2 weeks

(a) Materials

$$\frac{1,56,000 \times ₹\,90 \times 2}{48} = 5,85,000$$

(b) Wages

$$\frac{1,56,000 \times ₹\,40 \times 2}{48} = 2,60,000$$

(c) Overheads

$$\frac{1,56,000 \times ₹\,75 \times 2}{48} = 4,87,500$$

                                                          13,32,500   6,66,250 [50% complete]

(iii) Finished goods stock for one month

$$\frac{1,56,000 \times ₹\,205\,[\text{Total cost}] \times 1}{12}$$ 26,65,000

(iv) Debtors for 2 months [At cost]

$$\frac{1,24,800 \times ₹\,205 \times 2}{12}$$ 42,64,000

(v) Cash in hand and at bank   60,000

Total – A   **88,25,250**

[B] Current liabilities   **Amount (₹)**

(i) Creditors (1 month)

$$\frac{1,56,000 \times ₹\,90 \times 1}{12}$$ 11,70,000

(ii) Time lag in payment of wages

$$\frac{1,56,000 \times ₹\,40 \times 1.5}{48}$$ 1,95,000

(iii) Time lag in payment of overheads

$$\frac{1,56,000 \times ₹\,75 \times 1}{12}$$ 9,75,000

Total – B   **23,40,000**

[C] Net Working Capital [A – B]   **64,85,250**

FINANCIAL MANAGEMENT WORKING CAPITAL MANAGEMENT

Problem 2

ABC cements Ltd. sells its products on a gross profit of 20% on sales. The following information is extracted from its annual accounts for the current year ended on 31st March 2012.

	₹
Sales at 3 months credit	40,00,000
Raw materials	12,00,000
Wages paid-average time lag 15 days	9,60,000
Manufacturing expenses paid–one month in arrears	12,00,000
Administrative expenses paid-one month in arrears	4,80,000
Sales promotion expenses payable half year in advance	2,00,000

The company enjoys one month's credit from the suppliers of raw materials and maintains a 2 months stock of raw materials and one and half month's stock of finished goods. The cash balance is maintained at ₹ 1,00,000 as a precautionary measure. Assuming a 10% margin, find out the working capital requirements of the company.

Solution:

ABC Cements Ltd.
Statement showing the calculation of working capital requirements

Particulars	Amount (₹)
[A] Current Assets	₹
(i) Inventory:	
(a) Raw materials (₹ 12,00,000 × 2/12]	2,00,000
(b) *Finished goods $\left[\dfrac{₹\,32,00,000 \times 1.5}{12}\right]$	4,00,000
(ii) *Debtors $\left[\dfrac{₹\,36,80,000 \times 3}{12}\right]$	9,20,000
(iii) Prepaid sales expenses $\left[\dfrac{₹\,2,00,000 \times 6}{12}\right]$	1,00,000
(iv) Cash balance	1,00,000
Total – A	**17,20,000**
[B] Current liabilities	₹
(i) Creditors for goods $\left[\dfrac{₹\,12,00,000 \times 1}{12}\right]$	1,00,000
(ii) Wages $\left[\dfrac{₹\,9,60,000 \times 1}{2 \times 12}\right]$	40,000
(iii) Manufacturing expenses $\left[\dfrac{₹\,12,00,000 \times 1}{12}\right]$	1,00,000
(iv) Administrative expenses $\left[\dfrac{₹\,4,80,000 \times 1}{12}\right]$	40,000
Total – B	**2,80,000**
[C] Net working capital [A – B]	**14,40,000**

Add: 10% margin for contingencies	1,44,000
Total working capital requirement	**15,84,000**

*Finished goods are calculated on the basis of cost of production which is sales – gross profit [20% of sales].

	₹
Cost of production therefore in sales	40,00,000
Less: Gross profit	8,00,000
Cost of production	**32,00,000**

Debtors = ₹ 32,00,000 + ₹ 4,80,000 = ₹ 36,80,000

Cost of goods sold + Administrative expenses

Problem 3

A newly formed company has to prepare an estimate of working capital requirements for the coming year. The information about the projected Profit & Loss A/c. of the company is as under:

Particulars		Amount (₹)
Sales:		21,00,000
Less: Cost of goods sold		15,30,000
Gross profit		**5,70,000**
Less: Administrative expenses	1,40,000	
Selling expenses	1,30,000	2,70,000
Profit before tax		3,00,000
Provision for tax		1,00,000

Cost of goods sold has been derived as follows:

Materials used		8,40,000
Add: Wages and other manufacturing expenses		6,25,000
Add: Depreciation		2,35,000
		17,00,000
Less: Stock of finished stock		
[10% produced not yet sold]		1,70,000
		15,30,000

The figures above relate only to the goods that have been finished and not to those in process, goods equal to 15% of the year's production [in terms of physical units] are in process, requiring on an average full materials but only 40% of other expenses. The company believes in keeping two months consumption of material in stock.

FINANCIAL MANAGEMENT   WORKING CAPITAL MANAGEMENT

All expenses are paid in one month in arrears; suppliers of materials extend $1\frac{1}{2}$ months credit. Sales are 20% cash and the rest at two months credit, 70% of the income-tax has to be paid in advance in quarterly installments. Cash balance desired is ₹ 40,000.

Solution:

Statement showing working capital requirements

Particulars	Amount (₹)

[A] Current Assets

(I) Inventory:

(a) Raw materials $\left[\dfrac{₹\,8,40,000 \times 2}{12}\right]$ — 1,40,000

(b) Work in progress:

(i) Raw materials $\left[\dfrac{₹\,8,40,000 \times 15}{100}\right]$ — 1,26,000

(ii) Wages and other manufacturing expenses

$\left[\dfrac{₹\,6,25,000 \times 40 \times 15}{100 \times 100}\right]$ — 37,500

(c) Stock of finished goods:

[₹ 1,70,000 – 23,500 Dep] — 1,46,500

(II) Debtors – 2 months credit — 2,11,800

[See working note No. 1]

(III) Cash — 40,000

Total –A — **7,01,800**

[B] Current liabilities

(I) Lag in payment of expenses (1 month)

(i) Wages and manufacturing expenses	6,25,000	
(ii) Administrative expenses	1,40,000	
(iii) Selling expenses	1,30,000	
8,95,000/12	74,583	

(II) Creditors – $1\frac{1}{2}$ months credit

$\dfrac{8,40,000 \times 3}{24}$ — 1,05,000

Total – B — **1,79,583**

[C] Net working capital [A – B] — 5,22,217

Add: 10% contingency margin — 52,221

Total working capital requirements — **5,74,438**

FINANCIAL MANAGEMENT   WORKING CAPITAL MANAGEMENT

Working Note:

1. Calculation of Debtors ₹

Cost of goods sold:		15,30,000
Less: Depreciation		2,11,500
		13,18,500
Add: Administrative exp.		1,40,000
Selling exp.		1,30,000
Total		**15,88,500**
Credit Sales: 80% of ₹ 15,88,500	=	12,70,800
Debtors = $12,70,800 \times \dfrac{2}{12}$	=	2,11,800

2. Since depreciation is a non-cash expense, it is excluded from the cost of goods sold for determining work-in-process, finished goods and debtors.

Problem 4

The management of Gemini Ltd. has called for a statement showing the working capital needed to finance a level of activity of 3,00,000 units of output for the year. The cost structure for the company's product for the above mentioned activity level is detailed below:

Cost per unit	(₹)
Raw materials	20
Direct labour	5
Overheads	15
Total cost	**40**
Profit	10
Selling price	**50**

Past trend indicates that raw materials are held in stock, on an average for two months.

Work in progress [50% complete] will approximate to half a monthly production.

Finished goods remain in warehouse on an average for a month.

Suppliers for materials extend a month's credit.

For debtors two months credit is usually allowed. A minimum cash balance of ₹ 25,000 is expected to be maintained.

The production pattern is assumed to be uniform throughout the year.

FINANCIAL MANAGEMENT   WORKING CAPITAL MANAGEMENT

Solution:

Statement showing working capital requirements

Particulars		Amount (₹)

[A] Current Assets

(i) **Inventory:**

(a) **Raw materials:**

$\left[3,00,000 \text{ units} \times ₹\, 20 \times \dfrac{2}{12}\right]$ — 10,00,000

(b) **Work-in-progress:**

* Raw materials
  [12,500 units × ₹ 10]   1,25,000
* Direct labour
  [12,500 units × ₹ 2.5]   31,250
* Overheads
  [12,500 units × ₹ 7.5]   93,750   2,50,000
* 50% complete

(c) **Finished goods for one month:**

25,000 units × ₹ 40   10,00,000

(ii) Debtors: $3,00,000 \text{ units} \times ₹\, 40 \times \dfrac{2}{12}$ 20,00,000

(iii) Minimum cash balance   25,000

Total [A]   **42,75,000**

[B] Current liabilities

Creditors for one month:

$3,00,000 \text{ units} \times 20 \times \dfrac{1}{12}$ 5,00,000

[C] Net working capital [A – B]   **37,75,000**

Problem 5

Finix Ltd. has investigated the profitability of its assets and the cost of its funds.

The results indicate,

(i)   Current assets earn   10%
(ii) Fixed assets return   15%
(iii) Current liabilities cost   4%
(iv) Average cost of long-term funds   12%

The current balance-sheet is as follows:

Liabilities	₹	Assets	₹
Current liabilities	20,000	Current assets	40,000
Long-term funds	1,40,000	Fixed assets	1,20,000
Total	**1,60,000**	**Total**	**1,60,000**

(i) What is the net profitability?

(ii) The company plans to reduce its working capital by ₹ 10,000 by either (a) reducing current assets by ₹ 10,000 by shifting them to fixed assets or (b) by shifting ₹ 10,000 from long-term liabilities to current liabilities.

Advise the company about proper course of action.

Solution:

(i) **Net profitability** ₹

    (a) Earnings on current assets 10% on ₹ 40,000 = 4,000

    (b) Earnings on fixed assets 15% on ₹ 1,20,000 = 18,000

    Total   **22,000**

    (c) Cost of current liabilities 4% on ₹ 20,000 = 800

    (d) Cost of long-term funds 12% on ₹ 1,40,000 = 16,800

    Total   **17,600**

    (e) Profitability = [Earnings – Cost]   4,400

(ii) (a) Shifting ₹ 10,000 from current assets to fixed assets

    (b) Earnings on current assets 10% on ₹ 30,000   3,000

    (c) Earnings on fixed assets 15% on ₹ 1,30,000   19,500

    Total   **22,500**

    Less: Cost as calculated above   17,600

    Profitability   **4,900**

(iii) Shifting ₹ 10,000 to current liabilities from long-term funds.

    (a) Cost of current liabilities 4% on ₹ 30,000   1,200

    (b) Cost of long-term funds 12% on ₹ 1,30,000   15,600

    16,800

    Profitability = ₹ 22,000 – ₹ 16,800 = **5,200**

Conclusion: Shifting ₹ 10,000 to current liabilities from long-term funds are more profitable.

FINANCIAL MANAGEMENT   WORKING CAPITAL MANAGEMENT

Problem 6

A client of yours Swift Ltd. is about to commence a new business and finance has been provided in respect of fixed assets. They ask your advice about the working capital requirements of the company. The following information is available for your information:

Particulars	Average credit period	Estimate for first year (₹)
Purchase of materials	6 weeks	26,00,000
Wages	11/2 weeks	19,50,000
Overheads:		
Rent	6 months	1,00,000
Directors & Manager's salaries	1 month	3,60,000
Office salaries	2 weeks	4,55,000
Traveller's commission	3 months	2,00,000
Other overheads	2 months	6,00,000
Cash sales	–	1,40,000
Credit sales	7 weeks	65,00,000
Average amount of stock & WIP	–	3,00,000
Average amount of undrawn profits	–	3,10,000

Sales were made at an even rate throughout the year.

Calculate the working capital requirements for the company.

Solution:

Swift Ltd. statement showing working capital requirements

Particulars	Amount (₹)

[A] Current Assets

(i) Average amount of stocks and W.I.P.   3,00,000

(ii) Debtors for 7 weeks $\left[\dfrac{₹\,65,00,000 \times 7}{52}\right]$ 8,75,000

                                                    11,75,000

[B] Current Liabilities

(i) Lag in payment of expenses:

(a) Wages – (1½ weeks) $= \dfrac{19,50,000 \times 1.5}{52} = 56,250$

(b) Rent ₹ 1,00,000 × $\dfrac{6}{12}$ = 50,000

(6 months)

(c) Directors & Manager's salaries (1 month)

₹ 3,60,000 × $\dfrac{1}{12}$ = 30,000

(d)	Office salaries (2 weeks)				
	$\dfrac{₹\,4,55,000 \times 2}{52}$	=	17,500		
(e)	Traveler's commission (3 months)				
	$₹\,2,00,000 \times \dfrac{3}{12}$	=	50,000		
(f)	Other overheads (2 months)				
	$₹\,6,00,000 \times \dfrac{2}{12}$	=	1,00,000	3,03,750	
(ii)	Creditors – 6 weeks credit				
	$\dfrac{₹\,26,00,000}{52} \times 6$			3,00,000	
		Total B		**6,03,750**	
(C)	**Net Working Capital [A – B]**			**5,71,250**	

Note: In the above problems, debtors are calculated by taking the cost of sales. They can also be calculated by taking selling price.

4.12 Receivables Management / Management of Accounts Receivables

Introduction

Any business organisation, which is in manufacturing sector or in a service sector uses two types of capitals – fixed and circulating or working capital. Fixed capital is the amount of capital, which is invested in fixed assets. Fixed assets are those assets, which are not acquired for resale. In other words, the fixed assets are used in the business for enhancing the earning capacity. Plant and machinery, land and building, furniture, vehicles are some of the examples of fixed assets. Working capital is the amount of capital, which is required for running the day-to-day business. This capital is also called as circulating capital and it is defined as excess of current assets over current liabilities.

There are two concepts of working capital – gross and net. *Gross working capital is the total amount invested in the current assets of the firm while net working capital is the difference between the current assets and current liabilities.* Current assets are those assets, which are acquired or created in the business with an intention of converting them into cash or other current assets. Inventories, Debtors, Bills Receivables, Short- term investments, expenses prepaid and cash and bank balance are examples of current assets. Current liabilities are the liabilities, which are expected to mature within a period of one year from the date of creation and are expected to be paid either out of existing current assets or by creating a new current liability. Trade creditors, bank overdraft, cash credits, expenses outstanding and bills payable are the examples of current liabilities. The difference between the current assets and current liabilities is known as net working capital as mentioned above.

If we analyse the components of current assets, it will be observed that a substantial part of current assets is in the form of 'Trade Debtors'. In case of several Indian companies, it has been noticed that the 'Trade Debtors, after inventories are the major components of current assets. Though this proportion may vary from industry to industry and also on firm- to- firm basis, it is a fact that nearly 25% of the current assets are in the form of Trade Debtors. This amount is blocked in the Trade Debtors and if proper control is not exercised the firm may face shortage of working capital and it may result in the firm being caught in the debt trap. The management of Trade Debtors, which is also called as 'Credit Management' thus becomes of paramount importance for any management. The basic principle of managing the Trade Debtors is the tradeoff between liquidity and profitability or in other words it is striking balance between too liberal credit and too conservative credit. The basic principles of a sound 'Credit Management' are discussed in detail in this chapter in the subsequent paragraphs.

Trade Credit – Background

Let us trace the origin of 'Trade Debtors' and find out the cause behind the creation of this current asset. If we try to peep into the transactions of sale of any business organisation, whether in manufacturing sector or in service sector, we will realise that sales are basically of two types. The first one is cash sale where the transaction is settled then and there only. In other words, goods or services are sold and the cash is recovered on spot. Thus neither there is any risk in such transactions nor there is any need for creation of records as the transaction is over then and there only. However, all the sales cannot be on cash as customers are bound to expect some credit facilities from the firm. If the firm is in the seller's market, it can dictate terms with its customers and can insist on cash sales only. However in the present day era of cut-throat competition, a firm has to offer credit facilities to the customers and thus the credit offered by the firm creates Trade Debtors. Thus the Trade Debtors are created due to the credit offered by the firm to its customers. Trade Debtors are also called as Sundry Debtors or Book Debts. Accounts Receivables is yet another term used to describe the debtors. However Accounts Receivables include both, debtors on open account as well as debtors who have accepted bill of exchange drawn by the firm. A bill of exchange is a negotiable instrument drawn by the firm and accepted by the debtor. It contains an unconditional order given by the creditor [the firm] to the debtor to pay a certain sum of money on a certain date to a certain person or to his order. Thus a debtor who has accepted a bill of exchange is considered to be safer than the debtor on open account. It should be noted that wherever the word 'Trade Debtors' or 'Sundry Debtors' or 'Book Debts' has been used, it means both, debtors on open account and also debtors who have accepted the bill of exchange. It is also to be noted that the amount of Trade Credit will go on increasing if a firm follows liberal credit policy and on the other hand if a conservative credit policy is followed, the Trade Credit amount will be naturally on the lower side. However if a very liberal credit policy is followed, a firm will have to take the risk of bad debts as well as excessive investments in the debtors though the amount of sales may show an upward trend. On the other hand, a conservative credit policy may improve the liquidity position but there is a risk of losing some of the market share to the competitors. Hence there is a need of a well- defined credit policy, which will ensure a tradeoff between a very conservative policy and a liberal policy.

Causes Behind Granting Credit

As mentioned in the above paragraph, debtors are the result of trade credit granted by the firm. A question may be asked, why the firms grant credit at all? What benefits they are expecting out of the trade credit in spite of the risks associated with the same? It will be interesting to see the causes behind granting trade credit by various firms. These causes are discussed in the following paragraphs.

(a) Credit is granted to the customers to face the growing competition successfully. The market world over is becoming highly competitive and offering credit to customers can be additional selling point for a firm. Hence to obtain a sustainable competitive advantage, firms grant trade credit.

(b) It has been observed that in several business segments, buyers as well as the dealers prefer granting of credit, as they themselves have to extend credit to their customers. In other words they will not be able to operate without credit being extended to them and hence firms have to grant credit to such buyers. Credits are also offered to build up long- term relationship with dealers.

(c) When a new product is introduced, it requires some push in the beginning to establish its self. In such cases, credits are offered as a marketing policy to customers to attract them.

(d) Industry practices also play an important role in the decisions regarding granting of credit. If it is a regular practice in an industry to grant credit to customers, a firm has to follow that policy otherwise there is a danger of loosing customers.

(e) A firm uses credit policy as a leverage for growth. A judicious credit policy will definitely help a firm to magnify its sales and this can lead to enhanced market share. Thus credit policy can be used as a tool for improving the growth.

Objectives of Credit Policy

There are benefits and drawbacks of liberal credit and conservative credit as well. Allowing extremely liberal credit or following a very conservative credit policy are the two extremes of any credit policy and hence the objective of the credit policy of any firm will be to have a tradeoff between too liberal and too conservative credit policy. Accounts Receivables [debtors] of a firm depend on two things, first the volume of credit sales and second the collection period or the credit period allowed to the debtors. Thus for example, if the daily credit sales of a firm are ₹ 15 lakhs and the average collection period is 30 days, the amount of investment in debtors will be ₹ 15 lakhs × 30 days = ₹ 450 lakhs. In other words, daily credit sales will be blocked for 30 days and hence the investments in debtors will be so high. In the light of this, it is necessary to have a well- defined credit policy and follow the same so that balancing between liberal credit and conservative credit will be possible. Credit policy of a firm involves decisions regarding the following.

(a) **Credit Standards:** These standards represent the basic criteria for the extension of credit to customers. The standards involve decisions regarding granting credit to the customers. The quantitative basis of establishing credit standards are factors such as credit rating, credit references, average payment periods and certain financial ratios such as current ratio, liquidity ratio and debt equity ratio.

(b) **Credit Analysis:** Apart from credit standards, a firm should also conduct credit analysis. Credit analysis involves developing procedures for evaluation applications for credit. In other words, when customers apply for credit, there should be some mechanism for evaluation of these applications. Credit analysis precisely means this thing. The basis of this evaluation is obtaining information about credit standing of customers through various available sources and processing the same for evaluation of credit.

(c) **Credit Terms:** A firm has to take decision about the credit terms that are allowed to the customers. Credit terms include the credit period, quantum of cash discount to be allowed as well as the period of cash discount. The cash inflows will depend to a large extent on credit terms and hence these aspects should be evaluated carefully before a final decision is taken.

(d) **Collection Policies:** These policies involve laying down procedures to collect account receivables after the credit period is over. The collection of receivables should be made promptly and for this, there should be proper collection policy.

The points mentioned above are discussed in the following paragraphs in detail.

(a) **Credit Standards:** Credit standards are the criteria, which a firm follows in selecting customers for the purpose of credit extension. An important question that is to be answered is, what standards of credit the firm should follow? Whether credit should be granted to anyone and everyone or whether we should be extremely choosy in granting credit? Actually there are two extreme policies regarding granting of credit, the first one is to grant credit to anyone who demands the same and the second one is not to grant credit to any one irrespective of their credit standing. Between these extreme policies, lies the middle path, which really decides the credit standards that are to be followed. Therefore it becomes of paramount importance that a firm should fix credit standards so that decision making will be easier.

In order to determine the credit standards, careful analysis of alternate standards should be made. It should be remembered that if the credit standards were extremely liberal, there would be an impressive growth in sales. However due to the liberal standards, there will be huge losses due to bad debts as several customers may commit default in payment. The cost of collection as well as the cost of holding the investment in Accounts Receivables will also go up. On the other hand, if credit standards are extremely strict, there will be loss of sales but there will be substantial reduction in the bad debts. The collection costs and also the cost of holding the investments in Accounts Receivables will also be less. Therefore the cost/benefit analysis of alternate credit standards should be conducted to find out incremental sales and incremental cost of relaxing standards. If this analysis is favourable to the firm, i.e. if the incremental sales are more than the incremental costs, relaxation will be beneficial to the firm otherwise not. Thus, the choice of optimum credit standards involves a tradeoff between incremental return and incremental costs.

(b) Credit Analysis: Besides establishing credit standards, it is necessary for a firm to develop procedures for evaluating the credit applications. Thus the second aspect of credit policies of a firm is 'credit analysis and investigation'. For taking decisions regarding the grant of credit the first step is to obtain the credit information about the customers and secondly analysing the information. Decisions regarding the grant of credit are taken after carefully analysing information gathered from various sources. These steps are explained below.

  (I) Gathering Credit Information: Information about customers can be gathered from various sources. Sources of collecting information are mainly of two types.

   (i) **Internal Sources:** Information about customers is collected by asking them to fill up various forms and documents. Thus information about their financial transactions can be collected. Customers may also be asked to furnish trade references, which can be cross-verified for obtaining credible information. In addition to these sources, a firm can also verify past records of customers with them, i.e. their past transactions with the firm can be verified to obtain this crucial information.

   (ii) **External Sources:** In addition to the internal sources, a firm can use external sources for collecting information. External sources include financial statements of the customer's firm. Financial statements include Profit and Loss A/c and Balance sheet. These statements contain useful information and aspects like financial viability, liquidity, profitability, and solvency can be analysed. Though these aspect may not guarantee the future payments and also do not indicate the regularity of past payments, they can be useful in understanding the financial position of a firm. Another useful external

FINANCIAL MANAGEMENT | WORKING CAPITAL MANAGEMENT

source for collecting information is 'Bank References'. Information about the customer's financial position can be collected from the firm's bankers. Alternatively information about customer's financial position may be collected from the customer's bank. In addition, information can also be collected from specialist 'Credit Bureau Reports' from organisations specializing in supplying credit information.

(II) **Analysis of Credit Information:** After collecting information from various sources, the next step is to analyse the information. This is necessary to determine credit worthiness of the applicant. For analysing the information, the following methods can be used.

Quantitative Methods:

Under this method, use of quantitative methods is made for credit analysis. The following methods are used in this category.

- Ad hoc approach/ Numerical Credit Scoring: A firm may develop its own ad hoc approach of numerical credit scoring to determine the credit worthiness of the customers. Attributes assigned by the firm may be assigned weights depending on their importance and be combined to create an overall score or index. For example, a firm may list down desired attributes such as character, integrity, past record, profitability, and so on and weights may be assigned to each of this attribute. A total of these weights may be taken to decide the total score of the customer's firm and then a decision may be taken.

The following table shows the use of this procedure for assigning a rating index.

Factor	Factor Weight	Rating 5	Rating 4	Rating 3	Rating 2	Rating 1	Factor Score
Past Payment	0.30		✓				1.20
Net Profit margin	0.20		✓				0.80
Current ratio	0.20			✓			0.60
Debt-equity ratio	0.10		✓				0.40
Return on equity	0.20	✓					1.00
Rating Index							4.00

4.34

- **Simple Discriminant Analysis:** This is more objective method of analyzing customers. In this method a single discriminant factor is decided on the basis of which credit granting decision is taken. For example, empirical analysis may show that the ratio of earnings before depreciation, interest and taxes [EBDIT] to sales is a significant factor in discriminating between good and bad customers. The next step is to determine the cutoff point, which will distinguish between the good customers and bad customers. For this the good customers [paying] and bad customers [non paying] customers are arranged by the magnitude of EBDIT to Sales ratio. The next step will be selection of a cutoff point to divide the array into two parts with a minimum number of misclassification. The cutoff point is selected by visual inspection. The firm can consider granting credit to those customers who have the EBDIT to Sales ratio above the cutoff point.
- **Multiple-discriminant Analysis:** Credit worthiness of a customer depends on many factors that may interact with each other. This technique of multiple-discriminant analysis combines many factors according to the importance [weight] to be given to each factor and determines a composite score to differentiate good customers from bad customers. Altman, an expert financial analyst from USA, has developed and used a multiple discriminant analysis to predict bankruptcy of firms. His model is as given below.

$$Z = 0.012 [NWC/TA] + 0.014 [RE/TA] + 0.033 [EBIT/S] + 0.006 [MV/D] + 0.010[S/TA],$$ where,

NWC = Net working capital
TA = Total assets
RE = Retained earnings
EBIT = Earnings before interest and tax
S = Sales
MV = Market value of equity
D = Book value of debt

On the basis of statistical analysis, Altman's model established a cut-off score of Z of 2.675, which means that firms with a score above 2.675 are financially strong while those below this score have a very high likelihood of becoming bankrupt.

Example: You are considering extending credit to firms X and Y, which have the following financial rations. What are their Z scores if you use Altman's model?

Firms	NWC/TA	RE/TA	EBIT/S	MV/D	S/TA
Firm X	20%	10%	7.5%	360%	2.8
Firm Y	16%	12%	6.5%	210%	2.5

Z score for firm X and Y is computed as under,
Firm X = Z = 0.012 × 20 + 0.014 × 10 + 0.033 × 7.5 + 0.006 × 360 + 0.010 × 2.8 = 2.8155
Firm Y = Z = 0.012 × 16 + 0.014 × 12 + 0.033 × 6.5 + 0.006 × 210 + 0.010 × 2.5 = 1.8595

As mentioned above, the cut off score of Z is 2.675; firm X is above the cut off score and hence credit may be extended to them. Firm Y has a score less than the cut off score and hence credit may not be extended to them.

The quantitative models mentioned above no doubt give objective results. However it should be remembered that these models are based on past data and hence can be misleading. Therefore a firm will have to use their judgment also in addition to the models described above.

Risk Classification Scheme: On the basis of information and analysis in the credit management process, customers may be classified into various risk categories. A simple risk classification scheme is shown in the following figure.

Risk Class	Description
1	Customers with no risk of default
2	Customers with negligible risk of default [default rate of less than 2%]
3	Customers with little risk of default [default rate between 2% and 5%]
4	Customers with some risk of default [default rate between 5 and 10%]
5	Customers with significant risk of default [default rate in excess of 10%]

The risk classification scheme described above is one of the many risk classification schemes that may be used. Each firm would have to develop a risk classification scheme as per its need and requirements.

Qualitative Methods:

The quantitative methods described above should be supported by qualitative methods. These methods will include mainly subjective judgment and will mainly cover aspects relating to the quality of quality of management. Hence quantitative methods should be supported by the qualitative methods also. The assessment of prospective customers can be done on the basis of the 'five C's of credit'

- **Character:** Willingness of the customer to honor his obligations
- **Capacity:** Ability of customer to meet credit obligations
- **Capital:** Financial reserves of the customer
- **Collateral:** Security offered by the customer
- **Conditions:** The general economic conditions that affect the customer.

Credit Terms:

The stipulations under which a firm sells on credit to customers are called as 'Credit Terms'. These stipulations include I] Credit Period and II] Cash Discount. These are discussed in the following paragraphs.

[I] Credit Period:

The length of time allowed to customers for payment for their purchases is known as credit period. It is generally stated in terms of a net date. For example, if the firm's credit terms are 'net 35', it is expected that the customers will repay the credit obligations not later than 35 days. Normally the factors influencing the credit period are industry practices, severity of competition and also the cash flow position of the firm. However a firm may allow higher credit period in order to push up the sales while it may tighten the credit period if customers are defaulting too frequently and bad debts loses are mounting up. If the credit period is increased, sales will increase, however the operating profits will go up only when the cost of extending the credit period is less than the incremental profits. If sales increase, increase in the investment in accounts receivables will also increase, which will result in increased cost of investment in accounts receivables. Thus extending credit period will be beneficial only when the incremental sales will be more than the increased cost. The following example will clarify the point.

Illustration: XYZ Ltd. is considering increase its credit period from net 35 to net 50. The firm's expected sales to increase from ₹ 120 lakhs to ₹ 180 lakhs and average collection period to increase from 35 days to 50 days. The bad debts loss ratio and collection costs ratio are expected to remain at 5% and 6% respectively. The variable costs of the firm are 85% of the sales, corporate tax rate is 35% and the required post tax return is 20%. What are the implications of this decision?

The implications of these decisions are shown below.

Statement Showing Impact of Relaxation of Credit Policy

Particulars	Amount ₹ In Lakhs
1. Incremental Sales	60.00
2. Incremental Contribution 15% of sales	09.00
3. Incremental bad debts and collection costs	06.60
4. Incremental operating profit [2-3]	02.40
5. Incremental after tax operating profit [3-4]	01.56
6. Incremental investment in receivables *	13.33
7. Cost of investment in receivables	2.66
8. Net increase in operating profit	1.56 – 2.66 = 1.10

The proposed relaxation in credit period is not advisable as it will result in reduction in operating profits.

* Incremental Investment In Receivables:

Existing investments: 35/365 × ₹ 120 lakhs = ₹ 11.52 lakhs

Investments after increase in credit period: 50/365 × ₹ 180 lakhs = ₹ 24.65 lakhs

Incremental investments = ₹ 13.33 lakhs

FINANCIAL MANAGEMENT   WORKING CAPITAL MANAGEMENT

[II] Cash Discount:

A cash discount is reduction in the payment offered to customer in order to encourage prompt payment i.e. before the expiry of credit period allowed to customers. For example, if a firm sales on credit of ₹ 5 lakhs to customer 'A' on a credit of 30 days, it may offer a 2% cash discount if the payment is made within 15 days. Thus the customer may get motivated to make the payment before the due date in order to get a discount of 2%. A cash discount may be expressed as 2/15 net 30, which means that the customer can avail of the discount if he makes payment within 15 days and if he does not opt for the same, he can make the payment within 30 days.

Cash discount can be used effectively to increase not only the sales but also to expedite the payment. However before taking decision to allow cash discount, a firm will have to carefully think about the comparative costs and benefits of allowing cash discounts. The following illustration will clarify the point.

Illustration:

Rachana Ltd. currently makes all sales on credit and offers no cash discount. It is considering a 2% cash discount for payment within 10 days. The firm's current average collection period is 60 days. Sales at present are 200000 units, selling price ₹ 30 per unit, variable cost per unit ₹ 20 per unit and average cost per unit is ₹ 25 at the current sales volume.

It is expected that the change in credit terms will result in increase in sales to 225000 units and the average collection period will fall to 45 days. However due to increased sales, increased working capital required will be ₹ 100000 [it does not take into account the effect on debtors] Assuming that 50% of the total sales will be on cash discount and 20% is the required return on investment, should the proposed discount be offered?

Solution: Statement Showing Effect Of Extending Cash Discount To Customers

Particulars	Amount ₹
Increased sales revenue [25000 × ₹ 30]	7,50,000
Less: Variable cost [25000 × ₹ 20]	5,00,000
Incremental contribution	2,50,000
Add: Saving in cost due to decrease in investment in debtors *	29,167
Less: Cost of additional working capital required **	(20,000)
Less: Cost involved in cash discount ***	(67,500)
Profit	1,91,667

It is advisable that the firm should extend cash discount to its customers as it will result into an incremental profit of ₹ 1,91,667.

* Savings in cost due to decrease in investment in debtors

Present investment in debtors [without cash discount]

= ₹ 2, 00, 000 × ₹ 25/ 6 #

= ₹ 8, 33, 333

360 days/60 days average collection period = 6

**Cost of additional working capital = ₹ 1, 00, 000 × .20 = ₹ 20, 000

*** Cost involved in cash discount = 0.02 × 2, 25, 000 units × ₹ 30 × 0.5 = ₹ 67, 500

Note: In the above computation regarding the cash discount, it is given that 50% of sales will avail the cash discount and hence the same has been taken into computation.

(d) Collection Policies: Collection policies refer to the procedures followed for collecting accounts receivables when they become due after the expiry of credit period. There is a need of a well-defined collection policy because all the customers do not pay the firm's dues in time. Hence the main object of the collection policy is to accelerate the collections. If a firm analyzes the accounts receivables, it will be observed that some customers are slow payers and these customers need follow up. This follow up is ensured through the collection policy. The regular collection ensures regular cash flows, keeps collection costs and bad debts within limits and maintains overall collection efficiency. Debtors are also kept alert and they tend to pay their dues promptly. The collection program of the firm, which is aimed at timely collections of receivables, may consist of the following.

- Monitoring the state of receivables.
- Despatch of letters to customers whose due date is approaching.
- Telegraphic and telephonic advice to customers around the due date
- Threat of legal action to overdue accounts
- Legal action against overdue accounts.

The following aspects should be kept in mind while fixing the collection policy.

(i) There should be proper procedure laid down for collection. This procedure should be well defined and should be followed rigorously to ensure regular collections.

(ii) The responsibility for collection and follow-up should be fixed explicitly. Depending upon the requirements, either a separate credit department may be established or this responsibility should be assigned to sales or accounts department. It is necessary to have a close co-ordination among various departments, especially sales and accounts. Accounts department maintains the credit record and information while past information and current transactions are recorded by the sales department.

(iii) Though collection procedures should be established firmly, individual cases should be dealt with on their merits. There is a possibility that some customers might be in temporary difficulty and may not be able to pay due to their tight monetary position. This may be due to reversionary conditions or other factors, which are beyond the control of the customer. Special consideration is required in such cases.

For accelerating collections, the firm should chalk out a policy of offering cash discount to customers. Cash discount is a cost to the firm for ensuring faster recovery of cash. Some customers fail to pay within the specified discount period, yet they may make payment after deducting discount. Such cases must be identified promptly and necessary action should be initiated against them to recover full amount.

Illustration:

A firm is contemplating stricter collection policies. The following details are available.

1. At present, the firm is selling 36000 units on credit at a price of ₹ 32 each, the variable cost per unit is ₹ 25 per unit while the average cost per unit is ₹ 29, average collection period is 58 days, and collection expenses amount to ₹ 10000. Bad debts are 3%
2. If the collection procedures are tightened, additional collection charges amounting to ₹ 20000 would be required, bad debts will be 1%, the collection period will be 40 days, sales volume is likely to decline by 500 units.

Assuming a 20% rate of return on investments, what will be your recommendations? Should the firm implement the decision?

Solution:

(i) Bad debts expenses: Present plan: 3% of ₹ 11,52,000 = ₹ 34,500
Proposed plan: 1% of ₹ 11,36,000 = ₹ 11,360
Saving in bad debts expenses = ₹ 23,200

(ii) Average collection period/average investment in receivables.
Present plan = 36000 × ₹ 29/360/58 = ₹ 168200
Proposed plan = [36000 × ₹ 29] – [500 × ₹ 25] /360/40 = ₹ 114611
Savings in average investments = ₹ 168200 – ₹ 114611 = ₹ 53589
Assuming a 20% return, the firm will be able to earn ₹ 10718 on this saving.

(iii) Sales volume: since the sales volume will decline by 500 units, there would be a loss of ₹ 3500 [500 × ₹ 7]

(iv) Additional collection charges ₹ 20000

(v) Thus the total benefits from a tightening of the collection policy will be ₹ 33,918 [₹ 23200 + ₹ 10718] and the total cost will be ₹ 23500 [₹ 3500 + ₹ 20000] Therefore there would be a net gain of ₹ 10418 [₹ 33918 – ₹ 23500]. It is advisable therefore for the firm to implement the proposed strategy.

(E) Control Techniques:

A firm has to constantly monitor and control its receivables to ensure the success of the collection efforts. Methods used for controlling and monitoring the receivables are:

(i) Average Collection Period and
(ii) Aging Schedule and
(iii) Collection Experience Matrix.

These methods are discussed below in detail.

(i) Average Collection Period: Average collection period is the average number of days required for collection of the amount of receivables. In other words, it indicates the number of days of credit granted to the customers. For computing the average collection period, debtors turnover is computed and from the debtors turnover, average collection period can be computed. The debtors turnover is computed as follows.

Debtors Turnover Ratio = Credit Sales/Average Accounts Receivables.

Note: Average Accounts Receivables means opening balance of accounts receivables plus closing balance accounts receivables divided by 2.

Example: Credit Sales of a firm are ₹ 25,00,000 for a particular period. The Accounts Receivables at the beginning of the period were ₹ 6, 00, 000 and at the close of the period were ₹ 7, 00, 000. The debtors' turnover will be,

Debtors' turnover = Credit Sales /Average Accounts Receivables
= ₹ 25, 00, 000/ ₹ 6, 50, 000 * = 3.84 times or 4 times

* Average Accounts Receivables is computed as ₹ 600000 + ₹ 700000/2 = ₹ 650000

Now the turnover of debtors' is 4 times, which indicates that the debtors are paying the money 4 times in a year. It means that the average collection period is 12/4 = 3 months.

The average collection period thus computed is compared with the firm's stated credit period to judge the efficiency of the collection efforts. For example, if the credit period of the firm is 60 days, then a collection period of 4 months, i.e. 120 days is not at all satisfactory.

It should be remembered that an extended credit period delays cash inflows, thus affecting the liquidity position of the company. Besides this, the chances of bad debts losses also increase. Thus the average collection period is a fairly good indicator of the quality of receivables as it indicates the speed of recovery.

However one of the limitations of this method is that it provides an average picture of collection experience and is based on aggregate data. Secondly it is susceptible to sales variations and the period over which sales and receivables have been aggregated.

(ii) Aging Schedule: The aging schedule classifies outstanding accounts receivables at a given point of time into different age brackets. In other words, it breaks down receivables according to length of time for which they have been outstanding. An illustrative aging schedule is given below.

Age Group [In days]	% of Receivables
0-30	35
31-60	40
61-90	20
Above 90	5

The above aging schedule indicates that 40% of the receivables are outstanding for 31-60 days while 5% of the receivables are outstanding for more than 90 days. Thus the aging schedule helps to identify the slow-paying customers and is extremely useful for understanding the pattern of payment of the receivables. For better control, it is necessary to compare the actual aging schedule with some standard one to determine whether the accounts receivables are within control or not.

(iii) **Collection Matrix:** The average collection period and the aging schedule have traditionally been very popular measures for monitoring receivables. However they suffer from a limitation in that they are influenced by the sales pattern as well as by the payment behavior of the customers. If sales are increasing, the average collection period and the aging schedule will differ from what they would be if sales would have been constant. This holds even when the payment behavior of the customers remains unchanged. The reasons is quite simple, a greater portion of sales is billed currently. Similarly, decreasing sales leads to same results. The reason here is that a smaller portion is billed currently. Therefore in order to study the changes in the payment behavior of customers it is necessary to look at the pattern of collections associated with sales. This is illustrated in the following table.

Collection Matrix

% of Receivables collected during the	January Sales	February Sales	March Sales	April Sales	May Sales	June Sales
Month of sales	13	14	15	12	10	9
First following month	42	35	40	40	36	35
Second following month	33	40	21	24	26	26
Third following month	12	11	24	19	24	25
Forth following month	-----	------	------	5	4	5

The above matrix shows that credit sales during the month of January are collected as follows.

13% in January, 42% in February [the first following month], 33% in March [the second following month], and 12% in April [the third following month]

From the collection pattern, one can judge whether the collection is improving, stable or deteriorating. A secondary benefit of such an analysis is that it provides a historical record of collection percentages that can be useful in projecting monthly receipts for each budgeting period. Thus Collection Matrix is an extremely useful method of monitoring and controlling receivables.

Solved Problems

Management of Receivables

Problem 1

A firm has credit sales amounting to ₹ 32,00,000. The selling price per unit is ₹ 40, the variable cost is ₹ 25 per unit while the average cost per unit is ₹ 32. The average age of accounts receivable of the firm is 72 days.

The firm is considering to tighten the credit standards. It will result in a fall in the sales volume to ₹ 28,00,000 and the average age of accounts receivable to 45 days.

The firm expects a rate of return of 20%. Advise the firm whether the proposal is beneficial or not.

Solution:

In order to come to any conclusion, the present amount of profit will have to be compared with the expected profits from the proposal. The following statements of profits will help to find out the comparative profits.

I. Statement showing present profits:

Particulars		Amount (₹)
A. Sales [80,000 units × ₹ 40 per unit]		32,00,000
B. Variable cost [80,000 units × ₹ 25 per unit]		20,00,000
C. Contribution [A – B]		12,00,000
D. Fixed costs	5,60,000	
E. Investment costs [As per working note No. 1]	+ 1,02,400	6,62,400
F. Profit [C – D + E]		5,37,600

II. Statement showing profits from the proposed change in credit standards:

Particulars	Amount (₹)
A. Sales [70,000 units × ₹ 40 per unit]	28,00,000
B. Variable cost [70,000 units × ₹ 25 per unit]	17,50,000
C. Contribution [A – B]	10,50,000
D. Fixed costs	5,60,000
E. Investment costs [As per working note No. 2]	57,750
F. Profit [C – D + E]	4,32,250

Conclusion: It is clear from the above statements that the profit as per the revised proposed policy is less by ₹ 1,05,350 than the present profit. Therefore, it is advisable to continue existing policy.

FINANCIAL MANAGEMENT WORKING CAPITAL MANAGEMENT

Working notes:
1. Cost of investments in Accounts:
   Receivables: [Present plan]
   $$\frac{80,000 \text{ units} \times \text{Rs. } 25 \text{ [V/C]} + \text{Rs. } 7 \text{ [F/C.]}}{360 \text{ days} \div 72 \text{ days}}$$
   = 5,12,000 − 20% of 5,12,000 = 1,02,400
2. Proposed plan:
   $$\frac{70,000 \text{ units} \times \text{Rs. } 25 + \text{Rs. } 5,60,000}{360 \text{ days} \div 45 \text{ days}}$$
   = ₹ 2,88,750
   20% of ₹ 2,88,750 = ₹ 57,750

Problem 2

A company believes that it is possible to increase sales if credit terms are relaxed. At present, the sales are projected at ₹ 20,00,000 ; a profit/volume ratio of 30%, fixed costs at ₹ 1,00,000, bad debts 1% and an accounts receivable turnover of 10 times. The relaxed credit policy is expected to increase the sales upto ₹ 25,00,000. However, bad debts will rise to 2% of sales and accounts receivable turnover will decrease to 6 times.

The expected rate of return on investment is 20%. Advise the company about acceptance of the proposal.

Solution:
To come to any conclusion, the profit statements will have to be prepared.

I. Statement showing present profits:

Particulars	Amount (₹)
A. Sales	20,00,000
B. Variable cost [70% of sales]	14,00,000
C. Fixed costs	1,00,000
D. Bad debts [1% on sales]	2,00,000
E. Cost of investments [As per working note No. 1]	30,000
F. Total costs [B + C + D + E]	17,30,000
G. Profit / Loss [A − F]	2,70,000

II. Statement showing proposed profits:

Particulars	Amount (₹)
A. Sales	25,00,000
B. Variable cost [70% of sales]	17,50,000
C. Fixed costs	1,00,000
D. Bad debts [1% on sales]	2,50,000
E. Cost of investments [As per working note No. 2]	61,666
F. Total cost: [B + C + D + E]	21,61,666
G. Profit / Loss: [A − F]	3,38,334

FINANCIAL MANAGEMENT WORKING CAPITAL MANAGEMENT

Working Note No. 1:

Investment in Accounts Receivables:

$$\frac{14,00,000 + 1,50,000}{10}$$

$$= \frac{15,00,000}{10}$$

= 1,50,000

Cost of investments 20% of ₹ 1,50,000 = ₹ 30,000

Working Note No. 2

Investments in Accounts Receivables:

$$\frac{17,50,000 + 1,00,000}{6}$$

$$= \frac{18,50,000}{6}$$

= ₹ 3,08,333.33 or ₹ 3,08,333

Cost of investments 20% of ₹ 3,08,333 = 61,666

Conclusion: The proposal can be accepted as it is resulting into an additional profit of ₹ 68,334. [₹ 338,334 – ₹ 2,70,000].

Problem 3

XYZ Ltd., at present allows a credit of one month to its customers. The sales of the company at present are of ₹ 60 lakhs with selling price per unit of ₹ 100 and variable cost of ₹ 60 per unit. The fixed costs are ₹ 10 lakhs.

It is felt that the sales of the company can be increased if more liberal credit is extended to the customers. As per the projections sales can be increased by ₹ 10 lakhs if credit of two months is extended to the customers instead of one month. However, there is expectation of bad debts of ₹ 1,00,000.

Whether this relaxation is advisable? Assume rate of return of investment as 25%.

Solution:

Statement showing present profit

Particulars	Amount (₹)
A. Sales [60,000 units × ₹ 100 p/u.]	60,00,000
B. Variable costs [60,000 units × ₹ 60 p/u.]	36,00,000
C. Fixed costs	10,00,000
D. Cost of investments [As per working note No. 1]	95,833
E. Total cost: [B + C + D + E]	46,95,833
F. Profit / Loss: [A – E]	13,04,167

Statement showing profits from proposed change in credit policy

Particulars	Amount (₹)
A. Sales [70,000 units × ₹ 100 p/u.]	70,00,000
B. Variable costs [70,000 units × ₹ 60 p/u.]	42,00,000
C. Fixed costs	10,00,000
D. Bad debts	1,00,000
E. Cost of investments [As per working note No. 2]	2,16,667
F. Total cost: [B + C + D + E]	55,16,667
G. Profit / Loss: [A – F]	14,83,333

Conclusion: The profit is expected to increase by ₹ 1,79,166 and so the proposal can be accepted.

Working Note:

1. Investments in Accounts Receivables at present

$$\frac{36,00,000 + 10,00,000}{12 \text{ times}} = ₹ 3,83,333.33$$

or ₹ 3,83,333

Cost of investments – 25% of ₹ 3,83,333 = ₹ 95,833.33

or ₹ 95,833

2. Investments in Accounts Receivable as per the proposal

$$\frac{42,00,000 + 10,00,000}{6} = ₹ 8,66,666.66$$

or ₹ 8,66,667

Cost of investments – 25% of ₹ 8,66,667 = ₹ 2,16,666.66

or ₹ 2,16,667

Problem 4

Zenith Ltd. is considering to relax its present credit policy and is in the process of evaluating two proposed policies. Currently the firm has annual credit sales of ₹ 50 lakhs and accounts receivable turnover ratio of 4 times a year. The bad debts at present are ₹ 1,50,000. The variable costs are 70% of sales. The following additional information is available.

Particulars	Present policy	Option I	Option II
Credit Sales	₹ 50,00,000	₹ 60,00,000	₹ 67,50,000
Accounts receivable turnover ratio	4 times	3 times	2.4 times
Bad debts	₹ 1,50,000	₹ 3,00,000	₹ 4,50,000

The required rate of return is 25% Advise about the most profitable alternative.

FINANCIAL MANAGEMENT
WORKING CAPITAL MANAGEMENT

Solution:

Comparative statement showing profits under different policy options

Particulars	Present policy (₹)	Option I (₹)	Option II (₹)
I. Sales	50,00,000	60,00,000	67,50,000
II. Variable costs [70% of sales]	35,00,000	42,00,000	47,25,000
III. Bad debts	1,50,000	3,00,000	4,50,000
IV. Investment costs [As per working note]	2,18,750	3,50,000	4,92,188
V. Total costs [II + III + IV]	38,68,750	48,50,000	56,67,188
VI. Profit / Loss [I – V]	11,31,250	11,50,000	10,82,812

Conclusion: Policy option I is advisable as it results into highest profits.

Working notes:

Investments in accounts receivables:

$$\text{Present policy} = \frac{₹35,00,000}{4}$$

$$= ₹8,75,000$$

Cost of investments

25% of ₹ 8,75,000 = ₹ 2,18,750

$$\text{Policy Option I} = \frac{₹42,00,000}{3 \text{ times}}$$

$$= ₹14,00,000$$

Cost of investments 25% of ₹ 14,00,000

$$= ₹3,50,000$$

$$\text{Policy Option II} = \frac{₹47,25,000}{2.4 \text{ times}}$$

$$= ₹19,68,750$$

Cost of investments: 25% of ₹ 19,68,750

$$= ₹4,92,187.50$$

or   ₹ 4,92,188

Problem 5

Super Sports Company dealing in sports goods has an annual sale of ₹ 50 lakhs and currently extending 30 days credit to its dealers. It is felt that sales can pick up considerably if the dealers are willing to carry increased stocks but the dealers have difficulty in financing their inventory. Super sports company is, therefore, considering shift in credit policy. The following information is available.

FINANCIAL MANAGEMENT   WORKING CAPITAL MANAGEMENT

Average collection period at present = 30 days.
Costs: Variable costs 80% on sales.
Fixed costs - ₹ 6 lakhs p.a.
Required rate of return = 20%.

Credit policy	Average collection period	Annual sales (₹ lakhs)
A	45 days	56
B	60 days	60
C	75 days	62
D	90 days	63

Determine the most suitable policy.

Solution:

Comparative statement of profits under different alternatives [₹ in lakhs]

Particulars	Present [30 days]	Option A [45 days]	B [60 days]	C [75 days]	D [90 days]
I. Sales	50	56	60	62	63
II. Variable costs [80% of sales]	40	44.8	48	49.6	50.4
III. Fixed costs	6	6	6	6	6
IV. Cost of investments	.766	1.27	1.80	2.316	2.82
V. Total cost [II + III + IV]	46.766	52.07	55.80	57.916	59.22
VI. Profit / Loss [I – V]	3.234	3.93	4.20	4.084	3.78

Policy Option B is most suitable due to highest profits.

Working notes:

Cost of investment in accounts receivable is calculated as follows:

$$\frac{\text{Total cost}}{\text{Turnover ratio}} = \text{Investments}$$

Cost is 20% of investments.

For example:

$$\text{Present investment} = \frac{46 \text{ lakhs [Total costs]}}{12 \left[\frac{360 \text{ days}}{30 \text{ days}}\right]}$$

= 3.83

Cost = 20% of ₹ 3.83 lakhs
= ₹ 0.766 lakhs

For rest of the policies, the same method is followed.

4.13 Management of Cash

Cash is the most liquid asset in any business. It is a very crucial asset in the day-to-day operations of a business firm. Cash is the basic input required to run the business continuously and at the same time it is also the ultimate output expected to be realised by selling the service or product manufactured by the firm. A firm has to strike a balance between maintaining a very high cash balance and a very small amount of cash balance. If excessive cash balance is maintained, the excess cash will remain idle affecting the profitability of the business adversely. On the other hand, if too small amount of cash balance is maintained, it will lead to shortage of cash resulting into disruption of manufacturing operations of a business firm. Therefore, the major aspect of cash management is to keep a proper cash balance.

The term cash with reference to cash management is used in two senses. In a narrow sense, it is used broadly to cover cash [currency] and generally accepted equivalent of cash such as cheques, bank drafts and demand deposits in banks. The broader view of cash also includes 'near–cash assets' such as marketable securities and time deposits in banks. The main characteristic of these assets is that they can be readily sold and converted into cash. They also provide a short-term investment outlet for excess cash and are also useful for meeting planned outflow of funds.

Cash management thus is concerned with, the managing of,

(i) Cash flows into and out of the firm.

(ii) Cash flows within the firm.

(iii) Cash balances held by the firm at a point of time by financing deficit or investing surplus cash.

The management of cash assumes more importance because of the difficulties experienced in predicting cash flows, especially inflows. During some periods cash flows will be extremely erratic. It is also possible that at times cash outflows will exceed cash inflows while during some periods cash inflows will be quite higher than cash outflows. Due to these factors, considerable time of the management is to be devoted to cash management even though cash constitutes a small portion of the total current assets of the firm. This section, therefore, is divided into sections which are as follows:

(i) Objectives of holding of cash.

(ii) Cash planning and forecasting.

(iii) Monitoring collections and disbursements

(iv) Maintaining optimum cash balance.

These aspects are discussed in detail below:

Aspects of Cash Management

(i) **Objectives of holding cash:** A business firm needs cash for the following three objectives or motives.

  (a) **Transactions motive:** There are several transactions like purchases, sales, payment of expenses, wages and salary payments etc., taking place in the day-to-day business operations. For these transactions a firm needs cash. However, if there is perfect synchronisation between cash inflows and cash outflows, there would not be any need for maintaining cash. But in practise, this synchronisation is hardly possible. Therefore whenever cash payments exceed cash receipts, cash balance is to be maintained for meeting the payments. A firm may invest surplus cash in marketable securities, so that necessary cash can be available by disposing off these securities whenever required.

  (b) **Precautionary motive:** A business firm may face an emergency situation in future. In order to meet this situation in future, some cash may be held. The cash balance held will work as a cushion or buffer to face the unexpected emergency. If cashflows of the future can be predicted with reasonable accuracy, less cash balance will have to be maintained. Similarly, if the firm can borrow from outside the cash required, large amount of cash need not be maintained. The cash maintained for such purpose can be invested in high liquid and low risk marketable securities.

  (c) **Speculative motive:** If cash is held to take advantage of profit-making opportunities arising out of changes in the value of securities, the cash holding is called speculative holding of cash. The firm may also speculate on materials prices. If it is expected that material prices will fall in the future, the firm may purchase materials in the future by postponing the purchases at present.

(ii) **Cash Planning and Forecasting:**

  (a) **Cash planning:** It is quite possible that a business may suffer from shortage of cash inspite of satisfactory profits. On the other hand there may be surplus cash available remaining idle and thus affecting profitability adversely. These situations arise due to either poor planning of cash or no planning at all. Therefore, proper cash planning becomes absolutely necessary for any business. Cash planning is nothing but estimating future cash flows with reasonable accuracy. This helps in avoiding cash shortages as well as reduce the excessive cash balance by investing surplus cash. Cash planning can be done for short term, medium term or long term depending on the requirements of the firm. A cash planning can be for as short period as one week. A monthly cash planning, however, is more commonly followed.

FINANCIAL MANAGEMENT

WORKING CAPITAL MANAGEMENT

(b) **Forecasting of cash:** Cash budgeting or cash forecasting is the principal tool of cash planning as well as of cash management. A cash budget is a statement showing expected cash inflows and outflows for a specific future period. A cash budget can be prepared for a period of one year which is broken down to a budget for each month. The cash budget can also be prepared on weekly or even on daily basis. Generally, cash budgets upto one year is a short-term forecasting while if it exceeds one year, it is a long-term forecasting.

(A) Short-term forecasting:

The short-term cash forecasting, as explained above is in the form of cash budgets. Cash budgets are extremely helpful in (a) estimating cash requirements, (b) planning of short–term financing, (c) planning capital expenditure, (d) planning of purchasing materials and (e) developing credit policies.

The mostly used methods of short-term forecasting or cash budgeting are as follows. (1) The Receipts and Payments method and (2) The adjusted net income method.

1. The Receipts and Payments Method: In this method the receipts and payments are anticipated for a specific future period and the difference between the two is the expected cash balance at the end of that period. Both types of receipts i.e. revenue and capital are estimated while both types of payments i.e. revenue and capital are estimated. The basis of estimation of each item depends upon the nature of that item. e.g. Cash sales are dependent on estimated sales and its division between cash and credit sales while the payment for purchases depends on estimated purchases and its division between cash and credit purchases. The following illustration will clarify the method of preparation of this budget.

Problem 1

Summarised below are the income and expenditure forecasts for the months of March to August 2013.

Month	Sales (₹)	Purchases (₹)	Wages (₹)	Overheads (₹)
March	60,000	36,000	9,000	10,000
April	62,000	38,000	8,000	9,500
May	64,000	33,000	10,000	11,500
June	58,000	35,000	8,500	9,000
July	56,000	39,000	9,500	9,500
August	60,000	34,000	8,000	8,500

FINANCIAL MANAGEMENT　　　　　　　　　　　　　　　　　　WORKING CAPITAL MANAGEMENT

You are requested to prepare the cash budget for three months starting on May 1st, 1997 in view of the following information.
1. Cash balance as on 1st May, 2013 : ₹ 8,000.
2. Sales and purchases are all on credit.
3. Plant costing ₹ 16,000 is due for delivery in July, 1997, payable 10% of delivery and the balance after 3 months.
4. Advance tax instalments of ₹ 8,000 each are payable in March and June.
5. The period of credit allowed by suppliers is 2 months and allowed to customers is 1 month.
6. Lag in payment of all expenses is one month.

Solution: Cash Budget

Period: May – July 2013

Particulars	May (₹)	June (₹)	July (₹)
[A] Opening cash balance	8,000	16,500	13,000
[B] Expected cash receipts			
(i) Credit sales	62,000	64,000	58,000
[C] Total cash available [A + B]	70,000	80,500	71,000
[D] Expected cash payments:			
(i) Wages	8,000	10,000	8,500
(ii) Overheads	9,500	11,500	9,000
(iii) Purchases	36,000	38,000	33,000
(iv) Purchase of plant	–	–	1,600
(v) Advance tax	–	8,000	–
[E] Total payments	53,500	67,500	52,100
[F] Closing balance [C – E]	16,500	13,000	18,900

 2. **Adjusted Net Income Method:** In this method, there are three sections: sources of cash, uses of cash and the adjusted cash balance. In the preparation of this statement, items like dividends, depreciation, net profit etc. can be easily understood from financial statements. Major difficulties may be faced in estimating working capital requirements and changes. Ratio's relating to sales and receivables can be used conveniently to predict these changes. The major benefit of this method is that it keeps a control over working capital and anticipating financial requirements.

(B) Long-term cash forecasting:

The long-term forecasts of cash may be for a period of 2 yrs, 3 yrs or even for five years. These forecasts are prepared to give an idea about the financial requirements of the firm in the distant future. A firm requires finance for new product development as well as introduction of new product, purchase of new plant and machinery and other such needs arising in the future. The long-term cash forecasting helps the firm to make necessary provision of cash for these requirements.

Long-term cash forecasts may not be in as much details as short-term cash forecasting. But it definitely helps in improving corporate planning as well as evaluation of capital expenditure proposals.

(iii) Monitoring collections and disbursements:

To enhance the efficiency of cash management, collections and disbursements must be properly monitored. The following factors are of considerable importance in this respect.

- **(a) Efficient and prompt collections:** The collections from customers should be as prompt as possible. For this purpose the bills for goods sold should be sent as promptly as possible. Similarly cash collections can be accelerated by reducing the gap between the time and customer pays the bill and the cheque is collected and funds become available for the use of the firm. In addition to quick handling of cheques a firm receiving remittances by cheques from different parts of the country can decentralise its collections and reduce the delay in the conversion of cheques into cash. The customers may be asked to send their remittances to the regional or local offices rather than to the head office. The regional office of the bank may be asked to transfer the excess cash balance after keeping minimum cash balance in the regional office, to the head office. Periodic checking of these transactions will be helpful in ensuring smooth functioning of this system.

- **(b) Control of payables:** As far as payables are concerned, it should be ensured that the payments should be done only when they are due. The payables and their disbursements can be centralised. Delaying disbursements results in maximum availability of cash. However, care should be taken that the credit worthiness of the firm is not adversely affected by such delayed disbursements.

Playing the float: The technique of playing the float can be very usefully applied. When the firm's actual bank balance is greater than the balance shown by the firm's books, the difference is called as 'payment float.' The difference between the total amount of cheques drawn on a bank account and the balance shown on bank's books is caused by transit and processing delays. If the financial manager can accurately estimate when the cheques issued will be deposited and collected, he can invest the 'float' during the float period to earn a return.

(iv) Maintaining optimum cash balance:

In the above paragraphs, cash forecasting as well as controlling of cashflows are discussed. Another important aspect of cash management is to maintain an optimum cash balance which will be neither excessive nor in short. The question that arises is how to arrive at this balance? Which factors should be considered in determining the optimum cash balance?

To answer these questions, two models of optimum cash balance are discussed in the following paragraphs:

(a) Baumol Model: The model proposed by William J. Baumol is similar to the economic order quantity concept in inventory management. Baumol suggests that two types of costs are associated with the cash balance. The first type of cost is the transaction cost which is incurred when marketable securities are converted in cash. The second type of cost is the holding cost which is nothing but income foregone due to holding of cash balance. Both these costs are variable in nature but if one cost is reduced, the other type of cost will increase and vice versa. For example: if large cash balance is maintained, the transaction costs will be reduced while holding costs will increase and on the other hand if minimum cash balance is maintained, holding costs will be reduced while transaction costs will shoot up. The optimum size of cash balance will be reached when the total cost is minimised.

The optimum size of the cash balance can be found out either by preparing tables or the following formula can also be used for that purpose.

$$C = \sqrt{\frac{2bT}{I}}$$

where
- C = optimum cash balance,
- b = requirement of cash
- T = Transaction costs
- I = Interest

(b) Miller–Orr Model: As per this model there are upper control limits and lower control limits. The cash balance at any point of time is not allowed to go above the upper control limit while it is not allowed to fall below the lower control limit. In between these two levels, there is a 'returning point'. Upward changes in cash balances are allowed till the cash balance reaches the upper control limit as shown in the following figure. As this level is reached, the cash balance is reduced to the 'returning point' by investing in marketable securities. On the other hand, the downward changes are permitted till the cash balance is reached the lower control limit and once it touches that, enough marketable securities are disposed off to restore the cash balance to return point.

The following figure will explain this point.

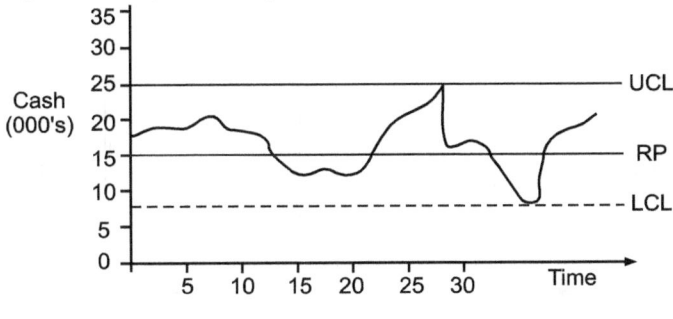

Fig. 4.8

Cash Budget

A Cash Budget is an estimate of the receipts and payments for each month or other period forming part of the whole budget period. It is essential to allow for the time-lag between certain transactions and the receipt or payment of the relative cash. The necessity and consequently, the objective of cash budget is to ensure that sufficient cash is available for both the revenue and capital expenditure to indicate when additional finance is required and how much and to show any expected surplus funds which may be invested profitably outside the business.

Important Functions of Cash Budget:

- To ensure that sufficient cash is available when required.
- To reveal any expected shortage of cash whether long-term or short-term.
- To reveal any expected surplus of cash, whether long term or short-term.
- To preserve the liquidity.
- To reveal the seasonal requirements such as payment of 'Income-Tax'.
- To assist in sound-investment policy.
- To indicate the availability of cash discounts.
- To indicate the availability of funds for replacement of assets, additions to assets, expansion schemes, new schemes, modification of existing plant etc.

Performa (Cash Budget)

		Jan. (₹)	Feb. (₹)	Mar. (₹)	April. (₹)	May (₹)	June (₹)	July (₹)	Aug. (₹)	Sept. (₹)	Oct. (₹)	Nov. (₹)	Dec. (₹)
(A)	Op. Cash Bal.:												
(B)	Cash Receipts												
	(i) Cash Sales												
	(ii) Collection from Debtors												
	(iii) Sale of Fixed Assets												
	(iv) Collection from B/R												
	(v) Loan from Banks												
	(vi) Interest on Investments												
	(vii) Issue of Shares												
	(viii) Issue of Debentures												
	[Receipts (A) + (B)]												
(C)	Cash Payments:												
	(i) Cash Purchases												
	(ii) Payment of Suppliers												
	(iii) B/P Payment												
	(iv) Payment of Exps. & Taxes												
	(v) Payment of Dividend												
	(vi) Interest on Loans												
	(vii) Purchase of Fixed Assets												
	(viii) Payment of Loans												
	Total Payments (C)												
	Closing Cash Bal. [(A) + (B) − (C)]												

FINANCIAL MANAGEMENT — WORKING CAPITAL MANAGEMENT

Solved Problems

Mangement of Cash

Problem 1

ABC company wishes to arrange for overdraft facilities with its bankers during the period April to June 2013. You are required to prepare a Cash–budget for the above period, indicating the extent of bank overdraft required, if any for each month.

Month	Sales (₹)	Purchases (₹)	Wages (₹)	Overheads (₹)
February	4,00,000	2,80,000	60,000	75,000
March	6,50,000	4,00,000	80,000	1,80,000
April	8,00,000	6,80,000	95,000	1,95,000
May	10,00,000	8,50,000	1,10,000	2,00,000
June	13,00,000	12,00,000	1,15,000	2,40,000

Additional information:
1. Expected cash balance as on 1st April, 2013 is ₹ 45,000.
2. Credit allowed to Debtors is 1 month and by creditors 2 months.
3. Wages and overheads are paid in the first week of the subsequent month.
4. All Sales and Purchases are on credit.

Solution:

ABC Comp. Cash Budget period 1st April to 30th June, 2013

Particulars		April (₹)	May (₹)	June (₹)
A. Opening balance		45,000	1,55,000	2,65,000
B. Expected cash receipts		6,50,000	8,00,000	10,00,000
C. Total cash available	[A + B]	6,95,000	9,55,000	12,65,000
D. Expected cash payments				
(i) Purchases		2,80,000	4,00,000	6,80,000
(ii) Wages		80,000	95,000	1,10,000
(iii) Overhead		1,80,000	1,95,000	2,00,000
Total – D		5,40,000	6,90,000	9,90,000
E. Closing balance [C – D]		1,55,000	2,65,000	2,75,000

Conclusion: From the above budget it is clear that overdraft facilities are not required in these three months. However, if any major expense arises, it may be required.

FINANCIAL MANAGEMENT

WORKING CAPITAL MANAGEMENT

Problem 2

From the following particulars, prepare a Cash budget from January to March, 2013.

Month	Sales	Purchases	Overheads		
			Administrative	Production	Selling
	₹	₹	₹	₹	₹
Oct. 2012	11,00,000	6,50,000	95,000	1,00,000	65,000
Nov. 2012	12,00,000	7,00,000	1,25,000	1,30,000	90,000
Dec. 2012	14,50,000	9,00,000	1,25,000	1,60,000	1,15,000
Jan. 2013	16,00,000	11,00,000	1,75,000	1,70,000	1,45,000
Feb. 2013	19,00,000	13,00,000	2,00,000	1,95,000	1,60,000
March 2013	19,00,000	14,00,000	2,10,000	2,00,000	1,70,000

Additional information:
1. Expected cash balance as on 1st January, 2013 is ₹ 80,000.
2. Out of the total sales 50% are Cash Sales. Credit allowed to debtors is one month.
3. All the purchases are on credit. The suppliers allow 2 months credit.
4. Capital expenditure proposed to be incurred on acquisition on Machinery in March, 2008 is ₹ 4,00,000.
5. Income–tax payable in March, 2013 is ₹ 90,000.
6. Interest receivable on Investment ₹ 35,000 in January, 2013.
7. Lag in the payment of overhead expenses is one month.

Solution:

ABC Company Period January to March, 2013

	Particulars	January (₹)	February (₹)	March (₹)
A.	Cash balance: opening	80,000	5,40,000	9,00,000
B.	Expected receipts:			
	(i) Cash Sales [50%]	8,00,000	9,50,000	9,50,000
	(ii) From Debtors	7,25,000	8,00,000	9,50,000
	(iii) Interest on Investments	35,000	–	–
C.	Total Cash available [A + B]	**16,40,000**	**22,90,000**	**28,00,000**
D.	Expected payments			
	(i) Purchases	7,00,000	9,00,000	11,00,000
	(ii) Administrative overheads	1,25,000	1,75,000	2,00,000
	(iii) Production overheads	1,60,000	1,70,000	1,95,000
	(iv) Selling overheads	1,15,000	1,45,000	1,60,000
	(v) Capital Exp. on Machinery purchases	–	–	4,00,000
	(vi) Income–tax payable	–	–	90,000
	Total [D]	11,00,000	13,90,000	21,45,000
E.	Closing Bal. [C – D]	5,40,000	9,00,000	7,45,000

FINANCIAL MANAGEMENT   WORKING CAPITAL MANAGEMENT

Problem 3

From the following information prepare a Cash budget for 6 months from January to June, 2008.

			₹
A.	Sales forecasts:	January' 2008	6,00,000
		February	8,00,000
		March	8,00,000
		April	12,00,000
		May	10,00,000
		June	8,00,000
B.	Actual sales:	November 2007	14,00,000
		December 2007	12,00,000

C. Gross profit margin is 20% on sales.
D. Wages and Salaries are ₹ 80,000 per month for first 3 months and thereafter expected to increase by ₹ 15,000 per month. They are to be paid in the same month in which they become due.
E. The company had expected that stock of goods as on 1st January, 2008, is ₹ 1,10,000. Thereafter the inventory level is to be kept at an uniform level of ₹ 1,15,000 per month.
F. Interest on ₹ 20,00,000 @ 14% on Debentures is due by March end and June end.
G. 40% of total sales are on Cash basis. Out of the remaining, 60% are recovered in the month following the sales and balance in subsequent month.
H. Creditors are paid in the same month.
I. Balance of Cash on 1st January 2008: ₹ 60,000.

Cash Budget of Period January – June 2008

	Particulars	Jan. [₹]	Feb. [₹]	March [₹]	April [₹]	May [₹]	June [₹]
A.	Opening balance	60,000	5,83,000	7,67,000	8,09,000	9,09,000	11,33,000
B.	Expected Cash receipts						
(i)	Cash Sales	2,40,000	3,20,000	3,20,000	4,80,000	4,00,000	3,20,000
(ii)	Collections from Debtors [Working note no. 1]	7,68,000	5,04,000	4,32,000	4,80,000	6,24,000	6,48,000
C.	Total cash available [A + B]	10,68,000	14,07,000	15,19,000	17,69,000	19,33,000	21,01,000
D.	Expected payments						
(i)	Purchases[Working note No. 2]	4,05,000	5,60,000	5,60,000	8,65,000	7,05,000	5,45,000
(ii)	Wages & salaries	80,000	80,000	80,000	95,000	95,000	95,000
(iii)	Interst on Deb.	–	–	70,000	–	–	70,000
	Total [D]	4,85,000	6,40,000	7,10,000	8,60,000	8,00,000	7,10,000
E.	Closing Balance [C – D]	5,83,000	7,67,000	8,09,000	9,09,000	11,33,000	13,91,000

Working notes: 1

1. Collections from Debtors

	₹
January 2008	
Cash Sales @40% of total sales	2,40,000
Therefore, credit sales	3,60,000
Cash received:	
60% of credit sales of Dec. 2007	4,32,000
40% of credit sales of Nov. 2007	<u>3,36,000</u>
	7,68,000
February 2008	
(i) 60% of credit sales in Jan. 2008	2,16,000
(ii) 40% of credit sales of Dec. 2007	<u>2,88,000</u>
	5,04,000
March 2008	
(i) 60% of credit sales of Feb.' 2008	2,88,000
(ii) 40% of credit sales of Jan.' 2008	<u>1,44,000</u>
	4,32,000
April 2008	
(i) 60% of credit sales of March 2008	2,88,000
(ii) 40% of credit sales of Feb.' 2008	<u>1,92,000</u>
	4,80,000
May 2008	
(i) 60% of credit sales of April 2008	4,32,000
(ii) 40% of credit sales of March 2008	<u>1,92,000</u>
	6,24,000
June 2008	
(i) 60% of credit sales of May 2008	3,60,000
(ii) 40% of credit sales of April 2008	<u>2,88,000</u>
	6,48,000

FINANCIAL MANAGEMENT   WORKING CAPITAL MANAGEMENT

Working Note No 2

Purchases are not given in the example. Therefore, from Gross Profit Margin and Cost of goods sold, purchases are found out as follows:

Particulars		Jan. [₹]	Feb. [₹]	March [₹]	April [₹]	May [₹]	June [₹]
Sales		6,00,000	8,00,000	8,00,000	12,00,000	10,00,000	8,00,000
Cost of goods sold [80% of sales]		4,80,000	6,40,000	6,40,000	9,60,000	8,00,000	6,40,000
Add: Closing stock		1,15,000	1,15,000	1,15,000	1,15,000	1,15,000	1,15,000
	Total	5,95,000	7,55,000	7,55,000	10,75,000	9,15,000	7,55,000
Less:							
Opening stock		1,10,000	1,15,000	1,15,000	1,15,000	1,15,000	1,15,000
Wages		80,000	80,000	80,000	95,000	95,000	95,000
Purchases		**4,05,000**	**5,60,000**	**5,60,000**	**8,65,000**	**7,05,000**	**5,45,000**

Observations: From the above calculations, it is seen that balance of cash is very high right from January 2008. The company is advised to invest at least a part of it, so that cash will not be idle.

Problem 4

From the following information and the additional information, prepare a cash budget for 6 months from January 2013.

Month	Purchases ₹	Salaries & Wages ₹	Prod. overheads ₹	Office & selling overheads ₹	Sales ₹
January	50,000	20,000	12,000	11,000	1,44,000
February	62,000	24,200	12,600	13,400	1,94,000
March	51,000	21,200	12,000	15,000	1,72,000
April	61,200	50,000	13,000	17,800	1,77,200
May	74,000	44,000	16,000	22,000	2,05,000
June	77,600	46,000	16,400	23,000	2,17,400

1. 50% of total sales are cash sales. Remaining are recovered in the subsequent month.
2. Suppliers allow one month's credit.
3. Dividend of ₹ 35,000 is to be paid in June.
4. Overheads are paid in the same month in which they become due.
5. Income tax payable in March ₹ 40,000.
6. Cash balance as on 1st January 2013 ₹ 80,000.

4.60

FINANCIAL MANAGEMENT — WORKING CAPITAL MANAGEMENT

Solution:

Cash Budget for January–June, 2013

Particulars	Jan. [₹]	Feb. [₹]	March [₹]	April [₹]	May [₹]	June [₹]
A. Opening balance	80,000	1,09,000	1,77,800	2,10,600	2,53,400	3,01,300
B. Expected cash receipts						
(i) Cash Sales	72,000	97,000	86,000	88,600	1,02,500	1,08,700
(ii) From Debtors	–	72,000	97,000	86,000	88,600	1,02,500
C. Total cash available [A + B]	1,52,000	2,78,000	3,60,800	3,85,200	4,44,500	5,12,500
D. Expected cash payments						
(i) Purchases	–	50,000	62,000	51,000	61,200	74,000
(ii) Salaries & Wages	20,000	24,200	21,200	50,000	44,000	46,000
(iii) Prod. overheads	12,000	12,600	12,000	13,000	16,000	16,400
(iv) Office & Selling	11,000	13,400	15,000	17,800	22,000	23,000
(v) Income–tax	–	–	40,000	–	–	–
Total – D	43,000	1,00,200	1,50,200	1,31,800	1,43,200	1,38,700
E. Closing balance [C – D]	1,09,000	1,77,800	2,10,600	2,53,400	3,01,300	3,73,800

4.14 Inventory Management

Introduction

One of the important constituents of current assets is the 'inventory'. In several business organisations, inventories account for nearly 50-60% if the total current assets of an organisation. The more the inventory, the more is the amount of funds locked in it and thus results in increase in the amount of the cost of the funds so locked up. Hence there is a need for effective management of the inventory so that the twin objectives of inventory management, i.e. minimizing the amount of investment in inventory and at the same time making sure that the production flow is not affected will be served. The various aspects of inventory management in the light of these objectives are discussed in detail in the following paragraphs.

Inventory – What is Included?

Inventories include the following:

(a) **Raw materials:** This is the material which is used for conversion into the finished product. For example, oil seeds will be raw material for the edible oil industry, cotton will be the raw material for the textile industry. Organisations purchase material after considering the production requirements and unused raw material at the end of a particular period, say at the end of an accounting year is the inventory of raw materials.

(b) Work-in-progress: At the end of an accounting year, there are some materials on hand which are neither fully raw, neither fully finished. Thus these material are in semi-finished stage and are called as work-in-progress.

(c) Finished goods: These are the finished goods remaining unsold at the end of a particular accounting period. The finished goods inventory ensures that the demand from the consumers is easily met and hence certain stock is required. However a large inventory of finished goods may indicate either sluggish demand or lack of demand.

(d) Stores and spares: Inventory also includes the stores and spares which are required for the running of machines. For example, stock of coolants, lubricating oil, spare parts of machinery etc are required to ensure that in they can be used in the repairs of the machinery.

Techniques of Inventory Control

The main objectives of inventory management are:

(i) To ensure that the investment in inventory is not too high. Thus overstocking of materials and other inventories should be avoided at any cost. This objective can be achieved by systematically reducing the level of inventory by careful planning of various activities. For example, the raw material inventory can be reduced by planning of the production and purchasing as per the exact production planning. The overstocking of material results in locking of funds and the business organisation may face shortage of working capital. For meeting the working capital needs, the firm may have to borrow and thus the interest cost will rise. There is a danger that the firm will be caught in the debt trap and it will be difficult to come out.

(ii) Another objective of inventory management is ensure that the supply of raw material to the production departments is smooth and uninterrupted. As for the finished goods, the stock should be sufficient to meet the demand of the customers.

For achieving the above conflicting objectives, a number of techniques are available. These techniques are as follows.

Economic Order Quantity

One important question that is to be answered by the Purchase Manager is how much to purchase at any one time? In other words, how much quantity is to be ordered at any one point of time? Whether there are any costs associated with the ordering quantity apart from the purchase price? It will be noticed that there are costs attached to the ordering quantity. These costs are of two types, the first is the ordering cost and the other one is the carrying cost. We will discuss about these costs. Ordering cost is the cost of placing an order. In other words, it can be said that when an order is placed, the company has to incur certain costs at the time of order. These costs include costs like handling and transportation costs, stationery costs, costs incurred for inviting quotations and tenders etc. The more is the frequency of order, the more are these costs.

On the other hand, there are certain costs that are called as carrying costs. The cost of carrying the inventory is the real out of pocket cost associated with having inventory on hand, such as warehouse charges, insurance, lighting, losses due to handling, spoilage, breakage etc, and another important component of carrying cost is the amount of interest lost due to the investment in the inventory. Carrying costs will go on increasing if the quantity of material in inventory goes on increasing.

Both, the carrying costs and the ordering costs are variable costs, however their behavior is exactly opposite of each other. It orders are more frequent, ordering costs will go on increasing but as the material ordered will be in less quantity, the carrying costs will decrease. On the other hand, if number of orders are reduced, the quantity per order will increase and the carrying cost will increase. The ordering cost will come down due to reduction of number of orders.

In this situation, the most desirable quantity to be ordered is that quantity at which both, the ordering costs and carrying costs will be minimum. This quantity is called as 'Economic Order Quantity'. This quantity can be calculated with the help of the following formula.

Economic Order Quantity = $\sqrt{2CO/I}$

Where,
- C = Annual consumption,
- O = Ordering cost
- I = Carrying cost

The Economic Order Quantity is an important concept as it guides the Purchase Manager regarding the quantity to be purchased of a particular material. However this concept is based on some assumptions. These assumptions are as follows.

- The concerned material will be available all the time without any difficulty.
- The price of the material will remain constant.
- Ordering cost and carrying costs are variable.
- Impact of quantity discounts on the prices is negligible.

Fixation of Level

Another important aspect of material procurement is not to purchase too much or too little. Similarly the timing of the purchase is also important. Fixation of levels of materials is done precisely with these objectives in mind. The following levels of materials are fixed for achieving objectives like avoiding overstocking, ensuring that the material is ordered at right time and also avoiding shortage of materials.

- **Maximum Level:** This is the highest level of material beyond which the inventory of material is not allowed to rise. Obviously this level is fixed with the objective of avoiding overstocking. This level is fixed after taking into consideration the consumption of material and the re-order period. Mathematically the level is fixed as under.

    Maximum Level = Re-order Level + Re-order Quantity –
    [Minimum Consumption × Minimum Re-order period]

- **Minimum Level:** This level is fixed with the objective of avoiding shortage of material. If production is held up due to shortage of material, there will be huge loss to the company. In order to avoid this, the minimum level is fixed. Care is taken that the stock do not fall below this level. The minimum level is fixed in the following manner.

    Minimum Level = Ordering Level – [Average rate of consumption × Re-order period]

- **Re-order Level:** This level is fixed for deciding the time of placing an order. If the stock of materials reaches this level, fresh order is placed so that by the time the material is procured, the level of material may fall up to minimum level but not below that. This level is fixed in the following manner.

    Re-order Level = Maximum Usage per Period × Maximum Re-order Period

- Average Level = This level is the average of the maximum and minimum level and computed in the following manner.

    Average Level = Maximum Level + Minimum Level / 2

- Danger Level = Generally the danger level of stock is indicated below the safety or minimum stock level. Sometimes, depending on the practices of the firm and circumstances prevailing, the danger level is determined between the re-order level and minimum level.

Perpetual Inventory System

Perpetual Inventory system means continuous stock taking. Chartered Institute of Management Accountants (CIMA) defines perpetual inventory system as *'the recording as they occur of receipts, issues and the resulting balances of individual items of stock in either quantity or quantity and value'*. Under this system, a continuous record of receipt and issue of materials is maintained by the stores department and the information about the stock of materials is always available. Entries in the Bin Card and the Stores Ledger are made after every receipt and issue and the balance is reconciled on regular basis with the physical stock. The main advantage of this system is that it avoids disruptions in the production caused by periodic stock taking. Similarly it helps in having a detailed and more reliable check on the stocks. The stock records are more reliable and stock discrepancies are investigated and appropriate action is taken immediately.

ABC System

In this technique, the items of inventory are classified according to the value of usage. Materials are classified as A, B and C according to their value.

Items in class 'A' constitute the most important class of inventories so far as the proportion in the total value of inventory is concerned. The 'A' items constitute roughly about 5-10% of the total items while its value may be about 80% of the total value of the inventory.

Items in class 'B' constitute intermediate position. These items may be about 20-25% of the total items while the usage value may be about 15% of the total value.

Items in class 'C' are the most negligible in value, about 65-75% of the total quantity but the value may be about 5% of the total usage value of the inventory.

The numbers given above are just indicative, actual numbers may vary from situation to situation. The principle to be followed is that the high value items should be controlled more carefully while items having small value though large in numbers can be controlled periodically.

Just In Time Inventory

This is the latest trend in inventory management. This principle envisages that there should not be any intermediate stage like storekeeping. Material purchased from supplier should directly go the assembly line, i.e. to the production department. There should not be any need of storing the material. The storing cost can be saved to a great extent by using this technique. However the practicality of this technique in Indian conditions should be verified before practicing the same. The benefits of Just In Time system are as follows,

- Right quantities are purchased or produced at right time.
- Cost effective production or operation of correct services is possible.
- Inventory carrying costs are eliminated totally.
- The stores function is eliminated and hence there is a considerable saving in the stores cost.
- Losses due to breakage, wastage, pilferage etc are avoided.

VED Analysis

This analysis divides items into three categories in the descending order of their criticality as follows.

- 'V' stands for vital items and their stock analysis requires more attention. The reason is that if these items are not available, the resulting stock outs will cause heavy losses due to stoppage of production. Thus these items are required to be stored adequately to ensure smooth operation of the plant.
- 'E' means essential items. Such items are considered essential for efficient running but without these items, the system will not fail. Care must be taken to see that they are always in stock.
- 'D' stands for desirable items, which do not affect production immediately but availability of these items will lead to more efficiency and less fatigue.
- Thus VED analysis can be very useful to capital intensive process industries. As it analyses items based on their importance and it can be used for those special raw materials which are difficult to procure.

FSND Analysis

Age of the inventory indicates the duration of inventory in the organisation. It shows the moving position of inventory during the year. This analysis divides the items of inventory into four categories in the descending order of their usage rate as follows.

(a) 'F' stands for fast moving items and stocks of such items are consumed in a short span of time. Stock of fast moving items must be observed constantly and replenishment orders be placed in time to avoid stock out position.

(b) 'N' means normal moving items and such items are exhausted over a period of time, i.e. say one year. The order levels and quantities for such items should be on the basis of a new estimate of future demand to minimise the risks of a surplus stock.

(c) 'S' indicates slow moving items, existing stock of which would last for two years or so. These items must be reviewed carefully before eliminating them.

(d) 'D' stands for dead stork which means that there will not be any further demand for the same. It is necessary to identify these items and if there cannot be any alternative use for the same, should be eliminated.

Inventory Turnover Ratio

There are several items in the store which are slow moving which means that they are issued to the production after a long time gap. Some items are such that they are never issued to the production as they have become obsolete or outdated and need to be disposed off. For identifying these items, it is necessary to compute the inventory turnover ratio. Inventory turnover ratio enables the management to avoid the capital being locked in such items. This ratio indicates the efficiency or inefficiency with which inventories are maintained. Inventory turnover ratio is calculated in the following manner.

Inventory Turnover Ratio: Cost of material consumed/Cost of average stock held during the year

The cost of average stock here is taken as the average of opening stock and closing stock. The inventory turnover ratio can also be calculated in days as below.

Days during the period / Inventory turnover ratio

Detection of Slow Moving and Non Moving or Obsolete Materials: It is essential for any business unit to detect slow moving and non moving or obsolete materials. Obsolete materials become useless or obsolete due to change in the product, process, design or method of production. Obsolete materials are different from slow moving materials and non-moving materials. Slow moving materials move at a slow rate. In the case of slow moving materials as well as non moving materials, capital remains blocked unnecessarily and also cost of storing continue to be incurred of these materials are kept in the store in excess of the requirements. Management should make proper investigations into slow moving and obsolete materials and try to minimise the capital investments in the same. It is necessary to have an efficient Management Information System which will enable to generate regular reports to examine the situations relating to these stocks so that the non moving and obsolete stocks can be disposed off in time.

Conclusion: Thus it can be seen that there are various tools and techniques that can be used to achieve the objectives of inventory management. By effectively controlling the level of inventory, a business organisation can manage the working capital effectively

Solved Problems

Inventory Management

Problem 1

From the following figures relating to two components X and Y, compute Re-order Level, Minimum Level, Maximum Level and Average Stock Level.

Particulars	Component X	Component Y
Maximum consumption per week	75 units	75 units
Average consumption per week	50 units	50 units
Minimum consumption per week	25 units	25 units
Reorder period	4 to 6 weeks	2 to 4 weeks
Reorder quantity	400 units	600 units

Solution:

The computation of various levels is shown below.

[A] Reorder Level = Maximum Consumption × Maximum Reorder Period
Component X = 75 units × 6 weeks = 450 units
Component Y = 75 units × 4 weeks = 300 units.

[B] Minimum Level = Reorder Level – Average Consumption × Average Reorder Period
Component X = 450 units – [50 units × 5 weeks] = 200 units
Component Y = 300 units – [50 units × 3 weeks] = 150 units

[C] Maximum Level = Reorder Level + Reorder Quantity –
[Minimum Consumption X Minimum Reorder Period]
Component X = 450 units + 400 units - [25 units X 4 weeks] = 750 units
Component Y = 300 units + 600 units – [25 units X 2 weeks] = 850 units

[D] Average Level = ½ [Maximum Level + Minimum Level]
Component X = ½ [750 units + 200 units] = 475 units
Component Y = ½ [150 units + 850 units] = 500 units

Problem 2

A manufacturer purchases 800 units of a certain component p.a. @ ₹ 30 per unit from outside supplier. The annual usage is 800 units, order placing and receiving cost is ₹ 100 per order and cost of holding one unit of the component for one year is ₹ 4. Calculate the Economic Order Quantity by tabular method. Also calculate the number of orders to be placed per year.

Solution:

The following table is prepared to compute the Economic Order Quantity.

Annual Consumption	Number of orders p.a.	Units per order	Average inventory Units	Carrying cost @ ₹ 4 per unit on average inventory	Order placing and receiving cost @ ₹ 100 per order	Total annual costs
800	1	800	400	₹ 1600	₹ 100	₹ 1700
	2	400	200	800	200	1000
	3	267	133	532	300	832
	4	200	100	400	400	800 *
	5	160	80	320	500	820
	6	133	67	268	600	868

* The total annual cost of ₹ 800 is the lowest when number of orders placed are 4 in a year. This means that the quantity per order of 200 [4 orders per year] is the Economic Order Quantity.

Points to Remember

- The amount invested by an organisation in fixed assets is called **'fixed capital'** and a business organisation invests some portion of its total capital in the fixed assets.
- **Working Capital** means current assets such as cash, accounts receivable and inventory and so on, minus the current liabilities.
- Management of the working capital of an organisation is extremely important as it decides the amount of current assets that are to be maintained in the business as well as that of the current liabilities.
- The concepts of working capital can be broadly divided into two categories Gross working capital and Net working capital
- **Operating cycle** means the time period that is required from the time cash is put in the business along with other inputs to the time it is recovered from the amount of sales made by the firm.
- The length of the operating cycle depends upon several factors.
- A firm has to strike a balance between maintaining a very high cash balance and a very small amount of cash balance.
- The basic objective of working capital management is that there should be an optimum investment in working capital.
- An aggressive current policy implies that there is a minimum investment in current assets in relation to sales.
- In conservative current asset financing policy, a firm relies more on long-term financing such as shares, debentures, preference shares, long-term debt and retained earnings.
- Exclusive long-term sources of funds can be used for financing working capital or exclusively short-term sources can also be used for financing the working capital.

Questions for Discussion

1. What is working capital? Explain the factors affecting working capital.
2. Explain: Financing of Working Capital Requirements.
3. Explain: Estimating of Working Capital Requirements.
4. State the nature and need for Working Capital Management.
5. What is Factoring? Explain its nature and types.
6. Explain the concept of Operating Cycle.
7. Write short notes:
   (a) Working capital budget
   (b) Working capital policy
   (c) Cash management
   (d) Inventory management
   (e) Average collection period
8. Explain: Accounts Receivables Management.
9. Explain: Assessment of Working Capital Requirements.
10. State the various types of Working Capital.

FINANCIAL MANAGEMENT

WORKING CAPITAL MANAGEMENT

Case Study

A Ltd. is a manufacturing company manufacturing wooden tables. The company has the installed capacity of manufacturing 100000 tables per annum. At present the capacity utilisation is 75%. The main raw material used to manufacture tables is the wood and plywood. The company wants to know the working capital requirement for the year 2013-14. From the following details, prepare a statement of working capital requirements for the company.

Cost Structure per table

Particulars	Amount [₹]
Raw material - wood	250
Raw material – plywood	150
Other material [nut bolts, polish etc]	100
Packing material	100
Direct labour	300
Factory overheads [Including depreciation ₹ 100]	250
Administrative overheads	200
Selling overheads	250
Total cost	**1600**

Additional information:

(i) The company expects the holding period of the raw material 2 months for wood, 2 months for plywood and 1 month for other material like nut bolts, and polish.

(ii) The estimated holding period for the work in progress is 0.5 months and there is 100% completion in respect of the raw material and 50% each for the labour and the overheads

(iii) The finished goods remain in stock on an average for about 1 month

(iv) Credit allowed to debtors is 2 months while the creditors for material purchases allow 1 month credit.

(v) On an average the delay in payment of wages is 1 week while in case of overheads it is 0.5 months.

(vi) Expected cash balance is ₹ 500000.

(vii) The company desires to add 10% contingency margin in the computation of the working capital.

Suggested Activity

Analyse Financial Statements of at least 5 companies out of which 3 should be in manufacturing and 2 in service sector to find out the amount of working capital and the way it is financed by the companies.

Questions from Previous Pune University Examinations

1. What are the Elements that Constitute the Working Capital of a Company : Write a note on Management of each Element. **[M.B.A. April 2006]**
2. Write Short Notes on:
   - (a) Factoring Services. **[P.G.D.B.M. April 2006, Dec. 2006]**
   - (b) Aspects of Cash Management. **[P.G.D.B.M. April 2006]**
   - (c) Cash Budget. **[M.B.A. Dec. 2006, 2007, April 2007]**
   - (d) Accounts Receivable Management. **[P.G.D.B.M. Dec. 2006]**
   - (e) Types of Working Capital. **[P.G.D.B.M. April 2006, Dec. 2006]**
   - (f) Factoring. **[P.G.D.B.M. Dec. 2007]**
3. Discuss fully Aspects of Cash Management. **[P.G.D.B.M. Dec. 2006]**
4. Which are the various factors that determine the Working Capital Requirements of a Firm? Explain. **[P.G.D.B.M. April 2007]**
5. Write Short Notes:
   - (a) Operating Cycle. **[P.G.D.B.M. April 2009]**
   - (b) Cash Budget. **[M.B.A. Dec. 2010, 2011, April 2011]**
   - (c) Management of Receivables. **[M.B.A. April 2011]**
   - (d) Factoring. **[M.B.A. Dec. 2011]**
   - (e) Gross Working Capital and Net Working Capital. **[M.B.A. Dec. 2010]**
6. What is Working Capital Management? Explain the Concept of Operating Cycle. **[M.B.A. Dec. 2010]**

■■■

Chapter 5...

Capital Structure and Firm Valuation

Contents ...

5.1 Introduction
5.2 Capital Structure: Meaning
5.3 Theories of Capitalisation
5.4 Overcapitalisation
5.5 Undercapitalisation
5.6 Cost of Capital
5.7 Meaning of Capital Structure and Theories of Capital Structure
5.8 Factors Affecting Capital Structure
5.9 Trading on Equity
- Solved Problems
- Points to Remember
- Questions for Discussion
- Suggested Activity
- Questions from Previous Pune University Examinations

Learning Objectives ...

After studying this topic, you should be able to,
1. Understand the meaning of Capital Structure of a Firm
2. Understand the Concept and Computation of Cost of Capital
3. Analyse problems associated with Capital Structure
4. Recount Factors that affect Capital Structure of a Firm

5.1 Introduction

A business organisation requires funds for various activities of the enterprise. Requirement of funds can be broadly categorised as:

(i) Long-term requirements
(ii) Short-term equirements.

The long-term requirements are for the purpose of fixed assets creation which is essential for improving the earning capacity of the business. Short-term funds are required for financing the day-to-day activities of the business. This is known as the working capital of the business.

Funds can be raised through various sources which are broadly classified into long-term sources and short-term sources. Long-term sources include funds raised through issue of shares and debentures and long-term loans while short-term sources include funds raised from bank credit, public deposits, and short-term loans and so on.

It is a fundamental principle of financial management that funds raised should be exactly as per the requirement of the business and they should be neither surplus nor inadequate from the requirements point of view. The aim of this chapter is, therefore, to discuss the meaning of 'capitalisation' and also the meaning of the terms like overcapitalisation and undercapitalisation as well as that of capital structure planning.

5.2 Capital Structure: Meaning

Capital structure refers to the way a company finances its assets through some combination of equity, debt, or hybrid securities. A firm's capital structure is therefore the composition or 'structure' of its liabilities.

The capital structure of a company may be highly complex and include many sources. An optimal capital structure, if there is one, is the one which maximises the value of the firm.

The term capitalisation means the total amount of funds raised through long-term sources. It includes funds raised from owned sources and from borrowed sources. Normally, capitalisation includes reserves and surplus of the company also. However, capital profits, which are available for distribution as much as dividends under certain conditions only, should be included in the capitalisation while reserves built out of revenue profits, can be included in capitalisation only if it is retained in the business.

As mentioned above, the amount of capitalisation should be exactly as much as the requirement of the company. If the amount raised is more than what the company can use effectively, it leads to overcapitalisation which is harmful to any business. On the other hand, undercapitalisation is also dangerous for a company.

Both the terms, overcapitalisation and undercapitalistion are explained in detail in subsequent paragraphs. However, prior to that, it is important for us to examine the theories of capitalisation which help to determine the exact amount of capital.

5.3 Theories of Capitalisation

The theories of capitalisation are given below:

(i) Cost Theory: This theory states that the amount of capitalisation should be determined according to the cost of the various assets required by the company. A business firm requires various assets, fixed and current for smooth running of the business. The total cost of acquiring these assets should be taken as the basis for determining the capitalisation of the company.

This theory is based on sound logic but the only precaution to be taken is that if the assets are acquired at inflated cost and also they include obsolete assets, the earnings may be on the lower side and the investments made in those assets may not be justifiable. This situation is known as 'overcapitalisation'.

(ii) Earnings Theory: This theory links capitalisation with the future earnings of the company. This theory states that the amount of capitalisation should be arrived at by capitalising the expected future earnings of the company by an appropriate capitalisation role. Thus, the first step in this method is to estimate the future earnings. This projection should be done carefully as it is not an easy task. The past earnings of the business as well as the trends in the future are to be taken into consideration while predicting the future profits.

The second step here is to apply a rate of capitalisation for capitalising the future earnings. The rate of capitalisation may be taken as the rate of earnings of similar organisations in the industry or alternatively it may be taken as the cost of capital. After determining the rate, the next step is to capitalise the earnings by this rate. The following example will clarify the theory.

Example: Suppose X Ltd. has estimated future earnings of ₹ 10,00,000 and the rate of capitalisation is 10 %. The amount of capitalisation will be ₹ 100,000,00 i.e. ₹ 10,00,000 × $\frac{100}{10}$.

The earnings theory of capitalisation is also based on sound logic as it relates the earning capacity to the capitalisation. However, in order to estimate the amount of capitalisation correctly, it is necessary to predict the future earnings and rate of capitalisation accurately, failing which, the amount of capitalisation will not be correct.

5.4 Overcapitalisation

Overcapitalisation means the existence of excess capital as compared to the requirements of the company. Over-capitalisation does not mean surplus or abundant capital. On the other hand, it may be a situation where there is a shortage of capital. Overcapitalisation implies that a company has raised capital which it can't utilise effectively in the business. This results in lowering the rate of return and fall in the value of shares in the market. The market price of the shares in fact, will be lower than the intrinsic value of the shares of the company.

Overcapitalisation may arise due to the following reasons:

(i) Assets may have been purchased at inflated rates that may not be in line with the rate of return generated by them. In other words, if assets are purchased in the inflationary period, the price paid will be too high and the rate of earnings on the lower side.

(ii) It is also possible that while forming of a company, huge amounts are paid on the acquisition of intangible assets like goodwill, patents, copyrights and so on. As a result, the earning capacity of the company may be adversely affected.

(iii) The top management of the company may have gone for raising funds through issue of securities though the company may not require the same. This may have been done to take advantage of the favourable market conditions.

(iv) If there is anything wrong in estimating either the amount of earnings or rate of earnings, the amount of capitalisation will also be based on wrong projections.

Overcapitalisation leads to lowering of the market value of the shares of the company. The shareholders of the company are affected adversely due to this as there may be an element of watered capital in the capitalisation which will reduce the asset backing of their shareholding. The rate of return on the shares of the company may also fall. This will affect the credit standing of the company and it may find it difficult to raise additional capital.

Overcapitalisation can be corrected through the following remedies.

(i) Repayment of debt either through existing earnings or by converting them into share capital.
(ii) Repayment of preference shares.
(iii) Reduction in the face value of equity shares.
(iv) Buy-back of equity shares.

5.5 Undercapitalisation

Undercapitalisation does not mean shortage or scarcity of capital; on the contrary, it means extremely efficient utilisation of funds which enables a company to earn a very high rate of return as the earnings are very high. Undercapitalisation indicates sound financial position and efficient management of the company. Undercapitalisation results in real worth exceeding over the aggregate of shares and debentures.

Undercapitalisation takes place due to the following:

(i) Wrong estimation of earnings or rate of capitalisation.
(ii) Unexpected or windfall profits are also responsible for undercapitalisation.
(iii) If the market conditions are consistently favourable, the earnings also reach a high level. Similarly, if a company is in a monopolistic market, profits achieved are very high.
(iv) A company may follow a conservative dividend policy which results in building up reserves and surplus. This leads to undercapitalisation.
(v) Constant modernisation and upgradation of fixed assets results in higher earnings which lead to the real value being more than the book value.

Undercapitalisation leads to higher profits which may give an indication that the line of business of the company is very lucrative and this leads to higher degree of competition. As the market prices of the shares are on the higher side, marketability of the shares is restricted. Employees of the company may be tempted to demand hike in wages and salaries due to increased profitability.

Undercapitalisation can be corrected by:

(i) Issue of bonus shares and

(ii) Splitting of shares.

5.6 Cost of Capital

A company raises funds from various sources for financing long-term requirements. These sources principally consist of, (i) Equity capital, (ii) Reserves and surplus, (iii) Long term loans and (iv) Debentures.

Each of the above sources cost the company something. Cost of capital, therefore, can be defined as cost of raising funds through different sources. Alternatively, it can also be defined as the rate of return that a company must earn on its investments so that the expectations of the investors are satisfied. In other words, the minimum rate of return mentioned above will maintain the existing position which means that if the present situation is not improved, at least it will not deteriorate further. This rate of return is in turn calculated on the basis of the cost of raising funds from different sources for financing the investments of the company.

Before discussing further the components of cost of capital and its components, it will be appropriate to view the cost of capital with respect to risk associated with a particular investment opportunity because the expected rate of return is bound to change with risk.

There may be three situations viz.

(i) Riskless rate of return may be offered from a particular proposed investment. This means that there is absolutely no risk involved from such investments. The rate of return expected in such cases is minimum which means cost of capital is also minimum.

(ii) In some investments, there is a risk known as business risk. Such risk arises out of the need to market the product successfully. For such proposals, expected rate of return is naturally high and, therefore, cost of capital is also high.

(iii) In addition to the business risk, there is a financial risk also in some proposals. This risk arises because of financing pattern of the project. If the major portion is financed through debt or preference capital, there will be an obligation on the part of the company to pay interest or preference dividend. This risk results into higher expected rate of return which implies higher cost of capital.

In view of the above discussion, it can be said that cost of capital can be stated as:

$k = k_0 + k_1 + k_2$ where,

k = Total cost of capital

k_0 = Riskless cost/rate of return

k_1 = Premium for business risk

k_2 = Premium for financial risk.

Uses of Cost of Capital

The cost of capital, which is a very useful concept, is used in the following decisions:

(i) Capital budgeting decisions: Capital budgeting decisions may be either: (a) accept or reject a particular proposal or (b) selection of a particular proposal from various alternative proposals available. For taking any of the above decisions, the cash inflows from various proposals are discounted at a rate of discount. This rate of discount can be decided on the basis of cost of capital of that capital expenditure proposal.

(ii) In planning of the capital structure also, cost of capital is a very relevant concept. According to traditional approach, cost of capital is very vital in determining the optimum capital structure of a company. In fact the optimum capital structure according to the traditional approach is such a combination of debt and equity that the aggregate cost of capital is minimum at that level.

Types of Cost of Capital

Cost of capital can be divided into the following types:

(i) **Specific Cost:** The specific cost of capital is the cost of specific source of capital i.e. equity capital, debt, retained earnings etc. It is measured as the rate of discount which equates the present value of the expected payments to that source of finance with the net funds received from that source of finance.

(ii) **Weighted Average Cost of Capital:** This cost of capital, which is the aggregate cost of capital, is calculated on the basis of the weights assigned to each source of capital based on either book values or market values. The following illustration will clarify the concept. Suppose, a company is using debt and equity for financing various investment proposals. The specific cost and weighted average cost is shown in the following table:

Source of capital	Book value [₹]	Weights on the basis of book value	Specific cost [%]	Weighted Average cost [%] [weights × specific cost]
Equity	40,000	.40	.16	.064
Debt	60,000	.60	.09	.054
	1,00,000	1.00		.118

Therefore, the weighted average cost is 11.8%

(iii) **Historical cost:** The cost of capital in relation to funds raised in the past is the historical cost of capital.

(iv) **Future cost:** The cost of funds that will be raised in future is the future cost of capital.

Calculation of Cost of Capital

(i) **Cost of debt:** The cost of debt capital is measured as the rate of discount which equates the present value of post–tax interest and principal repayments with the net proceeds of the debt issue. In the calculation of cost of debt, the annual debt interest payment is multiplied by the factor $(1 - t)$, where t = taxation rate. The reason is that the interest is a tax deductible expense.

The formula for calculation of cost of debt is as follows:

$$k_d = \frac{I(1-t) + \frac{F-P}{n}}{\frac{P+F}{2}}$$

where k_d = Cost of debt,
   I = Amount of interest,
   t = Taxation rate,
   F = Face value of debenture,
   P = Net amount realised,
   n = Number of years for maturity.

Illustration:

A company sells 15 years, 14% debentures of the face value of ₹ 1,000 at ₹ 970. In addition an underwriting fee of 1.5% of the face value is incurred. Rate of taxation is 50%.

The cost of debentures is calculated as follows:

$$k_d = \frac{140(1-.50) + \frac{1000-955}{15}}{\frac{1000+955}{2}} = 6.75\%$$

(ii) Cost of Term Loan: The term loans from financial institutions is also a very important source. These loans are generally repayable over a period of 8 to 11 years, equal annual or half yearly or quarterly installments after an initial grace period of 1 to 3 years. There is no question of repayment at premium and there is hardly any issue expense. The cost of such loan can be calculated as follows:

$$k_d = \text{Interest} (1 - \text{tax rate})$$

(iii) Cost of Preference Capital: Preference capital carries a fixed rate of dividend. However, this dividend is not a tax deductible expense. The formula for calculation of cost of preference capital is as follows:

$$k_p = \frac{PD + \frac{(F-P)}{n}}{\frac{F+P}{2}}$$

where
- k_p = Cost of preference capital,
- PD = Preference dividend,
- F = Repayable value,
- P = Net amount realised,
- n = Maturity period.

For example,

XYZ Ltd. issues ₹ 100 face value preference shares carrying 14% dividend which are repayable at par after 10 years. The net amount realised per share is ₹ 92.

The k_p is calculated below:

$$k_p = \frac{14 + \left(\frac{100-92}{10}\right)}{\frac{100+92}{2}} = 15.4\%$$

(iv) Cost of Equity Capital: There is a controversy regarding whether the equity capital has cost or not. However, it is now accepted that equity capital is not a cost-free source of financing. However, as compared to Pref. capital and debt where estimate of rate of return required by the suppliers of funds can be estimated fairly and easily, for equity capital it is a bit difficult. The reason is that the benefits expected by them cannot be measured easily. In order to remove this difficulty, several approaches have been proposed. These approaches are explained below.

    (a) Dividend/Price Approach: As per this approach, the market price per share is equal to the present value of the expected dividends discounted at the rate of return required by equity shareholders. In other words, from the given market price and expected dividends by equity shareholders, the rate of return required by equity shareholders can be calculated. The cost of equity capital in this case will be:

$$k_e = \frac{D}{P}$$

where D = Dividend per share,
P = Market price,
k_e = Cost of equity capital.

(b) **Dividend / Price + Growth rate approach:** In the above approach, the expected dividend per share by equity shareholders is presumed to be constant. However, if the rate of dividend is expected to grow in future, the cost of equity capital will be,

$$k_e = \frac{D}{P} + g$$

where g = growth rate.

Illustration: The market price per share of the equity capital of ABC Ltd. is ₹ 150. The expected dividend is ₹ 15 per share and expected growth rate is 7% p.a. The cost of equity capital will be

$$k_e = \frac{15}{150} + .07$$
$$= .10 + .07$$
$$= .17 \text{ or } 17\%$$

(c) **Earnings / Price approach:** As per this approach, earnings per share are more important than dividend per share. Therefore, cost of equity capital will be,

$$k_e = \frac{EPS}{P}$$

(d) **Realised yield approach:** According to this approach, the actual yield realised by equity shareholders in the past is taken as the cost of equity capital. In other words, it is the rate of discount which equates the cash outflow and the present value of cash inflows realised by investors.

(v) **Cost of retained earnings:** The cost of retained earnings is in the nature of opportunity cost for the investors. When the company prefers to retain the earnings rather than distribute it among the shareholders, the shareholders lose something in the form of return, which in turn is taken as the cost of retained earnings. The formula for calculation of this cost is as follows:

$$k_r = k_e \frac{1 - t_p}{1 - t_g}$$

where k_e = Cost of equity capital,
t_p = Ordinary personal income-tax rate,
t_g = Personal long-term capital gains.

5.7 Meaning of Capital Structure and Theories of Capital Structure

"Capital Structure is the make up of a firm's capitalisation i.e. it represents the mix of different sources of long term funds in the total capitalisation of the company."

— **C. W. Gerstenberg**

Capital Structure represents only long term funds, i.e., long term debts, shareholder's equity etc. and excludes all short term loans and advances. The selection of an appropriate capital structure is a very crucial decision and depends on a number of factors such as the nature of a company's business; the risks involved the requirements of the Government, regularity of earnings, condition of the money market and the terms relevant in the industry and the attitude of the investor etc. Theoretically, Capital structure of the company can be of the following four patterns:

(i) Capital structure with equity shares only.

(ii) Capital structure with both equity and preference shares.

(iii) Capital structure with equity shares and debentures.

(iv) Capital structure with equity shares, preferences shares and debentures.

Theories of Capital Structure: The following are the theories of capital structures.

(i) Net Income approach

(ii) Net Operating Income approach

(iii) Traditional approach

(iv) Modigliani – Miller approach (MM')

(i) Net Income Approach: This approach says that a relationship definitely exists between cost of capital and capital structure. The approach further says that cost of debt [k_d] is less than cost of equity [k_e]. Therefore, the aggregate cost of capital [k_a] will start decreasing when a firm increases the percentage of debt in its capital structure. Therefore, the valuation of a firm will increase because the aggregate cost of capital is falling down. [The valuation of a firm has inverse relationship with cost of capital].

In mathematical terms, the approach can be described as follows:

$$k_a = k_d \left[\frac{B}{B+S} \right] + k_e \left[\frac{S}{B+S} \right]$$

Where, k_a = Aggregate cost of capital

B = Borrowings

S = Share capital

k_e = Cost of equity capital

k_d = Cost of debt

The approach can also be presented in the form of a graph as follows:

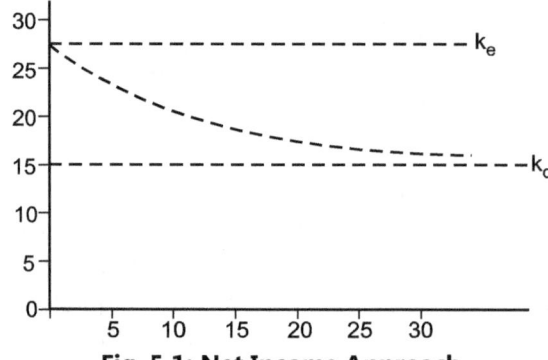

Fig. 5.1: Net Income Approach

Though it may be admitted that cost of debt [k_d] is less than cost of equity, the cost of debt may not remain the same at all levels of debts. In case of a company which is already loaded with debt, the cost of debt may be higher than a company, predominantly employing equity capital. Similarly, with the introduction of more debt, the hidden costs also increase. This hidden cost is not taken into consideration in this approach.

Therefore, it can be said that, though this approach quite rightly says, that cost of capital and capital structure are connected with each other, the assumptions are not that correct making the approach as a one sided.

(ii) Net Operating Income Approach: According to this approach, cost of capital and capital structure are not connected with each other. This means that the pattern of financing has no effect on overall cost of capital. The reason behind this is summarised in the following paragraph.

The graphical presentation of this approach can be as shown below:

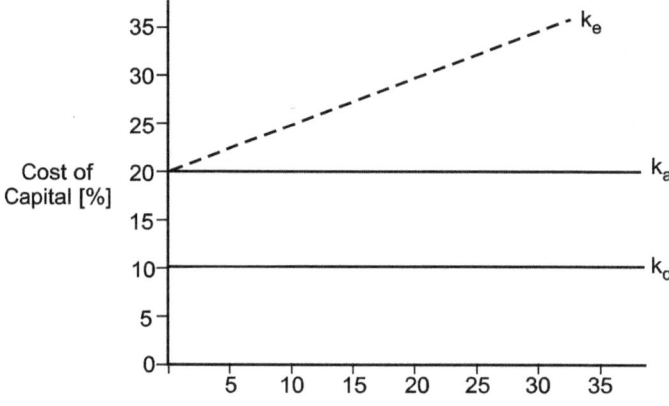

Fig. 5.2: % of Debt in Capital Structure

The approach says that in case a firm increases the proportion of debt in the capital structure, the initial reaction is that, aggregate cost of capital decreases because the cost of debt is less than cost of equity. However, this decrease is compensated by an increase in the cost of equity capital. The cost of equity capital increases because equity shareholders expect more from a risky firm. The firm becomes more risky due to increase in the proportion of debt in the capital structure. Therefore, the aggregate cost of capital remains at the same level as it was before the introduction of debt.

The approach is mainly advocated by **David Durand**, who argued that marked value of the firm depends upon its net operating income and not on the pattern of financing. The change in the leverage changes only the distribution of income. Therefore, the value of the firm remains unchanged, irrespective of the pattern of financing.

(iii) Traditional Approach: This approach resembles to a certain extent the Net Income approach. The similarity is that this approach also says that the aggregate cost of capital reduces with the introduction of more debt in the capital structure. However, this fall in the aggregate cost of capital is not unchecked. A stage comes when the aggregate cost of capital does not fall even after introduction of more debt in the capital structure. It remains constant for some time and after introduction of more debt, the aggregate cost again starts rising. The combination of debt and equity at which the aggregate cost of capital is minimum can be called as *optimum capital structure*. The graphical presentation of this approach can be shown as follows:

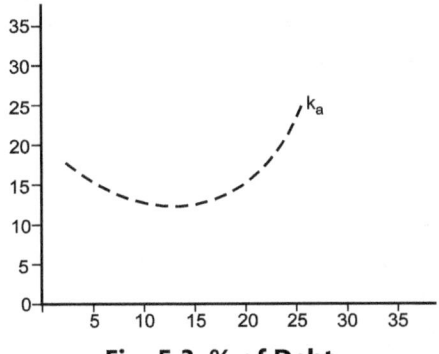

Fig. 5.3: % of Debt

(iv) Modigliani – Miller Approach (MM'): The basic aspect of MM' approach is that the total market value of a firm is equal to its expected operating income divided by the discount rate appropriate to its risk class. The market value, therefore, is not connected with the capital structure. According to MM' approach, a process called as arbitrage process, proves their argument. The arbitrage process is explained below:

Table 5.1: The Arbitrage Process

Particulars	X Ltd. (₹)	Y Ltd. (₹)
Total capital employed	20,00,000	20,00,000
Equity capital	20,00,000	12,00,000
Debt	nil	8,00,000
Net operating income	2,00,000	2,00,000
Interest on loan	nil	40,000 [5%]
Market value of debt	nil	8,00,000
Earnings for equity shareholders	2,00,000	1,60,000
Equity capitalisation rate	10%	12%
Market value of equity	20,00,000	13,33,333
Total market value of the firm	20,00,000	21,33,333

According to the table the value of levered firm Y Ltd. is more than that of levered firm X Ltd. As per the MM' approach, this solution cannot last for long because equity shareholders will sell their equity investments to Y Ltd., and invest in the equity of X. This will be done by substituting corporate leverage by personal leverage. The arbitrage process is explained below.

Suppose a person holds 1% of total equity of Company Y. He will sell this holding for ₹ 13,333.33. He will borrow ₹ 8,000 at 5% rate of interest [he will substitute his company's borrowings with his personal borrowings. Since he was holding 1% of the equity share capital in the company, he will borrow in the same proportion, i.e. 1% of the total borrowings of his company, i.e. ₹ 8000.] With ₹ 13,333.33 + ₹ 8,000 = ₹ 21,333 he will purchase the equity capital in Company X. It will result in the following income. ₹

Income on Investment in X Ltd.	2132
(–) Interest 5% on ₹ 8,000	400
Net income	1732

The net income of ₹ 1732 is higher than a net income of ₹ 1600 that is foregone by the shareholder when he sold shares in Y Ltd.

₹ 1600 being 1% of available profits.

Note: The person is holding 1% of total equity of Company Y. As he is selling that equity, he will borrow ₹ 8,000 which is 1% of the borrowings of Y Ltd. This is known as substitution of personal borrowings to corporate borrowings. As funds available with him are ₹ 21,333 [₹ 13,333.33 + ₹ 8,000] and they are approximately 1.066% of capital employed of company X, he will purchase 1.066% of the equity capital of company X. Therefore, he will be entitled for 1.066% of the earnings available for equity shareholders of company X. The amount comes to ₹ 2132 and after deducting ₹ 400 as interest on borrowings; his net income comes to ₹ 1732. To conclude, it can be said that by maintaining the same proportion of investments in X Ltd., the person can improve his net income from that company. This process is called as the Arbitrage process.

Criticism of MM' Approach: This approach is based on the assumption that the capital markets are perfect. However, in the real world perfections do not exist and, therefore, the capital structure of a firm may affect its valuation.

Another assumption of this approach is that there is an absence of corporate income-tax. This assumption is also unrealistic in the modern context. However, this assumption was removed later.

Conclusion: Due to corporate taxation, it can be said that the cost of capital is definitely by the financial leverage. Due to increase in financial leverage the cost of capital certainly is reduced. However, due to costs like bankruptcy costs and agency costs which increase due to financial leverage, the cost of capital increases. Therefore, it can be concluded that between cost of capital and capital structure, a relationship definitely exists.

5.8 Factors Affecting Capital Structure

Capital structure, which refers to the mix of long term sources of funds such as debentures, term loans, equity capital and reserves is said to be optimum when aggregate cost of capital is minimum. However, in practice, the determination of optimum capital structure is a very difficult task. In designing the capital structure of a company, several factors are to be taken into consideration. Finally, it is the judgement of the decision maker which plays a crucial role in planning of the capital structure.

One thing that must be admitted is that planning is required for designing the capital structure. Even though an optimum capital structure is very difficult to achieve, unplanned capital structure is very dangerous. Companies with unplanned capital structure may be successful in the short-run but in the long-run they may face considerable difficulties. These companies may also be unable to use their funds economically. Therefore, it is extremely necessary to plan their capital structure.

We will now look at the various factors that should be taken into consideration while planning of the capital structure.

(i) EBIT – EPS analysis

The *earnings per share* [EPS] are the amount of profit available per equity share for distribution. The EPS is calculated by dividing the amount of profit available for distribution amongst equity shareholders by the number of equity shares.

Under this approach, EPS is calculated under alternative financing plans, assuming a particular amount of *earnings before interest and tax* [EBIT]. The choice of combination of the sources [capital structure] would be one which results into the highest EPS at a given level of EBIT. This is explained with the help of the following illustration.

FINANCIAL MANAGEMENT — CAPITAL STRUCTURE AND FIRM VALUATION

Illustration:

Progressive company ltd. has the following capital structure

	₹
Equity Capital [₹ 10 each]	10,00,000
15% Debentures	8,00,000
Total	**18,00,000**

The company is planning to raise another ₹ 15,00,000 for modernisation and expansion. The following alternatives are considered:

(a) To raise the entire amount by equity capital [₹ 10 each].

(b) To raise the amount by term loan at an interest rate of 16%.

(c) To raise 50% amount by equity capital and the balance by 16% term loan.

(d) To raise ₹ 8,00,000 by equity capital, ₹ 4,00,000 by 16% term loan and the balance by 14% preference capital.

Assuming an income-tax rate of 50% and an EBIT of ₹ 8,00,000, advise the company about the proper alternative on the basis of EPS.

Solution:

Statement showing EPS under Alternatives I, II, III, IV

Particulars	I [All Equity]	II [All Loan]	III [Term Loan + Equity]	IV [Loan + Equity + Pref. Capital]
	[₹]	[₹]	[₹]	[₹]
A. EBIT	8,00,000	8,00,000	8,00,000	8,00,000
B. Interest [working note 1]	1,20,000	3,60,000	2,40,000	1,84,000
C. EBT [A – B]	6,80,000	4,40,000	5,60,000	6,16,000
D. Income–tax @50%	3,40,000	2,20,000	2,80,000	3,08,000
E. EAT [C – D]	3,40,000	2,20,000	2,80,000	3,08,000
F. Preference dividend	–	–	–	42,000
G. Earnings for equity shareholders [E – F]	3,40,000	2,20,000	2,80,000	2,66,000
H. No. of equity shares [Working note 2]	2,50,000	1,00,000	1,75,000	1,80,000
I. EPS (G ÷ H)	1.36	2.20	1.6	1.47

Since EPS under alternative II is the highest, that alternative can be selected.

FINANCIAL MANAGEMENT   CAPITAL STRUCTURE AND FIRM VALUATION

Working Notes:

1. The amount of interest is calculated as under:

Alternative I:	15% on ₹ 8,00,000	=	₹	1,20,000
Alternative II:	15% on ₹ 80,00,00	=	₹	1,20,000
	16% on ₹ 15,00,000	=	₹	2,40,000
Total			₹	**3,60,000**
Alternative III:	15% on ₹ 8,00,000	=	₹	1,20,000
	16% on ₹ 7,50,000	=	₹	1,20,000
Total			₹	**2,40,000**
Alternative IV:	15% on ₹ 8,00,000	=	₹	1,20,000
	16% on ₹ 4,00,000	=	₹	64,000
Total			₹	**1,84,000**

2. Number of equity shares:

Alternative	**I**	**II**	**III**	**IV**
Existing	1,00,000	1,00,000	1,00,000	1,00,000
New:	1,50,000	–	75,000	80,000
Total	**2,50,000**	**1,00,000**	**1,75,000**	**1,80,000**

Indifference point: An indifferent point is that amount of EBIT at which EPS under different financing plans is the same. If expected level of EBIT is more than the indifferent point, the use of debt would result in higher EPS, than equity. On the other hand if expected level of EBIT is less than the indifference point, alternative involving equity will result in higher EPS. This is illustrated below.

(ii) Cost of capital

As defined earlier, cost of capital is the minimum rate of return expected by the suppliers of a particular source of funds. In case of a risky situation, the expectations of the suppliers of funds are higher because of the risk taken by them. In case of a zero risk situation the expectations are naturally on a lower side.

The key question is whether there is a connection between cost of capital and capital structure? It has been accepted that the cost of debt is less than the cost of equity because of the tax deducibility of interest. Therefore, the aggregate cost of capital comes down if debt is employed in the capital structure. However, the aggregate cost of capital does not come down continuously with the introduction of debt.

After reaching a particular level, the introduction of further debt results in an increase in the aggregate cost of capital, because the debt becomes more costly as the risk increases. The creditors may demand a higher rate of interest to cover the risk which makes the debt more costly.

From the above discussion it can be concluded that at a particular combination of debt and equity, the aggregate cost of capital is the minimum. The combination is different from industry to industry and even from company to company. The aim of capital structure planning, therefore, should be to reach this level of combination. It can be added that other factors should also be considered before capital structure is planned.

(iii) Leverage

Another important factor to be taken into consideration is the analysis of leverages. The meaning, calculations and interpretations of leverages and the connection of leverages with capital structure are discussed below.

Leverage is a very general term which represents influence or power. In financial analysis it can be explained as the influence of one financial variable over the other related financial variable. Leverages are classified into three categories:

(a) Operating leverage

(b) Financial leverage

(c) Combined leverage.

These concepts are explained in the following paragraphs:

(a) Operating leverage: The operating leverage measures the change in the EBIT (Earnings Before Interests and Tax] as a result of change in sales. This leverage arises because of the presence of fixed cost in the cost structure. If fixed cost is nil in the total cost structure, the operating leverage will be nil and the EBIT will change in the same proportion of changes in sales.

The EBIT will change by a higher percentage than the percentage change in sales, if fixed costs are present in the cost structure. A higher operating leverage indicates that the proportion of fixed costs is higher. It also indicates that EBIT will increase at a higher rate than the rate of increase in sales. But at the same time it cannot be overlooked that if the sales decrease, the EBIT will decrease at a higher rate. Therefore, it can be said that operating leverage is a double edged weapon.

Operating leverage is calculated with the help of the following formula:

$$\text{Operating leverage} = \frac{\text{Contribution}}{\text{EBIT}}$$

FINANCIAL MANAGEMENT CAPITAL STRUCTURE AND FIRM VALUATION

Illustration:

Calculate operating leverage from the following information:
(i) Sales – 20000 units @ ₹ 8 per unit
(ii) Variable cost – ₹ 2 per unit
(iii) Fixed costs – ₹ 30,000.

Solution:

	₹
Sales 20,000 units @ ₹ 8 per unit	1,60,000
Less: Variable cost @ ₹ 2 per unit	40,000
Contribution	1,20,000
Less: Fixed costs	30,000
EBIT	90,000

$$\text{Operating leverage} = \frac{\text{Contribution}}{\text{EBIT}}$$

$$= \frac{1,20,000}{90,000}$$

$$= 1.33$$

Interpretation: Operating leverage in the above illustration is 1.33 which means that if sales increases by 1%, the EBIT will increase by 1.33% and if it [sales] decreases by 1%, EBIT will decrease by 1.33%. This can be proved as follows.

Suppose sales increases by 1%

Sales = ₹ 1,60,000 + 1% =	1,61,600
Less Variable costs ₹ 40,000 + 1% =	40,400
Contribution	1,21,200
Less Fixed costs	30,000
EBIT	91,200

The EBIT has increased by 1.33% due to change in sales by 1%.

(b) Financial leverage: Financial leverage measures the percentage change in EBT (Earnings Before Tax) as a result of changes in EBIT. Financial leverage will be higher if the difference between EBIT and EBT is higher. This difference will be higher if amount of interest is higher because the difference between EBIT and EBT is the amount of interest. Therefore, it indicates that if proportion of debt in capital structure is high, the amount of interest and also the financial leverage will be high.

Formula for calculation:

$$\text{Financial leverage} = \frac{\text{EBIT}}{\text{EBT}}$$

Illustration:

Calculate financial leverage from the following:

	₹
Interest	5,000
Sales	50,000
Sales	1000 units
Variable costs	25,000
Fixed costs	15,000

Solution:

	₹
Sales	50,000
Less Variable costs	25,000
Contribution	25,000
Less Fixed costs	15,000
EBIT	10,000
Less Interest	5,000
EBT	5,000

$$\text{Financial leverage} = \frac{\text{EBIT}}{\text{EBT}} = \frac{10,000}{5,000} = 2$$

Interpretation: Financial leverage in the above example is 2, which indicates that if EBIT increases by 1%, EBT will increase by 2%.

The degree of financial leverage [DFL] can be calculated as follows:

$$\text{DFL} = \frac{\Delta \text{EPS}/\text{EPS}}{\Delta \text{EBIT}/\text{EBIT}}$$

The degree of financial leverage explains changes in EPS in response to variations in EBIT. The financial risk refers to variability of EPS caused due to employment of debt capital. The degree of financial leverage as mentioned above helps to identify the financial risk.

(c) Combined leverage: It expresses the relationship between contribution and the taxable income. It helps in finding out the resulting percentage change in taxable income on account of percentage changes in sales.

Combined leverage = Operating leverage × Financial leverage

Illustration:

A company has sales of ₹ 2 lakhs. The variable costs are 40% of sales while fixed costs are ₹ 40,000. The amount of interest on long-term loan is ₹ 10,000. Calculate combined leverage.

Solution:

In order to calculate the combined leverage, fixed operating leverage and then financial leverage will have to be calculated.

	₹
Sales	2,00,000
Less Variable costs	80,000 [40% of sales]
Contribution	1,20,000
Less Fixed costs	40,000
EBIT	80,000
Less Interest	10,000
EBT	70,000

(i) Operating leverage $= \dfrac{\text{Contribution}}{\text{EBIT}}$

$= \dfrac{1,20,000}{80,000} = 1.5$

(ii) Financial leverage $= \dfrac{\text{EBIT}}{\text{EBT}}$

$= \dfrac{80,000}{70,000} = 1.142$

(iii) Combined leverage = Operating leverage × financial leverage
= 1.5 × 1.142 = 1.713

The conclusion that can be drawn from the above discussion is that if operating leverage as well as financial leverage is on the higher side, fresh capital should be raised preferably through equity shares rather than debt. Generally, it is said that one leverage should be low accompanied by the other higher leverage. If operating leverage is on the lower side, financial leverage can be kept on the higher side by employing more debt in the capital structure.

(iv) Analysis of Debt Capacity

Before planning the capital structure it will be highly beneficial to analyse the debt servicing capacity of a firm. The reason for this is that a firm should borrow only that much where it can serve even in adverse conditions. Employment of debt capital results into two types of obligations on a firm: (a) repayment of the principal amount and (b) interest on loan.

One of the tools used for the assessment of debt capacity of a firm is to calculate some key ratios, which are as follows:

(a) Interest coverage ratios: This ratio indicates the coverage of income before interest and tax to annual interest payments. In other words, this ratio indicates as to how many times the income is before interest and taxes as compared to the interest. This ratio is calculated with the help of the following formula.

$$\text{Interest coverage ratio} = \frac{\text{Earnings before interest and tax}}{\text{Annual interest on debt}}$$

The following illustration will clarify the point.

Suppose the EBIT for X Ltd. is ₹ 10,00,000 and the amount of interest is ₹ 2,00,000. The interest coverage ratio will be:

$$\frac{₹\ 10,00,000}{₹\ 2,00,000} = 5 \text{ times}$$

The indication given by the above ratio is that the EBIT is 5 times as compared to the interest.

The main drawback of this ratio is that it takes into consideration only the interest component and not the repayment of principal. Secondly, it takes into account the earnings before interest and tax and not the cash flows. Actually analysis of cash flows is more relevant than the earnings. Another aspect of the ratio is that there is no standard or ideal ratio against which the ratio of a particular firm can be compared.

In order to have a better idea about the debt servicing capacity of a firm, the following ratio is used.

(b) Cash flow coverage ratio: This ratio takes into account, both, the interest payment and the principal payments. The formula is as follows:

$$\text{Cash flow coverage ratio} = \frac{\text{EBIT + Depreciation + Non Cash Expenses}}{\text{Interest on debt} + \frac{\text{Loan repayment instalment}}{[1 - \text{tax rate}]}}$$

Illustration:

The EBIT of XYZ Ltd. is ₹ 25,00,000. Depreciation provided is ₹ 5,00,000. Interest on debt ₹ 2,00,000 and other non-cash expenses are ₹ 3,00,000. The annual installment of loan repayment is ₹ 8,00,000. The cash flow coverage ratio will be as follows:

$$\frac{25,00,000 + 5,00,000 + 3,00,000}{2,00,000 + \frac{8,00,000}{(1 - .50^*)}} = 1.83$$

* Income – tax rate.

This ratio indicates the coverage of cash flows for the interest as well as for principal repayments and, therefore, is definitely a better measure to assess the debt servicing capacity of a firm.

After analysing the above ratios, it can be concluded that if the ratios consistently show a declining trend, it will be dangerous to raise fresh debt. However, it must be mentioned that a cash flow analysis is also required before coming to any decision. Cash flow analysis is explained in the following point.

(v) Cash Flow Analysis

Many times it is seen that a high debt-equity ratio may not necessarily indicate a bad situation because the debt servicing capacity of the firm is quite satisfactory. On the other hand, a low debt ratio may be quite burdensome on a firm as the debt servicing capacity of the firm is quite inadequate. The debt servicing capacity of a firm, indicated by the ratios mentioned above, depends upon the cash flow position of a firm.

It is essential to predict the cash inflows under different situations. The different situations mean optimistic, pessimistic and most likely situations. That level of debt should be maintained, which the firm will be able to service even under pessimistic conditions.

(vi) Control

In designing capital structure of a company, the desire of management to retain control over the company should also be taken into consideration. The promoters of the company can retain their control on the company as long as their holding in the company is more than 50%. To retain the control over the company, it is suggested that there should be issue of debt as the holders of debt do not have any voting rights in the company. Similarly, issue of Preference shares will also not dilute the control of existing management. While raising the debt, care should be taken that it is not disproportionately high, otherwise there will be problems in repayment. The suppliers of debt may also put a lot of restrictions on the companies to protect their interests. A very excessive amount of debt may create liquidity problems which can result in the company being caught in a debt trap. This may invite sickness which means a total loss of control.

Therefore, the conclusion here is that to retain control it is advisable to go in for debt and preference capital but with proper caution so that the company does not turn into a debt loaded company.

(vii) Flexibility

Flexibility refers to the ability of a firm to raise capital from any source it wishes to tap. Flexibility ensures maneuverability to the finance manager. Flexibility can be ensured by keeping some of the debt raising capacity in reserve so that the firm can raise debt whenever need arises. Flexibility can also be ensured by early repayment of debt and preference capital if discretion is available to the company. This will result in replacing a cheaper source of finance with an expensive source of finance. However, flexibility has its own drawbacks especially for a growth firm. In order to keep reserve capacity of debt, a firm may issue equity shares at a time when the market is not favourable. This will not be beneficial to the company in the sense that the selling price of equity shares may be lesser than the intrinsic value based on expected growth.

To conclude, it can be said that the financial plan of the company should ensure such flexibility that the capital structure can be changed as per the operating strategy of the company.

(viii) Timings of the Issue

The situation in the capital market is also one of the important considerations in capital structure planning. The conditions in the capital markets may not be always favourable for tapping a particular source. If there is a general decline in the share prices [including its own share prices] in the stock markets and if the trend is expected to continue in the future, it will be advisable to raise debt from the market at present. In future, when the market is expected to improve, equity shares can be issued. If the situation in the capital market is quite encouraging i.e. shares trading at higher prices, it will be prudent to raise funds by equity shares rather than debt. A word of caution can be added here and that is, even if the situation is favourable for a particular type of issue, reserve capacity for that source should always be kept. For example, if the situation is favourable for debt issue, a company should not exhaust its borrowing powers totally. Similarly, the company should always take advantage of the present situation and not wait for improving the situation in future.

(ix) Growth Rate

Companies which are growing at a faster rate prefer more debt rather than equity. The reason for this is that due to the high financial requirements of the company, issue of shares may prove to be inadequate. Similarly, cost of equity tends to be more than the cost of debt and this is also one of the reasons for preference to debt.

(x) Stability of Earnings

Capital structure planning also depends on the stability of earnings of a company. The debt servicing capacity of a firm depends to a great extent on the cash flows of the firm and the cash flows in turn [operating cash inflows], depend on the stability of its earnings. If the earnings are expected to remain fairly stable in the future, a firm can afford to rely more on the debt than equity. The reason is that its debt servicing capacity is fairly high in such cases. On the other hand, if the earnings are expected to fluctuate violently in the future, conservative ways of financing like equity shares should be tapped.

(xi) Attitude of the Lenders

Sometimes, the attitude of the lenders may not be positive in sanctioning debts. In such cases, it is always better to rely on shares. In some cases, especially institutional lenders may put more and more restrictions on the borrowers. This also may lead firms to rely more on shares than on debt.

(xii) Taxation Structure in the Country

If the rates of taxes in the country are high, debt is cheaper than equity, as the interest on debt is a tax deductible item for calculation of taxable income. But as mentioned earlier, there should not be an overdose of debt only because it is cheaper. The debt servicing capacity of the firm should always be kept in mind while raising the debt.

FINANCIAL MANAGEMENT — CAPITAL STRUCTURE AND FIRM VALUATION

Conclusion: Planning of capital structure is a very crucial decision for a finance manager. Efforts should be made to achieve an optimum capital structure. But, optimum capital structure is very difficult to achieve in practice and, therefore, atleast capital structure should be designed after considering the above mentioned points.

5.9 Trading on Equity

A company earns profit on its total capital. On the borrowed capital, company pays interest or dividend at a fixed rate. If this fixed rate is lower than the general rate of earnings of the company, the ordinary shareholders will have an advantage in the form of additional profits. This may be referred to as *trading on equity*. This trading on equity is an arrangement under which a company makes use of borrowed funds including preference capital bearing a fixed rate of interest or dividend in such a way as to increase the rate of return on equity shares. The rate of dividend on equity shares could not otherwise go beyond the general rate of earning if whole of its capital is raised by the issue of equity shares.

For example, suppose a company requires a total sum of ₹ 5,00,000 which may fetch a return of 10 %.. If a company raises its entire capital by the issue of equity shares, it cannot declare a dividend at more than 10 %. But suppose the company raises ₹ 5,00,000 (the entire investment) in the following manner:

1. By issuing 6% debt - ₹ 2,00,000
2. By issuing 8% Preference share - ₹ 1,00,000
3. By issuing of equity share - ₹ 2,00,000

In this case the company will have to pay out of the profits of ₹ 50,000 (10% on total investment) earned by it, a sum of ₹ 12,000 as interest to the debt holders and ₹ 8000 as dividends to preference shareholders. A sum of ₹ 30,000 will be available for paying dividends to the equity shareholders. Since the amount of equity share capital is ₹ 2,00,000, the rate of dividend on such shares shall be 15%. In this way the rate of dividend on equity shares can be increased by issuing debentures or/and preference shares bearing a rate of interest/dividend below the general rate of return. Company will also have an advantage in the saving of income tax as interest paid on debentures is a deductible expense. This double advantage tempts management to trade on equity.

Solved Problems

Capital Structure

Problem 1

A limited company is considering different methods to finance its investment proposal. It is estimated that initially ₹ 40,00,000 will be needed. Two alternative methods are available for raising the funds:

(i) To raise ₹ 20,00,000 by sale of equity shares of ₹ 100 each and balance at 18% term loan.

(ii) To raise the entire amount by sale of equity shares of ₹ 100 each.

FINANCIAL MANAGEMENT

CAPITAL STRUCTURE AND FIRM VALUATION

The existing capital structure of the company consists of:

(i) 50,000 equity shares of ₹ 100 each and

(ii) 17% term loan of ₹ 20,00,000.

The expected EBIT (Earnings before interest and tax) is ₹ 15,00,000. Advise the company on the basis of EPS (Earnings per share) in each alternative. Income tax rate can be taken as 50%

Solution:

Statement showing earnings per share under different alternatives.

Particulars	Alternative I [₹ 20,00,000 Equity ₹ 20,00,000 Debt at 18%] ₹	II [All equity] ₹
A. EBIT (Earnings before interest and tax)	15,00,000	15,00,000
B. Interest on loan		
(i) Existing	3,40,000	3,40,000
(ii) Fresh	3,60,000	–
Total – [B]	**7,00,000**	**3,40,000**
C. Earnings before tax [A – B]	8,00,000	11,60,000
D. Income tax at 50%	4,00,000	5,80,000
E. Earnings after tax [C – D]	4,00,000	5,80,000
F. Number of equity shares [Existing + New]	70,000	90,000
G. Earnings per share [E ÷ F]	5.71	6.44

Conclusion: Since EPS is higher in case of alternative II involving sale of equity shares, it is advisable to use that source.

Problem 2

A new project under consideration by your company requires a capital investment of ₹ 150 lakhs. The required funds can be raised either through the sale of equity shares or borrowed from a financial institution. Interest on term loan is 15% and tax rate is 50%. If the debt–equity ratio of 2 : 1 is to be maintained calculate the indifference point of the project.

FINANCIAL MANAGEMENT   CAPITAL STRUCTURE AND FIRM VALUATION

Solution:

Capital investment of ₹ 150 lakhs is to be made. If a debt-equity ratio of 2 : 1 is to be maintained, equity will be 1/3rd i.e. ₹ 50 lakhs and debt will be 2/3rd i.e. ₹ 100 lakhs. The indifference point is calculated as follows:

$$\frac{x[1-t]}{N_1} = \frac{[x-I][1-t]}{N_2}$$

where,
x = EBIT at indifference level
t = Income tax rate
I = Interest
N_1 = No. of equity shares in alternative I
N_2 = No. of equity shares in alternative II

Therefore, $\quad \dfrac{x[1-.50]}{1,50,00,000} = \dfrac{[x-5,00,000][1-.50]}{50,00,000}$

x = **₹ 22,50,000**

Note: In the illustration, the value of equity shares on per share basis is not given and therefore, in N_1 and N_2 the total values of equity shares is taken instead of the number of shares.

Problem 3

XYZ Ltd. has currently an ordinary share capital of ₹ 250 lakhs consisting of equity shares of ₹ 100 each. The company is planning to raise another ₹ 200 lakhs for financing a major expansion programme. The following four options are available.

(i) Entirely through ordinary shares.

(ii) ₹ 100 lakhs through ordinary shares and the balance by 15% term loan.

(iii) ₹ 50 lakh through ordinary shares, ₹ 150 lakhs through long-term borrowing at 15% rate of interest.

(iv) ₹ 100 lakhs through ordinary shares, and ₹ 100 lakhs through preference shares with 14% dividend.

Expected EBIT of the company is ₹ 80 lakhs. Calculate EPS under each alternative and advise the company about the most beneficial alternative.

Income-tax rate can be taken as 50%.

FINANCIAL MANAGEMENT — CAPITAL STRUCTURE AND FIRM VALUATION

Solution:

EPS under different alternatives:

Particulars	Alternative I [Ordinary shares]	II [100 lakhs Ordinary Shares 100 lakhs balance term loan]	III [50 lakhs Ordinary Shares 150 lakhs term loan]	IV [100 lakhs Ordinary Shares 100 lakhs Pref.]
	[₹]	[₹]	[₹]	[₹]
A. EBIT	80,00,000	80,00,000	80,00,000	80,00,000
B. Interest	–	15,00,000	22,50,000	–
C. Earnings before tax [A – B]	80,00,000	65,00,000	57,50,000	80,00,000
D. Income-tax at 50%	40,00,000	32,50,000	28,75,000	40,00,000
E. EAT [C – D]	40,00,000	32,50,000	28,75,000	40,00,000
Less: Pref. Dividend	–	–	–	14,00,000
Earnings of equity	40,00,000	32,50,000	28,75,000	26,00,000
F. No. of equity shares	4,50,000	3,50,000	3,00,000	3,50,000
G. EPS [E ÷ F]	8.88	9.28	9.58	7.42

Conclusion: As per the above statement, earnings per share under Alternative III involving equity issue of ₹ 50 lakhs and term loan of ₹ 150 lakhs, is the highest. Therefore, it is advisable to follow that alternative:

---

*Pref. dividend

Problem 4

A company gives you the following figures:

Particulars	Amount (₹)
Profit before interest and tax	24,00,000
Less Interest on debentures @12.5%	2,00,000
Interest on long term loans @ 16%	2,00,000
Total Interest	**4,00,000**
Profit before tax	20,00,000
Less Income-tax at 50%	**10,00,000**
Profit after tax	10,00,000
Number of equity shares [₹ 10 each]	4,00,000
Earnings per share	2.50
Current market price	20.00
Price earnings ratio	8

FINANCIAL MANAGEMENT   CAPITAL STRUCTURE AND FIRM VALUATION

The company has undistributed reserves and profits of ₹ 81,50,000. The company needs to raise ₹ 36,00,000 for repayment of debentures and modernisation of plants. Two alternative sources are available for raising this money.

(i) Raising the entire amount through term loans @18% interest.

(ii) Raising partially by sale of ₹ 1,00,000 equity shares at an expected price of ₹ 18 per share and the balance through term loan @16% interest.

The company expects that the rate of return i.e. before tax and interest on funds employed will improve by 4% because of modernisation and if debt–equity ratio [debt/debt plus shareholders funds] exceeds 25% the P/E ratio will go down to 6.

Advise the company about the proper course of action.

Solution:

Statement showing Evaluation of Alternative Financing Plans

	Particulars	Plan I [Term loan @16%] ₹	Plan II [Equity ₹ 18,00,000 16% Debt ₹ 18,00,000] ₹
I.	Earnings before interest and tax [Working note no 1]	34,00,000	34,00,000
II.	Interest		
	(a) Existing	2,00,000	2,00,000
	(b) Fresh	5,76,000	2,88,000
	Total – (II)	**7,76,000**	**4,88,000**
III.	Earnings before tax (I – II)	26,24,000	29,12,000
IV.	Income-tax @50%	13,12,000	14,56,000
V.	Earnings after tax (III – IV)	13,12,000	14,56,000
VI.	No. of equity shares	4,00,000	5,00,000
VII.	Earnings per share [V ÷ VI]	**₹ 3.28**	**₹ 2.91**
VIII.	Price earnings ratio	6 times	8 times
IX.	Market price per share [VII × VIII]	₹ 19.68	R. 23.28

Plan No. II, involving combination of equity and term loan, is better than Plan I as it maximises market price of equity shares.

FINANCIAL MANAGEMENT

CAPITAL STRUCTURE AND FIRM VALUATION

Working Notes:

1. EBIT percentage on capital employed is expected to increase by 4% after modernisation. The capital employed is calculated as follows:

Particulars	Capital employed before modernisation ₹	Capital employed after modernisation ₹
Equity Capital	40,00,000	40,00,000
Reserves and Surplus	81,50,000	81,50,000
12.5% Debentures	16,00,000	Repaid
16% Term loan	12,50,000	12,50,000
Additional funds		36,00,000
Total	**1,50,00,000**	**1,70,00,000**

EBIT at present is ₹ 24,00,000 which is 16% on capital employed, i.e. ₹ 1,50,00,000. After modernisation it will be 20% on ₹ 1,70,00,000 i.e. ₹ 34,00,000.

2. Debt to equity ratio after raising debt of ₹ 36,00,000 will be as follows:

$$\frac{36,00,000 + 12,50,000}{36,00,000 + 12,50,000 + 40,00,000 + 81,50,000} \times 100 = 28.52\%$$

Since it is more than 25%, as per information given in the example, the P/E ratio is reduced to 6 from the present 8 times.

Problem 5

A company wants to have an optimum mix of debt and equity. The cost of debt and cost of equity at a different debt equity ratio is as follows:

Debt equity ratio	Cost of debt % [Post-tax]	Cost of equity [%]
—	—	12.5
10 : 90	.05	13.0
20 : 80	.05	13.6
30 : 70	.06	14.3
40 : 60	.07	16.0
50 : 50	.08	18.0
60 : 40	.10	20.0

What is the optimum capital structure of the company?

Calculation of combined cost of capital.

FINANCIAL MANAGEMENT

CAPITAL STRUCTURE AND FIRM VALUATION

Solution:

Debt–equity ratio	Cost of debt post–tax [%]	Cost of equity [%]	Combined cost [%]
–	–	12.5	12.5
10 : 90	.05	13.0	.10 × .05 + .90 × .13 = 12.2
20 : 80	.05	13.6	.20 × .05 + .80 × .136 = 11.88
30 : 70	.06	14.3	.30 × .06 + .70 × 14.3 = 11.81
40 : 60	.07	16	.40 × .07 + .60 × 16 = 12.4
50 : 50	.08	18	.50 × .08 + .50 × .18 = 13
60 : 40	.10	20	.60 × .10 + .40 × .20 = 14

From the above table at a combination of 30: 70 debt (–) equity the aggregate cost of capital is minimum and, therefore, it is an optimum capital structure.

Problem 6

A company needs ₹ 5,00,000 for modernisation. The following three plans are available. (i) Issue of 50,000 equity shares of ₹ 10 per share. (ii) Issue of ₹ 25,000 equity shares of ₹ 10 per share and 2,500 debenture of ₹ 100 each at 14% rate of interest. (iii) Issue of 25,000 equity shares and the balance through 10% preference shares.

If the company's earnings before interest and tax are ₹ 10,000, ₹ 20,000, ₹ 40,000, ₹ 60,000 and ₹ 1,00,000, what will be the earnings per share under each of the three financial plans? Assume an income–tax rate of 50%.

Solution:

Statement showing EPS

Financial Plan I

	₹	₹	₹	₹	₹
EBIT	10,000	20,000	40,000	60,000	1,00,000
Less: Interest	nil	nil	nil	nil	nil
Earnings before tax	10,000	20,000	40,000	60,000	1,00,000
Less: Income–tax at 50%	5,000	10,000	20,000	30,000	50,000
Earnings after tax	5,000	10,000	20,000	30,000	50,000
No. of Eq. shares EPS	50,000	50,000	50,000	50,000	50,000
[EAT ÷ No. of Shares]	.10	.20	.40	.60	1.00

FINANCIAL MANAGEMENT — CAPITAL STRUCTURE AND FIRM VALUATION

Financial Plan II

	₹	₹	₹	₹	₹
EBIT	10,000	20,000	40,000	60,000	1,00,000
Less: Interest	35,000	35,000	35,000	35,000	35,000
Earnings before tax	(25,000)	(15,000)	5,000	25,000	65,000
Less: Income–tax at 50%	(12,500)	(7,500)	2,500	12,500	32,500
Earnings after tax	(12,500)	(7,500)	2,500	12,500	32,500
No. of Eq. shares	25,000	25,000	25,000	25,000	25,000
EPS	(.50)	(.30)	.10	.50	1.3

Financial Plan III

	₹	₹	₹	₹	₹
EBIT	10,000	20,000	40,000	60,000	1,00,000
Less: Interest	nil	nil	nil	nil	nil
Earnings before tax	10,000	20,000	40,000	60,000	1,00,000
Less: Income–tax at 50%	5,000	10,000	20,000	30,000	50,000
Earnings after tax	5,000	10,000	20,000	30,000	50,000
Less: Pref. dividend	25,000	25,000	25,000	25,000	25,000
Earnings for Equity Shareholders	(20,000)	(15,000)	(5,000)	5,000	25,000
No. of Equity shares	25,000	25,000	25,000	25,000	25,000
EPS	(.80)	(.60)	(.20)	.20	1

Conclusion: The selection of a financial plan depends upon the EBIT. If sales are increasing, EPS under the second plan will be the highest. If sales are either remaining stagnant or reducing, equity shares will be the best alternative.

Problem 7

AB Ltd. needs ₹ 10,00,000 for expansion. The expansion is expected to yield an annual EBIT of ₹ 1,60,000. In choosing a financial plan, AB Ltd. has an objective of maximising earnings per share. It is considering the possibility of issuing equity shares and raising debt of ₹ 1,00,000 or ₹ 4,00,000 or ₹ 6,00,000. The market price per share currently is ₹ 50 and is expected to drop upto ₹ 40, if funds are borrowed in excess of ₹ 5,00,000. Funds can be borrowed at the rates indicated below:

(a) Upto ₹ 1,00,000 @ 8%,
(b) Over ₹ 1,00,000 upto ₹ 5,00,000 @12%
(c) Over ₹ 5,00,000 @ 18%

Assuming a tax rate of 50%, calculate EPS under the three financing plans.

FINANCIAL MANAGEMENT — CAPITAL STRUCTURE AND FIRM VALUATION

Solution:

Statement showing calculation of EPS

Particulars	Alternatives		
	I [Debt ₹ 1,00,000]	II [Debt ₹ 4,00,000]	III [Debt ₹ 6,00,000]
EBIT	1,60,000	1,60,000	1,60,000
Less: Interest	8,000	44,000	74,000
Earnings before tax	1,52,000	1,16,000	86,000
Less: Income tax 50%	76,000	58,000	43,000
Earnings after tax	76,000	58,000	43,000
No. of shares	36,000	24,000	20,000
EPS [EAT ÷ No. of shares]	2.11	2.42	2.15

EPS is highest in alternative II and so Alternative II should be selected.

Working notes:

The interest is calculated as follows:

Alternative II:	8% on ₹ 1,00,000	=	8,000
	12% on ₹ 3,00,000	=	36,000
	Total		**44,000**
Alternative III:	8% on ₹ 1,00,000	=	8,000
	12% on ₹ 4,00,000	=	48,000
	18% on ₹ 1,00,000	=	18,000
	Total		**74,000**

Leverages

Problem 8

From the following figures, calculate operating, financial and combined leverages of Aditya Ltd. and Amar Ltd.

Particulars	Aditya Ltd.	Amar Ltd.
Selling price per unit	₹ 75	₹ 75
Profit volume ratio	40%	60%
Fixed costs	₹ 40,00,000	₹ 60,00,000
Capital structure:		
Equity capital	₹ 20,00,000	₹ 35,00,000
Term loan	₹ 15,00,000 at 18%	₹ 10,00,000 at 17%
Production capacity	2,00,000 units p.a.	3,50,000 units p.a.
Capacity utilisation	90%	80%

Solution:

Profitability Statement of Aditya Ltd. & Amar Ltd.

Particulars	Aditya Ltd.	Amar Ltd.
Production units	1,80,000	2,80,000
Selling price per unit	₹ 75	₹ 75
Sales value (Production × Price p/u]	1,35,00,000	2,10,00,000
Contribution:		
40% of sales	54,00,000	
60% of sales		1,26,00,000
Less: Fixed cost	40,00,000	60,00,000
EBIT	14,00,000	66,00,000
Less: Interest	2,70,000	1,70,000
EBT	**11,30,000**	**64,30,000**

Operating leverage $= \dfrac{\text{Contribution}}{\text{EBIT}}$

Aditya Ltd. ₹ $\dfrac{54,00,000}{14,00,000}$ = 3.85

Amar Ltd. ₹ $\dfrac{1,26,00,000}{66,00,000}$ = 1.90

Financial leverage $= \dfrac{\text{EBIT}}{\text{EBT}}$

Aditya Ltd. $\dfrac{14,00,000}{11,30,000}$ = 1.23

Amar Ltd. $\dfrac{66,00,000}{64,30,000}$ = 1.02

Combined leverage: Operating × Financial leverage

Aditya Ltd. = 3.85 × 1.23 = 4.735

Amar Ltd. = 1.90 × 1.02 = 1.938

Conclusion: From the above calculations, it is clear that leverages for Aditya Ltd. are greater than that of Amar Ltd. Therefore, risk is higher for Aditya Ltd. than Amar Ltd. comparatively.

FINANCIAL MANAGEMENT   CAPITAL STRUCTURE AND FIRM VALUATION

Problem 9

From the following particulars, calculate the operating, financial and combined leverages.

Balance Sheet of Zenith Ltd. as on 31st March, 2013

Liabilities	₹	Assets	₹
Equity share capital		Fixed Assets [Net]	21,00,000
[₹ 10 each]	12,00,000	Current Assets	19,00,000
15% Debentures	8,00,000		
General Reserve	7,00,000		
Current liabilities	13,00,000		
Total	**40,00,000**	**Total**	**40,00,000**

Additional Information:

1. The earnings before interest and tax (EBIT) is 20% on sales for the year ended 31st March 2013.
2. The profit volume ratio is 40%.
3. The total asset turnover [Sales/Total asset] for the year is 2.

Solution:

The total asset turnover is 2 and therefore Sales are ₹ 40,00,000 × 2. ₹ 80,00,000 p/v ratio is 40%.

Therefore, contribution = ₹ 32,00,000 [40% of sales]

EBIT = 20% on sales = ₹ 16,00,000

(i) Operating leverage = $\dfrac{\text{Contribution}}{\text{EBIT}}$

= $\dfrac{32,00,000}{16,00,000}$ = 2

(ii) Financial leverage = $\dfrac{\text{EBIT}}{\text{EBT}}$ = $\dfrac{16,00,000}{14,80,000}$ = 1.08

[EBT = ₹ 16,00,000 − ₹ 1,20,000]

Interest on Debentures

(iii) Combined leverage = Operating leverage × Financial leverage

= 2 × 1.08

= 2.16

Comment: All the leverages for the company are quite low and, therefore, operating, financial and combined risks are quite low.

FINANCIAL MANAGEMENT — CAPITAL STRUCTURE AND FIRM VALUATION

Problem 10

From the following particulars, prepare income statements of Sure Ltd., Slow Ltd., and Fast Ltd., for the year ended 31st March 2013.

Particulars	Sure Ltd.	Slow Ltd.	Fast Ltd.
Operating leverage	5	6	4
Financial leverage	4	5	3
Interest [₹]	3,000	4,000	2,000
p/v ratio	40%	25%	50%
Income-tax rate	50%	50%	50%

Solution:

Income statements

Particulars	Sure Ltd.	Slow Ltd.	Fast Ltd.
A. Sales	50,000	1,20,000	24,000
B. Variable cost	30,000	90,000	12,000
C. Contribution [A – B]	20,000	30,000	12,000
D. Fixed cost	16,000	25,000	9,000
E. EBIT [C – D]	4,000	5,000	3,000
F. Interest cost	3,000	4,000	2,000
G. EBT [E – F]	1,000	1,000	1,000
H. Income-tax 50%	500	500	500
I. EAT [G – H]	500	500	500

Working notes:

$$\text{Operating leverage} = \frac{\text{Contribution}}{\text{EBIT}}$$

Contribution – Fixed cost = EBIT

$$\text{Financial leverage} = \frac{\text{EBIT}}{\text{EBT}}$$

EBIT – Interest = EBT

For Sure Ltd., Financial leverage is 4 which means EBIT is 4 times of EBT. In other words if EBIT is 4, EBT is 1 which means interest = 3 [4 – 1 = 3].

Now, if interest	= 3	= ₹ 3,000		
	4	= ₹ 4,000	= EBIT	
Similarly, for Slow Ltd.	= 4	= ₹ 4,000		
	5	= ₹ 5,000	= EBIT	
Fast Ltd.	2	= 2,000		
	3	= ₹ 3,000	= EBIT	

From operating leverage and EBIT, contribution for all the companies can be calculated.

Contribution = Operating leverage × EBIT

Sure Ltd.	5 × 4,000 =	₹ 20,000
Slow Ltd.	6 × 5,000 =	₹ 30,000
Fast Ltd.	4 × 3,000 =	₹ 12,000

Sales for all the companies can be calculated from p/v ratio and contribution.

Sure Ltd.: p/v ratio 40% contribution ₹ 20,000.

Sales = ₹ 50,000

Slow Ltd.   p/v ratio = 60%

Contribution = ₹ 30,000

Sales = ₹ 1,20,000

Fast Ltd.   p/v ratio = 50%

Contribution = ₹ 12,000

Sales = ₹ 24,000

Fixed cost is the difference between contribution and EBIT.

Note: EBIT = Earnings before interest and tax

EBT = Earnings before tax

EAT = Earnings after tax

Problem 11

Calculate the operating leverage, financial leverage and combined leverage from the following details:

Selling price per unit = ₹ 150

Variable cost per unit = ₹ 100

Fixed costs = ₹ 6,00,000

Production & sales = 20,000 units

The capital structure of the company under alternate financing plan is as follows:

Particulars	Plan I ₹	Plan II ₹
Equity Capital	20,00,000	10,00,000
16% Debentures	10,00,000	20,00,000
Total	**30,00,000**	**30,00,000**

Solution:

Calculation of leverages:

	Particulars	Plan I ₹	Plan II ₹
A.	Sales units	20,000	20,000
B.	Sales value [₹ 150 per unit]	30,00,000	30,00,000
C.	Variable cost [per unit ₹ 100]	20,00,000	20,00,000
D.	Contribution [B – C]	10,00,000	10,00,000
E.	Fixed costs	6,00,000	6,00,000
F.	EBIT [D – E]	4,00,000	4,00,000
G.	Interest	1,60,000	3,20,000
H.	EBT [F – G]	2,40,000	80,000

1. Operating leverage = $\dfrac{\text{Contribution}}{\text{EBIT}}$

   = $\dfrac{10,00,000}{4,00,000}$

   = 2.5

   Since fixed cost is the same for both, Plan I and Plan II, operating leverage is same for both the plans.

2. Financial leverage = $\dfrac{\text{EBIT}}{\text{EBT}}$

   Plan I = $\dfrac{4,00,000}{2,40,000}$ = 1.66

   Plan II = $\dfrac{4,00,000}{80,000}$ = 5

3. Combined leverage = Operating leverage × Financial leverage

   Plan I   2.5 × 1.66 = 4.15

   Plan II 2.5 × 5 = 12.5

Conclusion: In Plan II, since major amount is raised by debentures, the plan is more risky. It is clearly shown by the higher financial leverage accompanied by high combined leverage.

Problem 12

The income statement of a company is as follows:

Particulars	Amount [₹]
Sales	20,00,000
Variable costs [70%]	14,00,000
Contribution	6,00,000
Fixed costs	5,00,000
Earnings before interest & tax	1,00,000

FINANCIAL MANAGEMENT — CAPITAL STRUCTURE AND FIRM VALUATION

The capital structure of the company is as follows:

	₹
Equity Capital [₹ 10 each]	2,50,000
14% Debt	1,50,000
Total	**4,00,000**

Calculate:
1. The earnings per share
2. The percentage change in EPS as a result of 25% increase and decrease in sales.
3. Financial leverage. [Income–tax rate is 50%]

Solution:

1. Statement of EPS at existing level of sales

Particulars	Amount [₹]
Earnings before interest and tax	1,00,000
Less: Interest and debt	21,000
Earnings before tax	79,000
No. of equity shares	25,000
Earnings per share	3.16

2. Statement showing changes in EPS

Particulars	+ 25% in sales [₹]	– 25% in sales [₹]
Sales	25,00,000	15,00,000
Less: Variable costs [70%]	17,50,000	10,50,000
Contribution	7,50,000	4,50,000
Less: Fixed costs	5,00,000	(5,00,000)
EBIT	2,50,000	(50,000)
Less: Income–tax	1,25,000	(25,000)
EBT	1,25,000	(25,000)
EPS	5	(1)
Change in EPS	+ 58.22	—

3. Financial leverage $= \dfrac{\text{EBIT}}{\text{EBT}}$

At present $= \dfrac{1,00,000}{79,000} = 1.26$

Increase of 25% $= \dfrac{2,50,000}{1,25,000} = 2$

Cost of Capital

Problem 13

Annual net profit earned by a company amounted to ₹ 50,000. It is expected that retained earnings can be invested by the shareholders in a similar type of company @10%. If the same are distributed among the shareholders, the shareholders also have to incur by way of brokerage and commission @3% of the net dividends. Rate of tax is 40%. Calculate the cost of retained earnings.

Solution:

The calculation of cost of retained earnings can be done with the help of the following formula:

$$k_r = k_e (1 - t)(1 - b)$$

where
- k_r = cost of retained earnings
- k_e = cost of equity capital
- t = taxation rate
- b = brokerage and / or commission.

Therefore, $k_r = .10 (1 - .40)(1 - .03)$
= 5.82%

Problem 14

A company issues 10% debentures for ₹ 2,00,000. Rate of income tax is 40%. Calculate the cost of debt if the debentures are issued:

(i) at par,
(ii) at a discount of 10%, and
(iii) at a premium of 10%.

Solution:

The cost of debt is always post-tax cost.
The formula for calculating the same is as follows:

$$k_d = \frac{I}{P}[1 - t]$$

where,
- k_d = Cost of debt,
- I = Annual interest payment,
- P = Net proceeds
- t = Taxation rate.

(i) Debt issued at par

$$k_d = \frac{20{,}000}{2{,}00{,}000}[1 - .40] = 6\%$$

(ii) Debt issued at discount of 10%

$$k_d = \frac{20{,}000}{1{,}80{,}000}[1 - .40] = 6.6\%$$

FINANCIAL MANAGEMENT   CAPITAL STRUCTURE AND FIRM VALUATION

(iii) Debt issued at a premium of 10%

$$k_d = \frac{20,000}{2,20,000} [1 - .40] = 5.45$$

Note: Since the period of repayment is not mentioned, it is not taken into consideration.

Problem 15

X Ltd. has the following capital structure

	₹
Equity share capital [20,000 shares]	4,00,000
6% Preference shares	1,00,000
8% Debentures	3,00,000
	8,00,000

The market price of equity share is ₹ 20. It is expected that the company will pay a current dividend of ₹ 2 per share which will grow @ 7% forever. Rate of tax is 40%. Calculate the weighted average cost of capital.

Solution:

Before we calculate weighted average cost of capital, specific cost of capital will have to be calculated.

(i) Cost of Equity Capital $k_e = \frac{D}{P} + g$

where, D = Dividend per share
P = Market price
g = Growth rate

$$= \frac{2}{20} + .07 = .17$$

(ii) Cost of Debentures = $k_d = (1 - t) R$
$$= (1 - .40) .08$$
$$= .048 \text{ or } 4.8\%$$

(iii) Cost of Pref. Capital $= k_p = \dfrac{PD + \left[\dfrac{P - NP}{n}\right]}{\dfrac{P + NP}{2}}$

where PD = Preference dividend
P = Face value
NP = Net proceeds
n = Number of years

$$\therefore k_p = \frac{6 + \left[\dfrac{100 - 100}{10}\right]}{\dfrac{100 + 100}{2}} = .06$$

Note: It is assumed in the absence of information that the face value and net proceeds from the preference share are ₹ 100 each and their redemption period is 10 years.

FINANCIAL MANAGEMENT   CAPITAL STRUCTURE AND FIRM VALUATION

Weighted Average Cost of Capital:

Sources	Amount	Capital structure proportion [weights]	Specific cost	Weighted average cost
Equity Capital	4,00,000	.50	.17	0.085
Preference Capital	1,00,000	.125	.048	0.006
8% Debentures	3,00,000	.375	.060	0.0225
Total	**8,00,000**	**1.000**		**0.1135 or 11.35**

Weighted average cost = 11.35%

Problem 16

M/s. ABC & Co. has the following capital structure as on 31st March 2013.

Particulars	Amount (₹)
12% Debentures	3,00,000
9% Preference shares	2,00,000
Equity – 5,000 shares of ₹ 100 each	5,00,000
Total	**10,00,000**

The equity shares of the company are quoted at ₹ 102 and expected dividend is ₹ 9 per share for 2012-13. A growth rate of 7% was registered in the past which is expected to be maintained. On the assumption that the applicable income-tax rate for the company is 40%, calculate the weighted average cost of capital.

Solution:

The calculation of specific cost of capital will have to be done before calculating the weighted average cost of capital.

(i) Cost of Equity Capital:

$$k_e = \frac{D}{P} + g = \frac{9}{102} + .07 = .1582$$

(ii) Cost of Preference Capital

$$k_p = \frac{PD + \left[\frac{P - NP}{n}\right]}{\frac{P + NP}{2}} = \frac{9 + \left[\frac{100 - 100}{10}\right]}{\frac{100 + 100}{2}} = \frac{9}{\frac{200}{2}} = .09$$

Note: It is assumed that face value and net proceeds of preference shares are ₹ 100 each and the redemption period is 10 years.

(iii) Cost of Debentures:

$$k_d = [1 - t] R$$
$$= [1 - .40] \cdot .12 = .072$$

5.41

Calculation of weighted average cost of capital:

Source	Amount (₹)	Capital structure proportion [weight]	Specific cost	Weighted average cost
Equity Capital	5,00,000	.50	.1582	.0791
Pref. Capital	2,00,000	.20	.09	.018
12% Debentures	3,00,000	.30	.072	.0216
	10,00,000			.1187

Weighted average cost of capital = 11.87%

Problem 17

From the following data, calculate the value of each firm as per the Modigliani Miller approach.

Particulars	Firm A (₹)	Firm B (₹)	Firm C (₹)
Earnings before interest and tax	13,00,000	13,00,000	13,00,000
Number of shares	3,00,000	3,00,000	3,00,000
12% Debentures	–	9,00,000	10,00,000

Every firm expects 12% return on investments.

Solution:

According to Modigliani Miller approach, the market value of the firm is calculated by the following formula,

$$V_m = \frac{EBIT}{k_o}$$

where, EBIT = Earnings before interest and tax,
k_o = Overall cost of capital,
V_m = Total market value of the firm.

$$V_m = \frac{13,00,000}{.12} = ₹ 108.33 \text{ lakhs}$$

Since EBIT and overall cost of capital for each of the firm is the same, value of every firm will be the same. Number of shares and debentures are not relevant.

Overall cost of capital is equal to expected rate of return on investment.

Problem 18

Assuming that a company pays income-tax @ 40%, calculate the after-tax cost of capital in the following cases:

(a) A 8.5% preference share sold at par redeemable after 5 years.
(b) A perpetual bond with 8% rate of interest.
(c) A ten years 8% ₹ 1,000 debenture sold at ₹ 950 less 4% underwriting commission.
(d) A preference share sold at ₹ 100 with 9% dividend and redemption price of ₹ 110 and redemption period of 7 years.
(e) An ordinary share selling at a market price of ₹ 120 and current dividend of ₹ 9 per share which is expected to grow at 8%.

Solution:

(a) $$k_p = \frac{PD + \left[\frac{P - NP}{n}\right]}{\frac{P + NP}{2}} = \frac{8.5 + \left[\frac{100 - 100}{5}\right]}{\frac{100 + 100}{2}} = 8.5\%$$

Note: The par value and net proceeds are presumed to be ₹ 100 each.

(b) $k_d = [1 - t] R = [1 - .40] .08 = .048$ or 4.8%

(c) $$k_d = \frac{I + \left[\frac{P - NP}{2}\right]}{\frac{P + NP}{2}}$$

$$= \frac{80 + \left[\frac{1000 - 910}{2}\right]}{\frac{1000 + 910}{2}} = 13.08\%$$

This 13.08% is the pre-tax cost of debentures. The post-tax cost is calculated as follows:
$k_d = [1 - .40] . 13.08 = 7.84\%$

$$k_d = \frac{PD + \left[\frac{P - NP}{n}\right]}{\frac{P + NP}{2}}$$

$$= \frac{9 + \left[\frac{110 - 100}{7}\right]}{\frac{110 + 100}{2}} = \frac{10.42}{105} = .0992 \text{ or } 9.92\%$$

Note: P = Redemption value, if redemption value is different from face value.

(e) $k_e = \frac{D}{P} + g = \frac{9}{120} + .08 = .155$ or 15.5%

Problem 19

A company has the following long-term capital outstanding as on 31st March 2013.
(a) 10% Debentures with a face value of ₹ 5,00,000, [₹ 1000 each] redemption period of 10 years.
(b) Preference shares with a face value of ₹ 4,00,000 annual dividend 12%, redemption period 10 years.
(c) 60,000 equity shares of ₹ 10 each, the market price is ₹ 50 per share and growth rate of 12% realised. Dividend per share ₹ 7.

Calculate weighted average cost of capital. Assume income tax rate as 40%.

FINANCIAL MANAGEMENT — CAPITAL STRUCTURE AND FIRM VALUATION

Solution:

Calculation of specific cost of capital:

(i) Cost of Debentures $k_d = \dfrac{I + \left[\dfrac{P - NP}{n}\right]}{\dfrac{P + NP}{2}}$

$= \dfrac{100 + \left[\dfrac{1000 - 1000}{10}\right]}{\dfrac{1000 + 1000}{2}} = \dfrac{100}{1000} = 10\%$

Post-tax cost of debt $= [1 - .40] \, .10 = 6\%$

(ii) Cost of Preference Capital

$k_p = \dfrac{PD + \left[\dfrac{P - NP}{n}\right]}{\dfrac{P + NP}{2}} = \dfrac{12 + \left[\dfrac{100 - 100}{10}\right]}{\dfrac{100 + 100}{2}} = 12\%$

(iii) Cost of Equity Capital

$k_e = \dfrac{D}{P} + g = \dfrac{7}{50} + .12 = 26\%$

Calculation of weighted average cost of capital:

Sources of capital	Amount (₹)	Proportion in capital structure	Specific cost	Weighted average cost
Equity Capital	6,00,000	.40	.26	.104
Preference Capital	4,00,000	.2667	.12	.032
Debentures	5,00,000	.3333	.06	.0199
	15,00,000			.1559

Weighted average cost of capital = 15.59%

Problem 20

A company has the following specific cost of capital with the indicated book value and market value weights.

Type of capital	Cost	Book value weight	Market value market
Equity	18%	.40	.58
Preference shares	15%	.30	.17
Long term debt	7%	.30	.25

(i) Calculate the weighted average cost of capital.
(ii) Calculate the weighted average cost of capital, using marginal weights if the company intends to raise the needed funds using 50% long-term debt, 35% preference shares and 15% retained earnings.

Solution:

Weighted average cost according to book value weight

Sources of capital	Weight [%]	Specific cost [%]	Weighted average cost [%]
Equity	.40	.18	.072
Preference shares	.30	.15	.045
Long term debt	.30	.07	.021
			.138

Weighted average cost = 13.8%

Weighted average cost as per market value weight

Sources of capital	Weight [%]	Specific cost [%]	Weighted average cost
Equity	.58	.18	.1044
Preference shares	.17	.15	.0255
Long term debt	.25	.07	.0175
			.1474

Weighted average cost = 14.74%

Calculation of revised cost of capital

Sources of capital	Weight [%]	Specific cost [%]	Weighted average cost
Long-term debt	.50	.07	.035
Preference shares	.35	.15	.0525
Retained earnings	.15	.18	.0270
			.1145

Weighted average cost = 11.45%

Points to Remember

- **Funds** for a business organisation can be broadly categorised as long-term and short-term requirements
- **The long-term** requirements are for the purpose of fixed-assets creation which is essential for improving the earning capacity of the business.
- **Short-term** funds also called working capital of the business are required for financing the day-to-day activities of the business.
- Funds can be raised through various sources which are broadly classified into long-term sources and short-term sources.
- The term **capitalisation** means the total amount of funds raised through long-term sources.
- **Overcapitalisation** means the existence of excess capital as compared to the requirements of the company.
- Overcapitalisation leads to lowering of the market value of the shares of the company.
- **Undercapitalisation** means extremely efficient utilisation of funds which enables a company to earn a very high rate of return as the earnings are very high and results in real worth exceeding over the aggregate of shares and debentures.

- ➢ **Capital Structure** represents only long term funds, i.e., long term debts, shareholder's equity and so on and excludes all short term loans and advances.
- ➢ **Net Income Approach** says that a relationship definitely exists between cost of capital and capital structure.
- ➢ According to Net Operating Income approach, cost of capital and capital structure are not connected with each other.
- ➢ The basic aspect of MM' approach is that the total market value of a firm is equal to its expected operating income divided by the discount rate appropriate to its risk class.
- ➢ Many factors need to be considered while planning of the capital structure of a company.

Questions for Discussion

1. What is overcapitalisation? State is causes.
2. What is undercapitalisation? State is causes.
3. Explain the various theories of capitalisation.
4. Explain the various theories of capital structure.
5. Explain the various factors affecting capital structure planning.
6. What do you understand by cost of capital? What are the various types of cost of capital?
7. Explain the meaning of 'Weighted Average cost of capital'. How will you compute the same?
8. 'Equity capital is a cost free source of raising capital'. Do you agree? Explain with reasons.
9. What is Leverage? State it various types and significance.
10. Write short notes on:
    (a) Capitalisation
    (b) Remedies for over and undercapitalisation.
    (c) Capital structure.
    (d) Trading on Equity.

Suggested Activity

Collect the information about capital structure of various companies and analyse them to find out whether the capital structure is optimum or not.

Questions from Previous Pune University Examinations

1. Define Cost of Capital. How will you calculate cost of:
   (i) Debt
   (ii) Equity shares
   (iii) Preference shares   **[P.G.D.B.M. April 2009]**
2. How do you calculate cost of capital in respect to
   (a) Debenture
   (b) Equity shares
   (c) Preference shares.   **[M.B.A. Dec. 2011]**

Chapter 6...

Management of Profits (For PGDBM Only]

Contents ...
6.1 Introduction
6.2 Theories of Dividend
6.3 Dividend Policy Considerations / Factors Affecting Dividend Policy
6.4 Types of Dividend
6.5 Legal Provisions regarding Payment of Dividend
6.6 Procedural Formalities Involved in Dividend Payment
6.7 Bonus Shares
- Points to Remember
- Questions for Discussion
- Questions from Previous Pune University Examinations

Learning Objectives ...
After studying this topic, you should be able to,
1. Understand the concept of dividend
2. Know the different dividend theories
3. Know the legal provisions regarding the payment of dividend and issue of bonus shares

6.1 Introduction

The decision regarding the payment of dividend is another important decision in financial management. Dividend is an appropriation out of the divisible profits and is paid to the shareholders in proportion to their shareholdings in the company. The important question that is to be answered by a finance manager is that how much of the amount of divisible profits should be distributed as dividend and how much amount should be retained? Whether a high dividend policy or a low dividend policy should be followed? Keeping in mind the ultimate objective of financial management i.e. to maximise the wealth of the shareholders, what could be an optimum dividend payout ratio? Answers to these questions are not that easy because from shareholder's angle higher dividends are preferable while the company may see the retained earnings as the source of finance for future growth. Similarly, there are various legal and procedural aspects which have to be taken into account while fixing dividends and deciding dividend policy. The aim of this chapter is to discuss various theories of dividends as well as considerations to be taken into account while fixing dividend policy. At the end, legal aspects of dividends are also discussed. The various theories explaining relationship between dividends and market price are explained in the following pages.

6.2 Theories of Dividend

The theories of dividend can be broadly classified into: (i) Relevance and (ii) Irrelevance. The Relevance theories advocate that dividend decisions definitely affect market prices while Irrelevance theories say that between dividend and market price there is no connection at all. These theories are explained below:

(i) Relevance theories: Under these theories, the following theories or models are quite significant.

(A) Walter's Model: Prof. J. E. Walter advocates that between dividends and market prices of share, there is a definite connection. In order to explain this connection, Walter says that business firms can be classified into three categories on the basis of rate of return on investments [r] and cost of capital [k]. He further says that for a growth firm, the rate of return is more than the cost of capital i.e. $r > k$. If rate of return is less than k, the firm is called as declining firm. In case rate of return = cost of capital, the firms are called as indifferent firms. If $r > k$ i.e. for a growth firm, the optimum dividend policy will be 100% retention or zero percent payout. The market price of the shares will go on increasing when dividend payout ratio starts decreasing. On the other hand, market price will start reducing when payout ratio starts increasing. In the case of a declining firm the situation is exactly reverse. The optimum dividend policy for such firms will be 100% payout and nothing should be retained. It means that market price will start increasing when the dividend payout starts increasing. In case of indifferent firms when $r = k$, high or low dividend payout ratio will not make any difference. The reasons for these types of changes in the market prices of shares are that in case of a growth firm, there are a number of profitable opportunities outside and hence instead of declaring dividend, if the amount of profit is retained, the market price of shares will rise. In case of declining firms, exactly opposite things take place. As the opportunities outside are not available, instead of retaining profits, it is better to distribute the profits as dividends. In case of indifferent firms, whether dividends are declared or whether there is retention of profits, it will not make any difference. The model can be summarised as below:

r	>	k	Growth firm	–	100% retained will be optimum policy
r	<	k	Declining firm	–	100% payout will be optimum
r	=	k	Indifferent firm	–	100% payout or zero percent will not make any difference.

Walter's model can be expressed in a mathematical formula as given below:

$$P = \frac{D + \left[\frac{r}{k_e}\right](E - D)}{k_e}$$

P = Market price per share
D = Dividend per share
r = Rate of return
E = Earnings per share
k_e = Cost of capital (Equity)

The assumptions on which Walter's model is based are as follows:

(a) Retained earnings are the only sources of financing new investments.
(b) The rate of return i.e. 'r' as well as 'k_e' are always constant.
(c) The life of the firm is indefinite.

Illustrations:

Calculate the market price of share of a company if rate of return is 15% and cost of capital is 12%. The dividend payout is 40% while earnings per share is ₹ 30. What should be the optimum dividend policy of the company as per Walter's model?

Solution:

As per Walter's model,

$$P = \frac{D + \left[\frac{r}{k_e}\right](E - D)}{k_e}$$

$$= \frac{12 + \left[\frac{.15}{.12}\right](30 - 12)}{.12} = ₹ 287.5 = \text{Market price}$$

As per Walter's model, the firm is a growth firm because r > k_e. Therefore, the optimum dividend policy should be 100% retention. Market price will be the highest, if retention ratio is 100% or payout ratio is zero percent. This is shown below:

$$P = \frac{0 + \left[\frac{.15}{.12}\right](30 - 0)}{.12} = ₹ 312.5$$

Note: Dividend per share – 40% of ₹ 30 = ₹ 12.

The Walter's model has got a very limited application in real life situations due to the various assumptions. However, its usefulness cannot be denied in the sense that it shows the effect of dividends policy under varying profitabilities.

FINANCIAL MANAGEMENT — MANAGEMENT OF PROFITS

(B) Gordon's model: Gordon has also advocated a model which is similar to Walter's model. Gordon also agrees that market prices of shares are connected with the dividends declared by the firm. Like Walter's, Gordon also classifies firms into three categories. There are growth firms for whom rate of return [r] is greater than discount rate [k], for declining firms r < k while for indifferent firms r = k. The optimum dividend policies for these firms are as follows:

- r > k   Growth firm   — 100% retained is optimum
- r < k   Declining firm   — 100% payout is optimum
- r = k   Indifferent firm   — No change in price of shares inspite of dividend payout

The formula for calculation of market price, as suggested by Gordon is as follows:

$$P = \frac{E(1-b)}{k - br}$$

where
- P = Market price
- b = Retention ratio
- (1 − b) = Dividend payout ratio
- K = Rate of discount
- br = Growth rate of earnings and dividends
- r = Rate of return
- E = Earnings per share

Illustration of Gordon's Model:

Growth firm	Indifferent/ Normal firm	Declining firm
r > k	r = k	r < k
r = 30%	r = 30%	r = 20%
k = 20%	k = 30%	k = 30%
E = ₹ 10	E = ₹ 10	E = ₹ 10
b = 40%	b = 40%	b = 40%
$P = \frac{10(1-.40)}{.20 - (.40 \times .30)}$	$P = \frac{10(1-.40)}{.30 - (.40 \times .30)}$	$P = \frac{10(1-.40)}{.30 - (.40 \times .20)}$
$= \frac{6}{.20 - .12}$	$= \frac{6}{.18}$	$= \frac{6}{.22}$
$= \frac{6}{.08}$	= ₹ 33.33	= ₹ 27.27
= ₹ 75	b = 60%	b = 60%
b = 60%	$P = \frac{10(1-.60)}{.30 - (.60 \times .30)}$	$P = \frac{10(1-.60)}{.30 - (.60 \times .20)}$
$P = \frac{10(1-.60)}{.20 - (.60 \times .30)}$	$= \frac{4}{.12}$	$= \frac{4}{.22}$
$= \frac{4}{.02} = ₹ 200$	= ₹ 33.33	= ₹ 18.18

Gordon's model is based on the following assumptions:
   (a) Retained earnings represent the only source of financing for the firm.
   (b) The rate of return and the cost of capital of the firm is constant.
   (c) The growth rate of the firm is the product of its retention ratio and its rate of return.
   (d) The firm has an indefinite life.
   (e) Tax does not exist.

Revised model of Gordon's earlier model: Since Risk and Uncertainty factors have to be considered, Gordon has revised his earlier model. He says that discount rates in the future should be increased because risk and uncertainty increases with time. Gordon's revised equation is,

$$P_0 = \frac{D_0}{(1 + k_1)} + \frac{D_1}{(1 + k_2)} + \ldots \frac{D_t}{(1 + k_t)}$$

In this case is $k_1 < k_2$ and so on.

Gordon argues that dividend policy in such a case matters even when the rate of return on investment (r) is equal to the average of all ks.

(C) Traditional position: This theory advocated by **Graham** and **Dodd**, says that shareholders always prefer dividends to retained earnings. Therefore, market prices will tend to increase if dividend payout is on the higher side. According to this approach, "Given two companies in the same general position and with the same earning power, the one paying the larger dividend will always sell at a higher price."

(D) Radical Approach: Michael J. Brennan and other advocates of low payout position argue that a policy of low dividend payout ratio promotes the welfare of the shareholders. The reason for this is that, for taxation purposes capital gains are taxed more favourably [long-term capital gains] than the income from dividends. The investors, therefore, will prefer those shares which provide more capital appreciation and less dividend income. This is possible when the dividend payout ratio is on the lower side. If the shareholders of a company are from a higher income bracket, this model may be applicable. However, in the absence of any evidence, it is difficult to generalise this conclusion.

(ii) Irrelevance theory: Under this approach, the thought is that the market price of shares and the value of a firm is not at all dependent on the percentage of dividends declared. Modigliani and Miller are the strong advocates of this thought. Their arguments are as follows:

Modigliani - Miller Model: According to this model, the value of a firm is solely dependent on the earning capacity of the firm. How a firm is distributing its earnings is not the deciding factor in the valuation. The MM argument says that a firm may retain its earnings or it may distribute them. If the earnings are retained, it will lead to capital appreciation. On the other hand, if dividends are distributed, the shareholders will enjoy dividend income which is equal to the amount by which his capital would have appreciated if the company would have retained its earnings. The shareholders, therefore, do not make any differentiation between present dividend and retained earnings.

The MM' model is based on certain assumptions. These assumptions are as follows:
(a) There are perfect capital markets and investors are rational.
(b) Information is freely available and there are numerous transactions.
(c) An investor cannot influence prices.
(d) Floatation costs are nil.
(e) There are no taxes.
(f) The firm has a fixed investment policy.
(g) Risk of uncertainty does not exist.

Modigliani and Miller have has also given a mathematical proof for their argument. This is explained with the help of the following illustration.

Illustrations:

A company has a P/E (Price/Earnings) ratio of 10. The amount of share capital is ₹ 50,00,000 divided into shares of ₹ 100 each. The company expects declaration of dividend of ₹ 8 per share. On the assumption that the company pays dividend, its net income is ₹ 5,00,000 and it makes new investments of ₹ 10,00,000 during the period, prove under MM' assumption that the value of the firm remains unchanged when (a) dividends are paid and (b) dividends are not paid.

Solution:

(i) (a) Price P_1 when dividend is not declared.

$$P_0 = \frac{D_1 + P_1}{1 + k_e}$$

$$100 = \frac{P_1}{(1 + .10)}$$

$$= ₹ 110 = P_1$$

(b) **When dividends are declared**

$$P_0 = \frac{D_1 + P_1}{1 + k_e}$$

$$= 100 = \frac{8 + P_1}{1.10}$$

P_1 = ₹ 102
P_0 = Prevailing market price
k_e = Cost of capital
D_1 = Dividend to be received at the end of period one.
P_1 = Market price of a share at the end of period one.

FINANCIAL MANAGEMENT — MANAGEMENT OF PROFITS

(ii) (a) Amount required for new financing $I - [y - n D_1]$ that is,

$= ₹ 10,00,000 - [₹ 5,00,000 - ₹ 4,00,000]$

$= ₹ 9,00,000$

I = Amount of investment

y = Earnings

nD_1 = Amount of dividend [₹ 8 × 50,000 shares]

(b) New shares to be issued

$$An = \frac{₹ 9,00,000}{₹ 102 \begin{bmatrix} \text{Market price when} \\ \text{dividends are declared} \end{bmatrix}}$$

$= 8823.52$ or 8824

(iii) Value of the firm when dividends are declared

$$V = \frac{1}{(1 + k_e)} [nD_1 + (n + An) P_1 - I + y - nD_1]$$

$$= \frac{1}{(1 + .10)} \left[4,00,000 + \left(50,000 + \frac{9,00,000}{102}\right) 102 - 10,00,000 + 5,00,000 - 4,00,000 \right]$$

or

$$= \frac{4,00,000 + \left[\frac{50,000 + 9,00,000}{102} \times 102\right] - 10,00,000 + 5,00,000 - 4,00,000}{1.10}$$

or

$$\frac{55,00,000}{1.10}$$

$= ₹ 50,00,000$

(iv) Value of the firm if dividends are not declared:

$$V = \frac{1}{(1 + k_e)} [(N + An) p_1 - I + y]$$

$$= \frac{1}{1.10} \left[\left(50,000 + \frac{5,00,000}{110}\right) \times 110 - 10,00,000 + 5,00,000 \right]$$

$$= \frac{60,00,000 - 10,00,000 + 5,00,000}{1.10}$$

$= ₹ 50,00,000$

FINANCIAL MANAGEMENT　　　MANAGEMENT OF PROFITS

In the above formula, the explanations of the various terms are as follows:

- V = Value of the firm
- Ke = Cost of capital

$$\left[\text{P/E ratio is 10. Therefore, cost of capital is } \frac{1}{10} = .10 \right]$$

- N = Number of existing equity shares
- An = New shares
- nD_1 = Total dividends
- P_1 = Price of shares after dividend is declared or when no dividend is declared
- I = Amount of investment
- Y = Earnings

Conclusion: We have examined various approaches to dividend which explain the connection between dividends and market price of shares. The two theories i.e. relevance and irrelevance, are exactly contradictory to each other. The question that arises here is that which view can be taken as the correct one? One thought which has emerged in recent times is that if dividends declared are as per the expectations of the market, there will be no change in the market price after dividend declarations even if actual dividend declared is more than that of the previous year. If the dividend declared is higher than the expectations of the market, the market price of shares will definitely rise because higher dividends will give indication of a higher profitability. On the other hand, if actual dividends are lower than the expectations, market prices will fall.

The above analysis reconciles two extreme views of relevance and irrelevance. As per **Merton H. Miller**, "Both views are correct in their own ways. The academic is thinking of the expected dividends, the practitioner of the unexpected."

6.3 Dividend Policy Considerations / Factors Affecting Dividend Policy

The first question that has to be answered by a finance manager is how much payout ratio should be adopted? This decision is extremely tricky because it involves a conflict of interests between shareholders and the management. The shareholders will always expect a higher payout because they are interested in getting maximum return on their investments. On the other hand the management looks upon the divisible profits as a means for financing the requirements of the company. Instead of depending upon external sources to raise the finance, it will be always advisable to utilise the retained earnings which is the company's own source. Therefore, a dividend payout ratio will have to be decided after a careful consideration of the following factors:

(a) **Shareholders' expectations:** It is mentioned in the above paragraph that shareholders are always interested in high dividends. However, in case, the majority of the shareholders are from a higher income bracket, they may prefer lower rates of dividends. On the other hand, if a shareholder is a retired person with a small income, he will expect a higher amount of dividend. Though, it can be admitted that expectations of all the shareholders cannot be taken into considerations, at least a payout ratio which satisfies the expectations of majority of shareholders should be followed. Since, shareholders are the owners of the company, their wishes must be taken into account.

(b) **Liquidity:** As per the provisions of the Companies Act, 1956, dividends are to be paid in cash. Therefore, before deciding of a payout ratio, liquidity position of the company should be examined carefully. In case of a growing firm, liquidity may not be very high because of their substantial investments and other commitments. These firms may not be in a position to pay a high dividend even though they wish to do so. On the other hand, a mature firm may have greater liquidity as the investment opportunities have declined.

(c) **Projections of funds:** Another vital factor to be taken into account is the need of funds in the future. A forecast for the funds required in the future can be prepared and accordingly a payout ratio can be fixed. Firms which have substantial opportunities for investments require more funds than those firms whose opportunities are comparatively less. The firms having more investment opportunities can keep a low payout ratio and plough back the profits. If the firms do not see much of the requirements of funds in future, a high payout ratio can be adopted.

(d) **Capital structure:** Capital structure of a company is the combination of various sources like equity capital, preference capital and long-term loans. If the capital structure of a company is highly geared i.e. consisting a higher proportion of preference capital and term loans, there will be a heavy committment on the part of the company to pay preference dividend and interest on loan. This will force the firm to reduce the payout ratio as much of the earnings will be distributed for such committments. On the other hand, if in the capital structure, equity capital is higher than the other two sources, dividend committments are not high and, therefore, a high payout ratio can be maintained.

(e) **Control:** If finance is raised from external sources, there is a danger that the existing management will lose the control. The exception to this is the rights issue. If funds are raised from internal financing like retained earnings, there is no risk of losing control. In such cases, the payout ratio is kept low.

FINANCIAL MANAGEMENT   MANAGEMENT OF PROFITS

- **(f) Access to capital market:** If a firm has easy accessibility to the capital market, a high payout ratio can be adopted inspite of a lower liquidity. Easy accessibility to capital market ensures greater flexibility to the firm in paying dividends as well as in meeting the obligations of the firm. Thus, greater the ability of the firm to raise funds in the capital markets, the greater will be its ability to pay dividends even if it is not liquid.
- **(g) Restrictions by lenders:** The lenders may put some restrictions on the company. A firm may have to agree with the lender to restrict the payment of dividend payments. These restrictions may be in different forms. For example, a restriction can be, not to pay dividends unless some amount of the earnings are transferred to sinking fund. In such cases, the payout ratio will have to be kept low.
- **(h) Legal restrictions:** The legal provisions will have to be kept in mind before fixing a dividend policy. As per Companies Act, 1956, dividends shall be paid only out of profits and for this current profits as well as past profits can be used. The profits mentioned above should be profits after providing depreciation. In special cases, if it is in public interest, the Central Government may permit a company to declare dividends without providing for depreciation. The dividends are to be paid in cash but a company is allowed to capitalise its profits and issue bonus shares. The bonus issue should be done according to the guidelines issued by SEBI.

These legal restrictions will have to be taken into consideration before the dividend policy is fixed.

- **(i) Inflation:** Inflation actually can act as a constraint on paying dividends. Depreciation is provided on the original cost of an asset and, therefore, it may not be an adequate source for replacement of the asset. Therefore, some part of the earnings should be retained in order to maintain the capital intact.
- **(ii) Stability of Dividends:** Inspite of any dividend payout ratio fixed by a firm, the fact remains that the stability in dividend payments is considered as one of the desirable features in the dividend policy. This policy is desirable from the point of view of the shareholders also as they can plan their incomes accordingly. The question that arises is, what is stability? Whether it is stable payout ratio or stable dividend per share?

To answer this question, we will have to examine the different forms of stability. These forms are discussed in detail in the following paragraphs.

- **(a) Stable payout ratio:** According to this policy, a fixed payout ratio is decided and it is followed consistently year after year. For example, a firm may decide that payout ratio should be 40%. If the divisible profits are ₹ 7,00,000, the total dividend payment will be ₹ 2,80,000. If the profit figure changes to ₹ 6,00,000, the dividend payment will be 40% of ₹ 6,00,000 i.e. ₹ 2,40,000.

The stable payout ratio can be illustrated with the help of the following diagram.

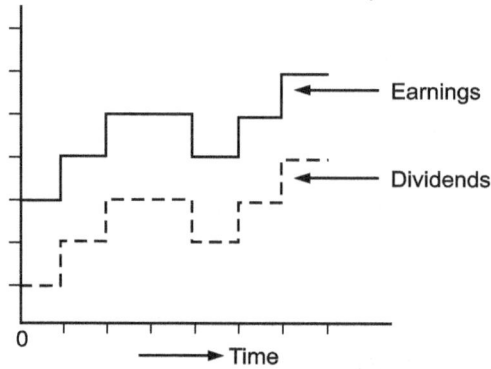

Fig. 6.1: Stable Payout Ratio

The feature of this policy is that if profits fluctuate, dividend per share also fluctuates. The stability of dividend per share, therefore, cannot be maintained. If amount of profits is nil, no dividends are paid to the shareholders. However, there is an inbuilt flexibility in this policy which ensures that if profits are high, dividends will be high and if profits are low, dividends are also very low.

(b) Stable dividend per share: In this policy, a stable dividend per share is paid irrespective of profits. For example, a company may decide that 20% dividend per share is to be paid. If the share is of ₹ 100 each, the amount of dividend per share is ₹ 20. If profits in a particular year are very high, the same dividend per share is maintained and the remaining amount can be ploughed back to profits. When profits decline, the past accumulated profits can be utilised to maintain the same dividend per share. This policy can be explained with the help of the following diagram.

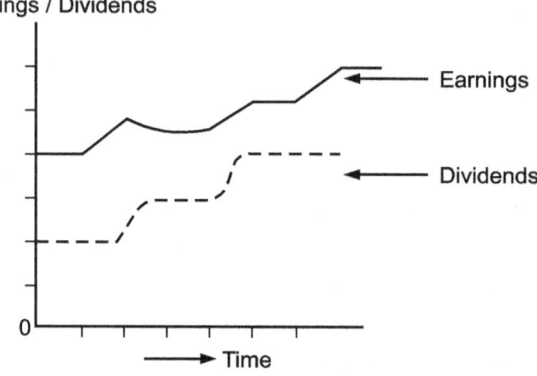

Fig. 6.2: Stable Dividend Per Share

In the diagram, the dividend line is shown as going up periodically. The indication given is that extra dividend per share can be paid if profits increase permanently.

This means that if profits increase temporarily, it may not be distributed as dividends. But if profits increase permanently, they should be distributed as extra dividend because otherwise there will be a stagnation in dividends.

To conclude, it can be said that stability of dividends is desirable from the investor's side because it eliminates uncertainty regarding dividend income. Similarly, it creates a faith in their minds about the return on their investments.

6.4 Types of Dividend

The dividends are to be paid in cash. One option is that it can be paid in the form of bonus shares or stock dividends. These types are discussed below:

(a) **Cash dividend:** Dividends are paid in cash as per Companies Act, 1956. For ensuring such payment, there should be sufficient bank balance in the account of the company. If such balance is not available, arrangements will have to be made for borrowings.

(b) **Bonus shares:** An issue of bonus share represents capitalisation of profits and issue of shares in addition to the cash dividends. The important advantage for issue of bonus shares is that there is no outflow of funds for the company. The liquidity position, therefore, is not affected. For the shareholders, no tax liability arises when bonus shares are issued. The tax liability may arise when bonus shares are sold out in the market.

However, the SEBI guidelines for bonus issue, have to be followed.

Corporate Dividend Behaviour: John Lintner, in 1956 surveyed the behaviour of corporate dividend and came out with the following conclusions:

(a) Most of the firms think primarily in terms of the proportion of earnings that should be paid out as dividends rather than in terms of the proportion of earnings that should be ploughed back.

(b) Firms try to reach the target payout ratio gradually over a period of time because shareholders prefer a steady rise in dividends.

John Brittian conducted an extensive study of corporate dividend behaviour and tested Lintner's basic model with some modifications. He substituted profits with cashflow and again splitted cashflows into two parts, profits and depreciation. It was found that the model has got considerable support.

6.5 Legal Provisions regarding Payment of Dividend

The following are the provisions of Companies Act 1956 regarding the payment of dividend.

(a) The Board of Directors should pass a resolution recommending the dividend to be paid in their meeting.

(b) The resolution of the Board should be approved by shareholders in the Annual General Meeting.

(c) The dividend is payable to shareholders whose names appear on the Register of Members.

(d) The actual payment must be made within 42 days. After 42 days have expired, within 7 days they should be transferred to unpaid dividends account.

(e) Dividend shall not be paid by a company for any financial year except out of the profits of the company for that year arrived at after providing depreciation in accordance with the relevant provisions of the Companies Act 1956. Dividend can also be paid out of the moneys provided by the State Government or Central Government in pursuance of a guarantee given by that Government.

(f) Dividend may be paid out of the accumulated profits of the previous years.

(g) The Board of Directors may declare interim dividends and the amount of dividend including interim dividend shall be deposited in a separate bank account within five days from the date of declaration of such dividend.

(h) Companies can pay only cash dividends (with the exception of bonus shares).

(i) Dividends can be paid only out of profits earned during the financial year after providing for depreciation and after transferring to reserves such percentage of profits as prescribed by law. The Companies (Transfer to Reserves) Rules - 1975, provide that before declaration of dividend, a percentage of profits as prescribed below should be transferred to the reserves of the company.

% of Dividend Declared	Transferred Amount to Reserves
1. More than 10%, but less than 12.5%	Not less than 2.5% of Current Profits
2. More Than 12.5%, but less than 15%	Not less than 5% of Current Profits
3. More than 15%, but less than 20%	Not less than 7.5% of Current Profits
4. More than 20%	Not less than 10% of Current Profits

(j) Dividends can not be declared for past years for which the accounts have been closed.

(k) When a dividend is declared by a company but not paid [claimed] within thirty days from the date of declaration, to any shareholder entitled to the payment of the dividend, the company shall within seven days from the date of expiry of the said period of 30 days, transfer the total amount of dividend which remains unpaid [or unclaimed] within the said period of 30 days, to a special account to be opened by the company in that befalf in any scheduled bank, to be called as 'Unpaid dividend account' of the company. Any such money transferred to the unpaid dividend account of a company as per this section, which remains unpaid or unclaimed for a period of seven years from the date of such transfer, shall be transferred by the company to a Fund established under sub section (1) of Section 205 C.

6.6 Procedural Formalities involved in Dividend Payment

Procedural Aspects

Generally speaking, it is presumed that every company has the main objective of earning huge profits and distributing them among the shareholders by way of dividends and hence the said organisation should try to make arrangement for procuring and accumulating capital in order to attract maximum number of investors by paying the highest dividend.

Rules: Generally speaking every procedure in order to become enforceable has to be governed by certain rules and regulations and hence even the said concept of dividend should be governed by certain fixed rules, which are as follows:

(a) It is mandatory to declare dividend by a resolution passed at the annual general meeting.

(b) The rate of dividend has to be fixed by the said Board after a meeting has been held but only after passing a said resolution in this connection.

(c) The rate so determined by the Board has to be sanctioned by the members of the company only by means of an annual general meeting.

(d) The said director should sign on the statement containing the rate of demand in the report attached to the said company' balance sheet.

(e) The director should also pay the dividend in proportion to the nominal value of the shares purchased by them but only in the absence of a clause to the contrary.

(f) The company should declare dividend for a particular year out of the profits of that particular year itself.

(g) To declare only that portion as dividend which is remaining after the expenses have been paid and after the company makes the provision for depreciation.

(h) It is also suggested that the company which fails to comply with the provisions of section 80-A dealing with redemption of redeemable preference shares shall not declare any amount as dividend on its equity shares.

The said dividend to be declared should be paid only in terms of cash and not in any other form. The most important rule is that Dividend should be paid only out of the current year's profits and not through any other source.

Thus, to conclude, it can be stated that the said company if it wants to progress further has to follow the said rules and regulations of the Companies Act.

6.7 Bonus Shares

Bonus shares are those shares which are issued to existing shareholders as a result of capitalisation of reserves.

Bonus shares can be defined as *"Shares issued by a company to its members, either fully paid up or partly paid-up, out of accumulated profits, in lieu of a dividend or bonus in cash, or. in other words instead of profits being paid in cash, they are capitalised, retained in the business the members benefiting by an allotment of shares instead of a payment of cash"*.

Companies which have large accumulated reserves may issue bonus shares to their equity shareholders. Bonus shares are given free of charge to the existing members. No consideration has to be paid by the member.

The amount equal to the face value of the bonus share is capitalised out of the accumulated reserves. The company may distribute dividend or issue bonus shares out of undistributed profit. All rights attached to equity shares are also applicable to bonus shares. The company may give bonus shares in a proportion to shareholder's existing holdings. The policy regarding issue of bonus shares is decided by the directors. In the general meeting, it is formally approved by a resolution. Issue of bonus shares may be called capitalisation of undistributed profits.

Conditions for Issue of Bonus Shares:
1. There should be a sufficient amount of accumulated general reserves.
2. Issue should be permitted by the Articles of Association of the company.
3. The Board should pass a Resolution proposing the issue of bonus shares.
4. Shareholders should give their formal approval to the directors proposal for the issue of bonus shares.
5. A share premium account and a capital redemption reserve account may be used for the declaration of bonus shares.

Reasons for the Issue of Bonus Shares:
1. The bonus issue tends to bring the market price per share within a more popular range.
2. It increases the number of outstanding shares. This promotes more active trading.
3. The nominal rate of dividend tends to decline. This may dispel the impression of profiteering.
4. The share capital base increases and the company may achieve a more respectable size in the eyes of the investing community.

Points to Remember

- Dividend is an appropriation out of the divisible profits and is paid to the shareholders in proportion to their shareholdings in the company.
- The theories of dividend can be broadly classified into:
  (a) Relevance and
  (b) Irrelevance
- A dividend payout ratio will have to be decided after a careful consideration of the following factors:
  (a) Shareholders expectations
  (b) Liquidity
  (c) Projections of funds
  (d) Capital structure

FINANCIAL MANAGEMENT   MANAGEMENT OF PROFITS

   (e) Control
   (f) Access to capital market
   (g) Restrictions by lenders
   (h) Legal restrictions
   (i) Inflation
➤ Dividends can be paid in the form of bonus shares or stock dividends.

Questions for Discussion

1. Describe the various Theories of Dividend.
2. Explain the Dividend Policy Considerations.
3. Explain the various Procedural Formalities involved in Payment of Dividend.
4. Write short notes:
   (a) Type of Dividend.
   (b) Legal Procedure for Payment of Dividend.
   (c) Bonus Shares.

Theory Questions from Past Pune University Question Papers

1. What is Dividend? What are the Types of Dividend? Explain the Legal and Procedural Aspects of Dividend Payment. **[P.G.D.B.M. Dec. 2004]**
2. What are the Various Factors that are to be taken into account while deciding upon the dividend policy? **[P.G.D.B.M. Dec. 2007]**
3. Discuss in detail the Procedural and Legal Formalities involved in the Payment of Dividend. **[M.B.A. April 2009]**
4. Discuss in detail the Various Factors Affecting the Dividend Policy of the Company. **[M.B.A. Dec. 2009]**
5. What is Over Capitalization? Why Over Capitalization Arise? Explain the Corrective Remedies for Over Capitalization. **[M.B.A. Dec. 2010]**
6. Write Short Notes:
   (a) Over and Under Capitalization. **[P.G.D.B.M. April 2006]**
   (b) Over Capitalization. **[P.G.D.B.M. Dec. 2007]**
   (c) Determinants of Dividend Policy. **[P.G.D.B.M. April 2006]**
   (d) Constant Dividend Policy. **[M.B.A. Dec. 2006, 2010 and April 2011]**
   (e) Bonus Shares.
      [M.B.A. Dec. 2006, 2007, April 2007 and P.G.D.B.M. April 2007, Dec. 2007]
   (f) Under Capitalization. **[M.B.A. Dec. 2011]**
   (g) Factors Affecting Dividend Policy. **[M.B.A. Dec. 2011]**
7. Discuss in detail the Merits and Limitations of Under and Over Capitalization.
   [M.B.A. April 2009]
8. Differentiate: Over Capitalization Vs. Under Capitalization. **[M.B.A. April 2010]**

■■■

MULTIPLE CHOICE QUESTIONS

[1] Select the correct answer from the choices given below and complete the sentence.

1. The objective of financial management is:
   - [a] Profit maximisation
   - [b] Wealth maximisation
   - [c] Maximisation of earnings per share
   - [d] Maximisation of Return on Capital employed

   Ans. [b]

2. Capital budgeting is
   - [a] preparing a capital expenditure budget
   - [b] planning capital expenditure
   - [c] planning and evaluation of capital expenditure
   - [d] planning of expenditure

   Ans. [c]

3. Ratio analysis is used for:
   - [a] analysing the profit and loss account
   - [b] analysing the balance sheet
   - [c] analysing funds flow statement
   - [d] analysing and interpretation of financial statements

   Ans. [d]

4. Ideal current ratio is
   - [a] 1:1
   - [b] 2:1
   - [c] 3:1
   - [d] 1.5:1.

   Ans. [b]

5. In the computation of liquid ratio, excluded from the current assets is
   - [a] cash in hand
   - [b] bank balance
   - [c] accounts receivables
   - [d] inventory

   Ans. [d]

6. Net worth means
   - [a] share capital plus reserves
   - [b] equity capital plus reserves
   - [c] total assets minus current liabilities
   - [d] total assets minus long term liabilities

   Ans. [a]

FINANCIAL MANAGEMENT MULTIPLE CHOICE QUESTIONS

7. Earnings per share is
   - [a] amount of profit distributed as dividend to equity shareholders
   - [b] amount of profit available for distribution to preference shareholders
   - [c] amount of profit available for distribution per equity share
   - [c] amount of profit distributed as preference dividend

Ans. [c]

8. A stock turnover ratio of 12 indicates that the stock holding period is
   - [a] 2 months
   - [b] 1 month
   - [c] 3 months
   - [d] 12 months

Ans. [b]

9. A debtors turnover ratio of 6 times indicates that the collection period is
   - [a] 3 months
   - [b] 6 months
   - [c] 1 month
   - [d] 2 months

Ans. [d]

10. An increase in inventory and no change in the current liabilities will
    - [a] increase
    - [b] decrease
    - [c] not change the current ratio
    - [d] None of these

Ans. [a]

11. Operating net profit ratio is computed as per the formula of
    - [a] net profit before income tax/ Sales × 100
    - [b] net profit after income tax / Sales × 100
    - [c] operating net profit / Sales × 100
    - [d] net profit before interest / Sales × 100

Ans. [c]

12. If current assets of a company are ₹ 54 lakhs and current liabilities are ₹ 18 lakhs, the current ratio will
    - [a] increase
    - [b] decrease
    - [c] will not change
    - [d] will be negative if the company purchases machinery of ₹ 10 lakhs and pays the amount by cheque

Ans. []

13. Gross profit ratio is calculated by dividing
    - [a] gross profit
    - [b] net profit
    - [c] cost of goods sold
    - [d] net profit after tax by sales

Ans. [a]

14. If, at present the debt-equity ratio of a company is 2:1, issue of additional equity shares will
    - [a] not change
    - [b] Increase
    - [c] decrease the debt-equity ratio
    - [d] None of these

    Ans. [c]

15. Current assets minus current liabilities is
    - [a] gross working capital
    - [b] net working capital
    - [c] fluctuating working capital
    - [d] fixed working capital

    Ans. [b]

16. A high capital gearing ratio will indicate
    - [a] high risk
    - [b] low risk
    - [c] zero risk
    - [d] none of these

    Ans. [a]

17. Working capital turnover ratio is calculated by dividing net sales by
    - [a] gross working capital
    - [b] permanent working capital
    - [c] fluctuating working capital
    - [d] net working capital

    Ans. [d]

18. Fixed assets turnover ratio indicates
    - [a] amount invested in fixed assets per rupee of sales
    - [b] amount of sales per rupee invested in fixed assets
    - [c] movement of fixed assets
    - [d] sales of fixed assets

    Ans. [b]

19. A creditors turnover ratio of 10 indicates that the credit period allowed by suppliers is
    - [a] 2 months
    - [b] 3 months
    - [c] 1.2 months
    - [d] 1 month

    Ans. [c]

20. Interest coverage ratio is calculated by dividing the net profit + non cash expenses by
    - [a] total interest payments
    - [b] interest on long term loans
    - [c] interest on short term loans
    - [d] interest on accounts payables

    Ans. [a]

21. Operative leverage is calculated by dividing contribution by
    - [a] earnings before interest and tax
    - [b] sales
    - [c] fixed cost
    - [d] variable cost

    Ans. [a]

FINANCIAL MANAGEMENT   MULTIPLE CHOICE QUESTIONS

22. Operating leverage measures
    [a] operating risk   [b] financial risk
    [c] combined risk   [d] foreign exchange risk
Ans. [a]

23. Financial leverage is calculated by dividing the earnings before interest and tax by
    [a] earnings after tax   [b] earnings before tax
    [c] contribution   [d] sales
Ans. [b]

24. Return on capital is calculated by dividing
    [a] net profit after tax   [b] net profit after interest and tax
    [c] net profit before tax   [d] net profit before interest and tax
Ans. [d]

25. The ideal liquid ratio is
    [a] 2:1   [b] 1:1
    [c] 3:1   [d] 1.5:1
Ans. [b]

26. Earnings per share is calculated by dividing the net profit after interest, income tax and preference dividend [if any] by
    [a] total number of equity shares and preference shares
    [b] number of equity shares
    [c] amount of equity capital
    [d] total amount of equity and preference capital
Ans. []

27. Dividend payout ratio indicates
    [a] percentage of dividend paid out of the divisible profits
    [b] amount of profit available per equity share
    [c] amount of dividend paid
    [d] amount of dividend recommended
Ans. [a]

28. Return on equity is calculated by dividing the net profit after taxes and preference dividend [if any] by
    [a] equity plus preference capital
    [b] number of equity shares
    [c] total number of equity and preference shares
    [d] equity shareholders funds
Ans. [d]

29. Total assets turnover ratio indicates the
    [a] ability of the firm to generate sales per rupee of current assets
    [b] ability of the firm to generate sales per rupee of the fixed assets
    [c] ability of the firm to generate sales per rupee of the total assets
    [d] ability of the firm to generate sales per rupee of the capital employed
Ans. [c]
30. If the raw material inventory turnover ratio of a manufacturing company is 6, it indicates that the holding period of raw material inventory is
    [a] 6 months   [b] 4 months
    [c] 2 months   [d] 3 months
Ans. [c]

[2] Complete the sentence by selecting the correct answer from the options given
1. In capital budgeting, the techniques based on the present value of money are known as
    [a] non discounted cash flow techniques
    [b] discounted cash flow technique
    [c] cash flow techniques
    [d] techniques based on accounting profits
Ans. [b]
2. In the Average Rate of Return method of evaluation of capital expenditure, the
    [a] net profit
    [b] net profit before interest and income tax
    [c] operating net profit
    [d] net profit after income tax
    (is divided by the average investments made in the project)
Ans. [d]
3. Internal rate of return is the rate of return at which the net present value is
    [a] positive   [b] negative
    [c] zero   [d] none of these
Ans. [c]
4. A project requires an initial investment of ₹ 10,00,000 with a life of 5 years. The estimated cash inflows per year are ₹ 4,00,000. The pay back period for this project is
    [a] two years   [b] three years
    [c] two and half years [d] five years
Ans. [c]
5. The rate of discount applied for discounting the cash inflows in a capital expenditure project is normally synonymous with
    [a] cost of capital   [b] internal rate of return
    [c] rate of interest   [d] net profit percentage
Ans. [a]

6. Pay back period indicates the number of years in which
   [a] the initial investment made in the project is recovered
   [b] the number of years in which the projected cash inflows will be more than the initial investments
   [c] the number of years in which the projected cash inflows will be less than the initial investments
   [d] none of these

Ans. [a]

7. Profitability index in a capital expenditure proposal is calculated by dividing the
   [a] net present value
   [b] the total present value of cash inflows
   [c] the expected life of the project
   [d] the net profit after income tax by the initial investments

Ans. [b]

8. A project requires an initial investment of ₹ 25 lakhs and an estimated life of 5 years. The projected cash inflows for the first five years are respectively ₹ 7 lakhs, ₹ 12 lakhs, ₹ 15 lakhs, ₹ 13 lakhs and ₹ 9 lakhs. The pay back period will be
   [a] 2 years   [b] 3 years
   [c] 2.24 years   [d] 4 years

Ans. [c]

9. Discounted pay back period takes into consideration
   [a] cash inflows after tax   [b] cash inflows before tax
   [c] net profits after tax   [d] discounted cash inflows

Ans. [d]

10. For calculating the net present value, the initial investments are compared with
    [a] pay back period
    [b] the internal rate of return
    [c] total present value of the cash inflows
    [d] cash inflows after income tax

Ans. [c]

11. The amount of working capital which changes according to seasonal fluctuations is called as
    [a] fixed working capital   [b] net working capital
    [c] gross working capital   [d] fluctuating working capital.

Ans. [d]

12. If the production cycle is longer, the working capital requirements are
    [a] lower   [b] normal
    [c] higher   [d] fluctuating

Ans. [c]

13. If a firm follows a liberal credit policy for its debtors, the working capital requirements will
    - [a] increase
    - [b] decrease
    - [c] remain the same
    - [d] none of these

    Ans. [a]

14. The net working capital is
    - [a] total of current assets
    - [b] current assets minus the current liabilities
    - [c] total current liabilities
    - [d] total fixed assets

    Ans. [b]

15. The hedging approach suggests that
    - [a] long term funds should be utilised for financing the fixed portion of current assets
    - [b] short term funds should be utilised for financing the total current assets
    - [c] long term funds should be utilised for financing total current assets
    - [d] long term funds should be utilised for financing the temporary current assets

    Ans. [a]

16. Liberal dividend policy
    - [a] reduces the working capital requirements
    - [b] increases the amount of working capital
    - [c] do not affect the working capital requirements
    - [d] none of these

    Ans. [b]

17. Transaction, precautionary and
    - [a] liquidity
    - [b] profitability
    - [c] solvency
    - [d] speculative are the three motives of holding cash

    Ans. [d]

18. A cash budget is a statement of estimated
    - [a] cash receipts and cash payments
    - [b] cash receipts
    - [c] cash payments
    - [d] profits

    Ans. [a]

19. Cash, in a narrow sense implies
    - [a] cash in hand
    - [b] cash at bank
    - [c] currency and bank balance
    - [d] currency, cheques, bank balance and investments

    Ans. [c]

20. Economic order quantity of material takes into account ordering costs and
    - [a] carrying costs
    - [b] lead time
    - [c] re-order level
    - [d] maximum level

Ans. [a]

21. Relaxation of credit standards will result in
    - [a] higher risk of bad debts
    - [b] higher liquidity
    - [c] higher profitability
    - [d] none of these

Ans. [a]

22. Re-order level of inventory is calculated by taking into consideration maximum consumption and
    - [a] minimum lead period
    - [b] maximum lead period
    - [c] minimum lead period
    - [d] average lead period

Ans. [b]

23. In ABC system of inventory control, the material is divided in A, B and C categories on the basis of
    - [a] material quantity
    - [b] consumption value of material
    - [c] re-order level of each material
    - [d] maximum level of material

Ans. [b]

24. VED analysis of material involves classification of inventory into vital, essential and
    - [a] demand
    - [b] delivery
    - [c] desirable
    - [d] decline

Ans. [c]

25. While calculating maximum level of inventory
    - [a] minimum consumption X minimum re-order period
    - [b] maximum consumption X maximum re-order period
    - [c] normal consumption X normal re-order period
    - [d] economic order quantity is deducted from the total of re-order level and re-order quantity

Ans. [a]

26. Inventory turnover ratio indicates
    - [a] holding period
    - [b] maximum quantity
    - [c] economic order quantity
    - [d] minimum quantity

Ans. [a]

27. Order cost and carrying cost are
    - [a] fixed
    - [b] variable
    - [c] semi variable
    - [d] indirect costs

Ans. [b]

28. In factoring service, if the loss of bad debts is borne by the factor, it is called as
    - [a] with recourse service
    - [b] normal factoring service
    - [c] without recourse factor
    - [d] no risk factoring service

Ans. [c]

29. The combined cost of capital is known as
    - [a] marginal cost
    - [b] implicit cost
    - [c] weighted average cost
    - [d] explicit cost

    Ans. [c]

30. A company will be advised to raise fresh capital through debt if
    - [a] operating leverage is high
    - [b] financial leverage is high
    - [c] operating leverage is high and financial leverage is low
    - [d] operating leverage and financial leverage are high

    Ans. [c]

31. In the Net Income theory of capital structure cost of debt is assumed to be lower than the cost of
    - [a] current liabilities
    - [b] equity
    - [c] preference share capital
    - [d] reserves and surplus

    Ans. [b]

32. As per the traditional theory of capital structure, the aggregate cost of capital falls with the introduction of
    - [a] equity
    - [b] preference share capital
    - [c] debt
    - [d] retained earnings

    Ans. [c]

33. Overcapitalisation can be corrected by
    - [a] consolidating the shares
    - [b] splitting the shares
    - [c] issue of new equity shares
    - [d] buy back of shares

    Ans. [a]

34. If the rate of corporate income tax increases, the cost of debt
    - [a] increases
    - [b] do not change
    - [c] decreases
    - [d] becomes higher than the cost of equity

    Ans. [c]

35. The decrease in the rate of corporate income tax will
    - [a] not change the cost of equity
    - [b] decrease the cost of equity
    - [c] increase the cost of equity
    - [d] none of these

    Ans. [a]

36. Capital structure theories explain the theoretical relationship between capital structure and
    - [a] cost of debt
    - [b] cost of equity
    - [c] cost of retained earnings
    - [d] aggregate cost of capital

    Ans. [a]

37. Capital structure means
    [a] total amount of capital raised
    [b] total amount of equity capital
    [c] the proportion of various sources of raising capital
    [d] total amount of debt capital
Ans. [c]

38. Capitalisation means
    [a] amount of equity capital   [b] amount of debt
    [c] total amount of capital   [d] retained earnings
Ans. [c]

39. While calculating cost of preference capital the increase in the corporate income tax rate will
    [a] increase the cost of preference capital
    [b] decrease the cost of preference capital
    [c] will not change the cost of preference capital
    [d] will increase the rate of dividend
Ans. [c]

40. In case of net operating income theory of capital structure, the increase in the proportion of debt in the capital structure will
    [a] increase in the aggregate cost of capital
    [b] decrease the aggregate cost of capital
    [c] will not change the aggregate cost of capital
    [d] will increase the cost of equity
Ans. [c]

41. Any increase in the current assets will result in
    [a] increase in working capital   [b] decrease in working capital
    [c] no change in the working capital [d] increase in current liabilities
Ans. [a]

42. Decrease in current liabilities will result in
    [a] decrease in working capital   [b] no change in the working capital
    [c] increase in working capital   [d] increase in current assets
Ans. [c]

43. In funds flow statement, funds in a broader sense mean
    [a] cash   [b] working capital
    [c] all financial resources   [d] cash inflows
Ans. [c]

44. Issue of shares for purchase of assets is treated as
    [a] application of funds
    [b] sources of funds
    [c] neither sources nor application of funds
    [d] funds from operations
Ans. [b]

45. Any decrease in working capital results in
    [a] sources of funds
    [b] application of funds
    [c] neither source nor application of funds
    [d] increase funds from operations

    Ans. [a]

46. Any increase in the current liability as compared to the previous year results in
    [a] decrease in working capital   [b] increase in working capital
    [c] no change in working capital   [d] decrease in funds from operations

    Ans. [a]

47. In the calculation of funds from operations, all non cash expenses are
    [a] added in the net profits
    [b] deducted from the net profit
    [c] neither added nor deducted from net profits
    [d] added in the working capital statement

    Ans. [a]

48. In preparing cash flow statement, any decrease in current assets as compared to the previous year is
    [a] cash inflow   [b] cash outflow
    [c] increase in funds from operations [d] none of these

    Ans. [a]

49. Any increase in working capital as compared to the previous year is
    [a] application of funds
    [b] source of funds
    [c] neither source nor application of funds
    [d] increase in funds from operations

    Ans. [a]

50. In preparing funds flow statement, goodwill written off will
    [a] increase the funds from operations
    [b] decrease the funds from operations
    [c] have no change in the funds from operations
    [d] increase the working capital

    Ans. [a]

[3] Answer the following by choosing the correct answer from the alternatives given

1. Current assets of a firm are ₹ 25,00,000 and current liabilities are ₹ 15,00,000. The current ratio at present is 1.67. If there is a decrease in the current assets and current liabilities by ₹ 5,00,00 each, the current ratio will
    [a] increase   [b] decrease
    [c] remain the same   [d] None of these

    Ans. [a]

2. According to earnings price approach of calculating the cost of equity shares, if the earnings per share is ₹ 12 and the market price is ₹ 20, the cost will be
   [a] 6% [b] 12%
   [c] 15% [d] 18%
Ans. [a]

3. A debt collection period of 3 months indicates that the debtors turnover ratio is
   [a] 3 times [b] 2 times
   [c] 4 times [d] 6 times
Ans. [c]

4. The liquid ratio of a company is at present 1:1. If the company is able to convert its inventory into sales by 20%, the liquid ratio will
   [a] not change [b] increase
   [c] decrease [d] None of these
Ans. [b]

5. Credit sales of a firm are ₹ 15,00,000. The credit period allowed is 3 months. The amount of debtors will be
   [a] ₹ 3,50,000 [b] ₹ 5,00,000
   [c] ₹ 3,75,000 [d] ₹ 4,00,000
Ans. [c]

6. The gross profit ratio of a firm is 20%. The cost of goods sold is ₹ 45,00,000. Amount of sales will be
   [a] ₹ 40,00,000 [b] ₹ 56,25,000
   [c] ₹ 60,00,000 [d] ₹ 50,00,000
Ans. [b]

7. Total current assets of a firm are ₹ 60,00,000 and the current ratio is 2:1. The liquid ratio is 1:1. The liquid current assets will be
   [a] ₹ 40,00,000 [b] ₹ 20,00,000
   [c] ₹ 10,00,000 [d] ₹ 50,00,000
Ans. [b]

8. The fixed assets to proprietary funds ratio in case of a firm is 0.75. The amount of net working capital is ₹ 30,00,000. The amount of fixed assets will be
   [a] ₹ 22,50,000 [b] ₹ 30,00,000
   [c] ₹ 90,00,000 [d] ₹ 100,00,000
Ans. [c]

9. The gross profit ratio of a firm is 25% while the amount of sales is ₹ 40,00,000. The inventory turnover ratio [in relation to cost of goods sold] is 6 times and the opening stock is more than the closing stock by ₹ 50,000. Cost of goods sold includes purchases only apart from opening stock and closing stock. The amount of purchases will be
   [a] ₹ 30,00,000 [b] ₹ 25,00,000
   [c] ₹ 29,50,000 [d] ₹ 27,00,000.
Ans. [c]

10. Credit purchases of a firm are ₹ 60,00,000 and the average credit period is 4 months, the creditors turnover ratio is
    [a] 2 times
    [b] 4 times
    [c] 3 times
    [d] 5 times

Ans. [c]

11. The initial investments in a capital budgeting proposal is ₹ 20,00,000. The total present value of the cash inflows over the effective life of the project is ₹ 34,00,000 and the net present value is ₹ 14,00,000. The profitability index will be
    [a] 1.7
    [b] 2.42
    [c] 0.70
    [d] 0.58

Ans. [a]

12. Sales of a firm are ₹ 35,00,000, current assets are ₹ 20,00,000 and current liabilities are ₹ 15,00,000. The working capital turnover ratio will be
    [a] 5 times
    [b] 6 times
    [c] 7 times
    [d] 8 times

Ans. [c]

13. If the operating expenses to sales ratio of a firm is 85%, the operating net profit ratio is
    [a] 20%
    [b] 25%
    [c] 15%
    [d] 10%

Ans. [c]

14. If the maximum level of stock is 15000 units while the minimum level of stock is 5000 units, the average level will be
    [a] 10000 units
    [b] 20000 units
    [c] 12000 units
    [d] 7000 units

Ans. [a]

15. If operating leverage of a firm is 6 and the earnings before interest and tax is ₹ 1200000, the contribution will be
    [a] ₹ 72,00,000
    [b] ₹ 2,00,000
    [c] ₹ 5,00,000
    [d] ₹ 10,00,000

Ans. [a]

16. Operating leverage of a firm is 9 while the financial leverage is 6. The combined leverage will be
    [a] 15
    [b] 54
    [c] 1.5
    [d] .67

Ans. [b]

17. The market price of a company's equity share is ₹ 15 while the dividend per share is ₹ 10. The cost of equity according to Dividend/Price [D/P] approach will be
    [a] 1.5%
    [b] 15%
    [c] 10%
    [d] 0.66%

Ans. [d]

18. If the rate of interest on debt is 14% and the corporate income tax rate is 35%, the cost of debt will be
    - [a] 12%
    - [b] 15%
    - [c] 9.1%
    - [d] 10%

Ans. [c]

19. The dividend per equity share is ₹ 1 expected to grow by 6%. If the market price of the share is ₹ 25 per share, the cost of equity capital will be
    - [a] 15%
    - [b] 10%
    - [c] 9%
    - [d] 8%

Ans. [b]

www.ingramcontent.com/pod-product-compliance
Lightning Source LLC
Chambersburg PA
CBHW080740230426
43665CB00020B/2812